D0820829

A LAYPERSON'S GUIDE TO CRIMINAL LAW

Raneta Lawson Mack

Greenwood Press
Westport, Connecticut • London

Library of Congress Cataloging-in-Publication Data

Mack, Raneta Lawson, 1963–
A layperson's guide to criminal law / Raneta Lawson Mack.
p. cm.
Includes bibliographical references and index.
ISBN 0–313–30556–0 (alk. paper)
1. Criminal law—United States—Popular works. I. Title.
KF9219.6.M33 1999
345.73—dc21 98–53382

British Library Cataloguing in Publication Data is available.

Library of Congress Catalog Card Number: 98–53382
ISBN: 0–313–30556–0

First published in 1999

Greenwood Press, 88 Post Road West, Westport, CT 06881
An imprint of Greenwood Publishing Group, Inc.
www.greenwood.com

Printed in the United States of America

The paper used in this book complies with the Permanent Paper Standard issued by the National Information Standards Organization (Z39.48–1984).

10 9 8 7 6 5 4 3 2

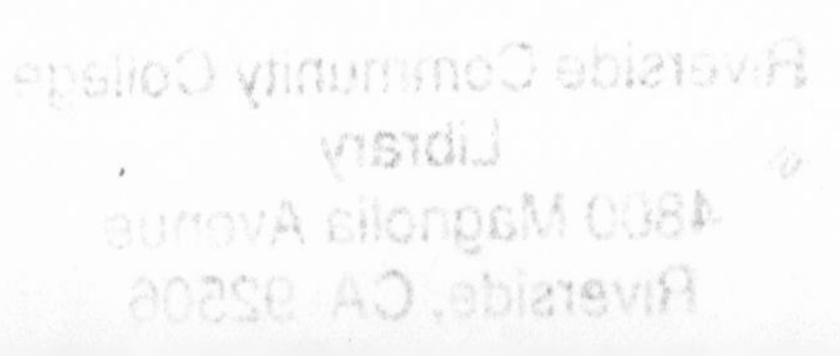

To Helen and Ernest Lawson, Jr.,
with love and appreciation for your
guidance, patience, and understanding

Contents

Preface ix

Introduction xi

1. A Brief History of Crime and Punishment in America 1

2. Basic Concepts of Criminal Law 19

3. Unlawful Killings 43

4. Sexual Assault and Related Offenses 65

5. Preparatory Criminal Conduct 87

6. Theft Offenses 111

7. Criminal Law Defenses 131

8. Miscellaneous Criminal Offenses 157

9. The Criminal Process 175

Glossary 191

Bibliography 197

Index 199

Preface

My fascination with crime and criminal law began as a young "layperson" growing up in Chicago watching crime dramas and reading true-crime novels. That fascination continues today in academia, although considerably more focused on the intricacies and subtleties of the criminal law. For me, and perhaps for many others, the "whys" and "hows" of crime and punishment raise very basic yet compelling questions of morality and choices—choices that society has made in criminalizing certain conduct and choices that individuals make when their conduct violates the criminal law.

This book endeavors to provide readers with a greater awareness and understanding of how these choices overlap in the American criminal justice system. Because a large part of the criminal law deals with the application of discrete crimes, it is possible to begin by reading the later chapters that discuss specific crimes. However, I highly recommend first exploring the chapters on the history and basic concepts of criminal law because these chapters place the criminal law in a broader historical context and explain the foundation underlying many of the specific crimes discussed later.

Speaking of foundation, one does not typically get to the point of writing a book without a significant personal and professional foundation. I owe a debt of gratitude to many people who have served as mentors and advisers along the way. I would especially like to recognize the efforts of several people who went the extra mile for me. My special thanks to Dr. Steve McConnell at the University of Toledo and to Chris Richardson at Davis, Graham and Stubbs in Denver, who each took the time to offer advice and encouragement at different stages in my professional development. In addition, my professional career has been and continues to be profoundly influenced by the wisdom, guidance and example of my mentor and friend Don Lively, Dean of Florida Coastal School of Law.

During my time at Creighton University School of Law, I have had the benefit of financial and academic support for my research and writing projects. I would like to thank Dean Larry Raful for ensuring the necessary support. I would also like to thank my colleague and friend Joe Allegretti, who willingly took the time to share his insights and advice concerning the book writing and publishing process.

Families are, of course, our first foundation. The love and encouragement of my parents, Helen and Ernest Lawson, Jr., has enabled me in so many positive ways that I cannot begin to repay them. This book is dedicated to them as a small step toward repayment. A special thanks also to my sister, Martita, and my nephew, Derrick, whose influence over the years has kept me grounded and "normal." And last, but certainly not least, my love and gratitude to my husband, John, who encouraged me on this project and sacrificed countless hours together so that I could complete the book on time. Thank you.

Introduction

When I initially developed the idea for a book explaining some of the complexities of criminal law, the O.J. Simpson "trial of the century" had recently concluded in a controversial acquittal verdict, the second Menendez trial had resulted in first-degree murder convictions and the Oklahoma bombing trial was gearing up. Although each trial was unique, they were also similar in the sense that they were intensely scrutinized by the media and generated hours of commentary by pundits attempting to explain the legal wranglings both inside and outside the respective courtrooms. While much of the commentary was timely and accurate, the time limitations (and somewhat sensationalistic nature) of network television programming simply did not accommodate detailed, context-rich explanations of the law in action. As a result, many followers of these media intense trials may have been left with feelings of confusion and skepticism concerning the American criminal justice system.

For example, at the conclusion of the Simpson criminal trial, ardent followers reached dramatically different conclusions as to whether the prosecution had met its burden-of-proof standard of "beyond a reasonable doubt." Some appeared to believe that this standard was just another way of saying, "apply your common sense to the evidence." Yet others seemed to interpret "beyond a reasonable doubt" to mean "beyond all possible doubt." Is either interpretation correct? Or does the answer lie somewhere between the two? Furthermore, how did we arrive at such a seemingly ambiguous standard for determining a person's guilt?

In addition to exposure to high-profile criminal trials through the media, in today's society many Americans are increasingly experiencing the criminal law on a more personal level, either as direct participants (e.g., defendants), through relatives or friends or from the unfortunate position of victims. In many instances, it is likely that these encounters with the criminal law have been fraught with the type of fear and anxiety that is often associated with journeys into the unknown. For criminal defendants, these feelings are perhaps a natural result of the basic understanding that criminal liability can and often does result in punishment. Moreover, depending upon the particular crime and the level of punishment, there may also be a severe societal stigma attached to a criminal conviction. From a victim's perspective, however, much of the fear and anxiety may result from the complexity and confusion that often surrounds the criminal process. In most criminal trials, the defendant is a passive participant while lawyers argue about such things as "mental states," "burden of proof" and "first degree versus second degree." These terms typically have very little or no meaning to a victim who has been injured or lost a loved one and simply wants to ensure that justice is done.

This book is intended to explain the origin and substance of American criminal law. What is unique about this book is that it explains the criminal law in terms understandable to the layperson who is interested in demystifying the criminal law without wading through legal jargon. Thus, this book will be of particular interest to those who follow local or national criminal proceedings, whether for personal, educational or professional reasons. Additionally, anyone who has had firsthand involvement in the criminal process will find this book useful for explaining some of the confusing terms and processes that are an inevitable part of our complex criminal justice system. Although this book is not intended to serve as a substitute for the advice of a competent attorney, it can provide supplementary information to assist in gaining a basic understanding of criminal law and the criminal trial process.

The book begins with an explanation of the origins of criminal law to provide readers with an awareness and understanding of the historical development of criminal statutes. Next, some of the fundamental concepts of criminal law are explained in detail, since those concepts form the foundation upon which most criminal statutes are constructed. The book then explores different categories of specific criminal offenses, beginning with homicide, and also examines some of the more popular criminal law defenses. A chapter is also devoted to an explanation of the criminal trial process from arrest through the final verdict, to acquaint readers with some of the procedural mechanics of a typical criminal trial and to place the criminal law in an appropriate procedural context. Finally, a glossary of terms at the end of the book provides concise definitions of some of the criminal law terms introduced and discussed within the chapters.

Explanatory (and sometimes humorous) hypotheticals are also used throughout the book to help analyze some of the more difficult concepts in an everyday, understandable context. While some of the hypotheticals describe violent circumstances, I hope readers will understand that these examples are necessary to explore the relevant criminal law concepts. It is, after all, a bit difficult to fully explore premeditated and deliberate murder without an example that adequately describes that kind of conduct. Readers are encouraged to analyze the hypotheticals with an eye toward fully understanding the issues they raise.

After each hypothetical, suggested "answers" to the questions raised by the example are discussed in detail. Although some of the answers are more clear-cut than others, practically all of the answers are open to some debate. The fact that there are no final answers or solutions to many of the questions raised illustrates both the complexity and the uncertainty of our criminal justice system. Readers who may encounter real-life circumstances that mirror those of an example should not assume that their situations will be resolved in the same manner.

At the end of each chapter, case studies analyze how actual cases interpreted and/or applied some of the concepts discussed in the chapter. Examining the criminal law as it is applied to real people and issues provides some sense of how the practice and the theory of the law interact (and sometimes conflict) in the criminal justice system. Following the case studies, a series of discussion questions challenge readers to further explore and expand upon issues discussed in the chapter. These questions raise fundamental issues concerning the hows and whys of the criminal law, which sometimes gets lost amid the study and application of the technical rules.

It should be noted at the outset that this book is not patterned after the criminal statutes of any particular jurisdiction. Instead, it provides a general explanation of the most common criminal statute components. Those who wish to learn more about federal or state criminal statutes should consult their local libraries.

Finally, it bears repeating that this book is not intended to provide legal advice. Those facing the possibility of criminal prosecution or concerned about their rights as victims should seek the advice of a competent attorney.

1

A Brief History of Crime and Punishment in America

History is no more than the portrayal of crimes and misfortunes.

—Voltaire

THE COMMON LAW

U.S. Supreme Court Justice Oliver Wendell Holmes once remarked that "the life of the law has not been logic; it has been experience." That observation has never been more accurate than when applied to the development of the criminal law. Although most of the laws defining crime and punishment are now incorporated into modern federal or state statutes, the criminal law has a rich and diverse historical tradition. Early settlers of America, fleeing the tyranny of the English monarchy, brought with them a fierce desire for independence from the mother country. In order to quickly establish a basic foundation for their emerging legal system, those pioneers also imported portions of the English legal system. Once imported, however, the laws did not remain static or tied to English tradition. Instead, since the American colonies were as diverse as modern states are today, each colony shaped and utilized different aspects of English law according to its particular needs and interests.

The English law imported by the colonies was generally referred to as the "common law." Since the common law of England was, for the most part, based upon the decisions of judges in particular cases, it was sometimes also referred to as "judge-made" law. When rendering decisions, judges using the common law were expected to rely upon basic principles of law, which reflected the societal customs and values of the period. Over time, the judiciary developed specialized approaches for dealing with particular types of issues, and each successive factually similar case was decided in a similar fashion. These specialized methods for dealing with particular issues formed a body of legal *precedent*. This meant that judges did not have to "reinvent the wheel" when cases arose that were factually similar and that prior decided cases had precedential value in assisting the judges in determining future cases. Of course, cases maintained precedential value only as long as societal customs and values supported the application of such precedent to particular issues.

For example, much of the early colonial criminal law focused on regulating and punishing crimes that offended the "morals" of society. This standard led to the infamous Salem witch trials, as well as to numerous prosecutions for "crimes" such as fornication, profanity and failure to attend church. Gradually however, as a result of industrial and economic expansion, the criminal law began to shift its focus away from the regulation of morals to the regulation of property and economic relationships. In light of this new economic emphasis, many of the laws and decisions relating to crimes against morality were overshadowed and rarely enforced. Nonetheless, it is interesting to note that criminal statutes outlawing fornication and adultery can still be found in many state statutes today, although most are rarely if ever enforced. Perhaps one explanation for the continued presence of these statutes is that few state legislators relish the idea of going on the public record in calling for the repeal of these morality-based statutes.

Another example of the gradual evolution of the common law is the crime of theft (discussed later). English legal historian and jurist William Blackstone, in his classic statement of the common law, *Commentaries on the Laws of England*, defined larceny as the "felonious taking and carrying away of the personal goods of another." This definition was adequate as long as economic relationships were simple. However, as capitalism grew and as banks and corporations entered the economic picture, it became clear that Blackstone's definition was far too specific to encompass new forms of property such as bank notes and stock certificates. Therefore, theft laws had to be modified to meet the changing demands of economic progress and the new forms of criminality that accompanied that progress. To a certain extent, this evolutionary process is still apparent in modern theft statutes. For example, modern theft statutes were not broad enough to address the enormous growth in the area of computer technology. Specifically, as the definition of property in many theft statutes did not encompass the theft of computer services or time, law enforcement officials were for a while left without statutory weapons to deal with the theft of this new genre of "property." The adoption of comprehensive computer-crime statutes addressing the specifics of computer technology provided the necessary statutory basis for prosecuting these offenses.

Although the common law formed the foundation for much of the colonial legal system, it had several distinct disadvantages. First, because it was "judge-made" and developed as a result of specific cases, it was not widely knowable and accessible to the majority of people. In fact, given the limited means for widespread communication during the colonial period, it is unlikely that decisions in particular cases were known to many people beyond the individuals involved in the cases and perhaps the local legal community. Second, the common law was reactive in the sense that the judiciary could not respond to or resolve issues until the specific facts were presented to the courts. As a result, the common law did not provide a mechanism for addressing future problems and concerns. Finally, outcomes under the common law were uncertain. Unless a similar set of facts had come before the court on a previous occasion, citizens could not know or predict the outcome of a particular case. These shortcomings were particularly troublesome in the area of criminal law because they conflicted with the basic belief that citizens should have prior notice as to which types of conduct are considered criminal and know the punishment associated with that conduct. These difficulties led some colonies to begin drafting and enacting written codes that specifically defined criminal conduct and punishment.

CRIMINAL CODES

Early criminal codes incorporated the traditional common law felonies of murder, manslaughter, arson, robbery, burglary, larceny and rape. Additionally, many of these early codes included what might be considered "nontraditional" criminal offenses and punishments, many of which seem either barbaric or comical when compared with contemporary standards. For example, the Law and Liberties of Massachusetts (1648), one of the earliest statutory codifications, included the crime of burglary. As part of the punishment for this crime, the code specified that if the burglary occurred on the "Lord's Day," the convicted burglar would lose an ear. Also, as a reflection of the continuing concern with witchcraft and immorality, many statutes provided that anyone found to be "consulting with familiar spirits" would be put to death. On the lighter side, early Indiana statutes made it a crime to sell skimmed milk or shoot hens or prairie chickens out of season.

Despite the idiosyncrasies of these early statutes, the codification process was significant because it placed the law-making function in the hands of legislators, thereby making the law knowable, accessible and capable of responding to future circumstances. These characteristics were particularly important for the criminal law in light of the severe punishment handed out for some offenses and the continually evolving nature of criminal activity. Codification also allowed flexibility in classifying conduct and defining punishment. At common law, crimes such as murder, manslaughter, robbery, arson, larceny and burglary were felonies, and a felony conviction often resulted in the death penalty. Codifying these crimes eventually allowed for the inclusion of specific degrees of criminal conduct (e.g., first-degree murder and second-degree murder), which permitted the imposition of less severe penalties in instances when leniency was warranted.

At the conclusion of the Revolutionary War, the move toward codification of laws expanded to the federal level with the ratification of a national constitution. There was such a concern about the rights of criminal defendants vis-à-vis the government that the U.S. Constitution contains what is sometimes referred to as a "national criminal code." The provisions of this national criminal code are contained in the Bill of Rights. For example, the Fourth Amendment protects against unreasonable searches and seizures (a seizure typically means an arrest or detention of the person). The Fifth Amendment grants protection against compelled self-incrimination, while the Sixth Amendment provides for the right to the assistance of counsel for one's defense in a criminal case. The Constitution made each of these rights applicable in federal criminal cases; eventually, the states were also constitutionally required to provide the same protections to suspects and defendants.

As the codification process continued on the federal and state levels, there was a simultaneous expansion in the development of criminal statutes. This growth was enhanced by the enactment of a new breed of regulatory or economic crime, which was introduced into many statutory schemes as a means for regulating industry conduct. For example, in Illinois, it was a crime to practice barbering without a license. Although many of these regulatory crimes were rarely enforced, they demonstrated that society viewed the criminal law as a means to distribute the social costs of industrial expansion. Thus, the government, through the criminal justice system, bore the responsibility and burden for prosecuting the errant barber for practicing without a license instead of requiring private individuals to bring civil suits after the fact for bad haircuts.

The use of the criminal law as a means to protect society and regulate industrial expansion meant that more and more statutes were created to keep pace with rapid industrial development. At the same time, very few statutes were repealed even though they had obviously outlived their usefulness. What resulted in many states was a statutory structure that contained a hodgepodge of common law–based crimes, regulatory/economic crimes and piecemeal statutory amendments to address new types of criminal conduct. Little attention was paid to maintaining overall consistency and cohesiveness throughout the criminal code. This failure to focus on the big picture resulted in inconsistent definitions and penalty structures. One of the well-known maxims of criminal law is that the punishment must fit the crime. Implicit in this statement is that like crimes will be punished in a like fashion. With ad hoc and often hasty amendments to criminal statutes, internal consistency in penalty structures suffered and similar crimes were often punished in a dissimilar fashion.

Concerns about the scope and inconsistent nature of criminal codes prompted several states to begin reforming their criminal statutes. This effort was aided by the development of the Model Penal Code (MPC) in 1962. The MPC was drafted and approved by the American Law Institute (ALI), a private organization of lawyers, judges and legal academics that independently undertook the task of drafting a model criminal code that was comprehensive, cohesive and consistent. Although the MPC is not law itself, it serves as an influential model or example for states drafting or revising criminal codes. The ALI hoped that the MPC would provide a worthy example for states seeking to reform their criminal codes. By 1982, at least thirty-seven states had reformed their criminal codes in accordance with the MPC provisions, although the degree of incorporation of MPC components varied by state. Some states incorporated practically all of the MPC provisions while others incorporated only select portions. Nevertheless, given the level of influence that the MPC has had on state codes, it is fair to say that its provisions are representative of most criminal codes in the United States.

COMMON CHARACTERISTICS OF CRIMINAL CODES

As states continued the process of statutory reform using the MPC as an example, most criminal codes began to exhibit common characteristics in terms of prohibited conduct and penalties. For example, most statutes eliminated the stark common law distinction between felonies (for which a conviction meant certain death) and misdemeanors in favor of a more flexible classification system based upon the potential for incarceration. Under this statutory structure, if a crime is punishable by at least one year in jail, it is typically considered a felony. If the punishment is less than a year, the crime is classified as a misdemeanor.

With respect to specific code provisions, most modern criminal statutes begin with a general definitional section that outlines the basic principles of criminal liability. This section usually describes when individuals may be criminally responsible for the acts of others (e.g., accomplice liability) and may also include a description of some defenses that may excuse criminal liability (e.g., the insanity defense).

Following the definitional section, an overwhelming majority of criminal statutes contain general provisions incorporating the basic common law crimes of murder, manslaughter, robbery, larceny, burglary, arson and rape. These crimes are now separated into different degrees with different levels of punishment based upon the severity of the offense. For example, first-degree murder might carry a maximum punishment of death or life imprisonment, while a conviction for second-degree murder might result in a maximum punishment of 40 years in prison.

As a reflection of modern changes in the nature of criminality, today most statutes also include sections outlawing narcotics possession or distribution, gambling and domestic violence. It is also noteworthy that many states have recognized the importance of victim and witness rights with the incorporation of statutory provisions that specifically protect those rights. For example, some statutes provide that victims may recover any profits that a convicted defendant receives as a direct result of the crime. Additionally, and perhaps more important, many statutes provide that victims and witnesses are entitled to notification in the event that violent offenders are released from prison.

Finally, most statutes contain sections on penalties and sentencing. These sections typically outline the maximum and minimum penalties for crimes according to their classification. The penalties for a given offense may include a specified period of incarceration, a fine or a combination of the two.

Generally speaking, since there is no uniformity requirement among the various state criminal codes, each state is free to decide which statutory components to emphasize or de-emphasize. Thus, each state, through its legislative process, is free to adapt its code in accordance with the changing nature of criminal conduct within its borders.

FEDERAL CRIMINAL LAW

Federal criminal law covers most of the same types of conduct included in state criminal codes. What distinguishes federal crimes from their state counterparts is the requirement that, on the federal level, the criminal conduct must involve a "federal interest." The federal interest provides the federal government with legal jurisdiction to prosecute the offense. For example, bank robbery becomes a federal crime if the robbery occurs at a federal bank (the federal interest). Similarly, if the victim of a homicide is a federal official or employee, then the federal homicide provisions apply. Additionally, if the criminal conduct extends beyond state borders (e.g., mailing fraudulent material from one state to another state, or mail fraud), then the federal government has jurisdiction because the conduct is said to affect interstate commerce. In addition to these traditional offenses, other high-profile federal criminal statutes were enacted because the federal government determined that certain criminal conduct was so widespread and harmful that federal efforts were necessary to combat the activity. Examples of these statutes include the Racketeer Influenced and Corrupt Organizations Act (RICO), which is designed to eliminate long-term organized criminal activity; securities fraud statutes, which regulate insider trading; and environmental statutes, which criminalize certain conduct that is harmful to the environment.

In terms of punishment, federal law provides that judges follow sentencing guidelines to reduce the potential for disparity in the sentencing process. These guidelines utilize a point system to calculate sentences based upon the nature of the offense and the offender. Federal sentencing guidelines have engendered a great deal of criticism and controversy because they severely restrict the authority and discretion of the judiciary in the sentencing process. Judges no longer have the freedom to be harsher or more lenient if particular situations require such treatment. The guidelines have also been sharply criticized because of the perception that they produce biased outcomes. The most notable example of this is the sentencing structure for possession of cocaine. A person convicted for possession of a small amount of crack cocaine will receive a much harsher sentence than a person convicted for possession of a much larger quantity of powdered cocaine. This outcome is thought to be biased because a disproportionate number of arrests and convictions for possession of crack cocaine involve members of minority communities. This controversial issue will be further explored in a case study in Chapter 8.

PROCEDURAL VERSUS SUBSTANTIVE LAW

Procedural criminal law defines the relationship between the government (e.g., police and prosecutor) and the individual in matters of criminal law. It sets limits on how far the government may intrude upon a person's rights when that person is suspected of or charged with a crime. If the government fails to follow appropriate procedure, then, in some instances, the criminal case may be dismissed without regard to the suspect's guilt or innocence. Procedural criminal law is derived from various sources. One source is the U.S. Constitution. As discussed above, the Fourth, Fifth and Sixth amendments to the Constitution provide numerous procedural protections to individuals during their interactions with the police. Other sources of criminal procedural law include state constitutions, state law and police procedural manuals. Each of these sources defines procedures that the government must follow when investigating, detaining, arresting or prosecuting individuals for criminal conduct.

In contrast, substantive criminal law is the set of laws that defines the types of conduct considered illegal and outlines the categories of punishment to be imposed for violations of the substantive laws. As previously discussed, substantive criminal law is rooted in the common law and has been gradually reduced over the years to written codes and enacted by legislative bodies. For the most part, this book will be devoted to explaining the substantive criminal law, although procedural issues will be addressed as they arise.

PUNISHMENT

A discussion of the development of criminal law would be incomplete without an examination of the role of punishment in the American criminal justice system. A system of criminal laws would be hollow and ineffective without a corresponding system of punishment. To prevent citizens from doing what society considers undesirable, this system of punishment must contain certain components. First, the nature of the punishment must be well defined so that citizens have fair notice of the potential punishment for criminal conduct. This means that for every crime, the statute must specify a punishment or range of punishments. Today, almost every statute outlines maximum and minimum sentences for specific criminal conduct. Second, the statutory punishment must be proportionate to the crime. For example, a first-time offender who shoplifts a seventy-five-cent candy bar from a grocery store should not face the threat of life imprisonment for her conduct. Third, there must be a perception of fairness and a certain degree of flexibility in terms of how the punishment system is structured and allocated. This notion of fairness means that any system of punishment should take into account the nature of the offense, the harm to society and any mitigating circumstances. These factors will allow flexibility in imposing harsher or more lenient sentences when circumstances dictate such treatment. For instance, a bank officer who embezzles $1,000,000 from a bank over a five-year period will perhaps have fewer mitigating factors in his favor than an unemployed father of four who, in a moment of desperation, robs a bank at gunpoint and gets away with $2,000. However, the father may nevertheless be subject to harsher punishment because his use of a deadly weapon to commit the robbery unnecessarily jeopardized the lives of innocent people. Finally, there must be some degree of certainty that the punishment will be carried out upon conviction. The criminal law can achieve its goal of preventing citizens from engaging in undesirable conduct only if there is a high likelihood that offenders will be punished fairly and swiftly.

Each of these components is critical and ultimately assists in reinforcing the fairness, effectiveness and moral legitimacy of our criminal justice system. The question remains, however, what overall goals are we seeking to promote with a system of punishment? Why do we punish? In response, several theories have been advanced.

One theory is that punishment very simply is meant to deter individuals from committing further crimes. Since people react differently to the threat of punishment depending upon social class, age and offender status, the judge is often given discretion to adapt the punishment to maximize its deterrent effect. For example, in the case of a teen offender who, while driving recklessly, unintentionally kills a woman, the judge might sentence the teen to a period of incarceration. As further punishment, the judge might also order the teen to visit the grave of the victim every year on the anniversary of the crime. Such a unique punishment seeks to provide the teen offender with an unpleasant experience that he will not want to endure again. Furthermore, it is hoped that this "personalized" form of punishment will have an even more profound deterrent effect because it reinforces the tragic human consequences of the crime. Finally, in a broader sense, it is also anticipated that upon witnessing the loss of liberty and societal stigma suffered by convicted defendants, others will be deterred from engaging in unlawful conduct.

Another theory of punishment is restraint. This theory urges that society receives the most benefit if convicted defendants are removed from society and can no longer present a threat to society. Sentences such as imprisonment and confinement to mental institutions illustrate this theory of punishment. Of course, to maximize its effectiveness, the period of restraint must be of sufficient length to ensure that the offender no longer presents a danger to society upon release.

The rehabilitation theory of punishment holds that if criminal conduct has been caused by certain factors and if those factors can be identified and appropriately remedied, then the offender can eventually be returned to society. The rehabilitation theory has met with limited success and has provoked a great deal of skepticism primarily because of the inherent difficulties associated with isolating factors that lead to criminal conduct. Additionally, the limited financial resources available to many prison and mental health facilities make it difficult, if not impossible, to devote significant personnel, research and time to the rehabilitative effort.

Last, the oldest theory of punishment, and one that is still widely respected, is retribution. In its purest form, retribution holds that a person who has voluntarily chosen to violate societal laws deserves to be punished because, by violating the rules, the offender has obtained an unfair advantage. Society then restores the proper balance by obtaining revenge against the offender. According to this theory, the father of four who robs a bank at gunpoint in a moment of desperation would be punished just as any other armed bank robber without regard to the particular factual (and perhaps mitigating) circumstances contributing to his criminal conduct. Critics of the retribution theory argue that this "eye for an eye" model of punishment encourages a lust for vengeance without any real corresponding societal benefit. They further argue that if we are to have a criminal justice system based upon morality, fairness and justice, then that system must dispense punishment in a manner that comports with those goals. Thus, while those who engage in criminal conduct deserve to be punished, that punishment must ultimately be fair, just and morally defensible.

CASE STUDIES

"Undesirable Conduct" and Criminality

As explored in this chapter, American criminal law has its origins in English common law. However, because the criminal law cannot remain static and must adapt to the changing needs of society, new laws defining and punishing what is deemed morally blameworthy conduct are enacted regularly. Once enacted, these laws often attract constitutional scrutiny, particularly if they appear to expand the scope of the criminal law to cover innocent or involuntary behavior, or if they conflict with other constitutional rights.

In the early 1960s, in an apparent effort to stem the flow of illegal narcotics trafficking and use within its borders, the state of California enacted a criminal statute that made it a misdemeanor for a person either to *use* narcotics or to *be addicted to the use* of narcotics while present in the state. The mandatory penalty for conviction of this offense was a sentence of not less than 90 days in jail.

In one precedent-setting case prosecuted under this statute, Lawrence Robinson was arrested after Los Angeles police searched him and discovered that he had several needlemarks and discolorations on his arms that were consistent with prior drug use. At the time of his arrest, Robinson also allegedly told the police that he had used narcotics in the past. At trial, however, he denied ever using narcotics and told the jury that the needlemarks resulted from an allergic condition rather than narcotics use or addiction.

The trial judge instructed the jury that they could find Robinson guilty if they determined that he either used narcotics or was addicted to their use. The judge further explained that being addicted to the use of narcotics was a status or condition that is chronic and continuing and therefore subjects the offender to arrest and prosecution at any time before he reforms. The judge concluded the instructions by explaining that for a conviction, the jury need only find that the defendant was addicted to the use of narcotics while in the city of Los Angeles. Robinson was convicted of being addicted to narcotics and sentenced to 90 days in jail. Robinson appealed this conviction, arguing that the California statute, which punished and stigmatized individuals based solely upon the status of being an addict, inflicted a cruel and unusual punishment in violation of the Constitution.

The Supreme Court agreed. The Court first acknowledged that the state of California has wide authority and latitude in protecting the health and welfare of its citizens through the use of criminal statutes and sanctions addressing the manufacture, possession or sale of narcotics. However, the Court observed that this particular criminal statute went beyond that scope and punished defendants for the mere status of being narcotics users, whether or not actual use of narcotics had ever occurred within the borders of the state of California. Perhaps most important, the Court explained that narcotics addiction is an illness or condition that may be contracted innocently or involuntarily. In that regard, the Court noted that the narcotics addict falls into the same category as the mentally ill or those persons afflicted with leprosy or a venereal disease. The Court concluded that while all of these individuals may be legally required to undergo some form of compulsory treatment for their condition, laws that create criminal offenses and punishments based upon these conditions are cruel and unusual and therefore unconstitutional.

It is clear from this case that California had chosen a novel and aggressive approach to curtail the spread of illegal narcotics within its borders. Undoubtedly, the legislative choice to pursue those who were addicted to narcotics was motivated in part by a desire to cut off the demand for illegal narcotics by using the deterrent effect of the criminal law. While that might be a desirable goal, this case illustrates that the criminal law was not the most appropriate tool to pursue that objective constitutionally. Because of the potential stigma and loss of liberty associated with a criminal conviction, the criminal law must be confined to conduct that is voluntary and to some degree controllable by the defendant. When these conditions are met, there is a degree of certainty that the defendant has acted in a morally blameworthy manner and deserves the punishment and stigma associated with a criminal conviction. In contrast, if behavior is largely beyond the defendant's control (as in the case of narcotics addiction and a host of other diseases), then punishing him for that "status" or condition does little to further the goal of punishing the morally blameworthy. Moreover, enacting and utilizing criminal laws as a method for controlling this conduct may ultimately shift the focus and limited resources away from more effective alternatives such as compulsory treatment and drug awareness education. Although the states may not impose criminal sanctions for the mere status of being addicted to narcotics, courts have given the states much wider latitude when that addiction has the potential to impact others—particularly the unborn fetus.

In recent years, several states have begun to aggressively prosecute pregnant women who use illegal drugs during their pregnancies. These prosecutions are designed both to deter the use of illegal narcotics and to prevent harm to the fetus by significantly reducing the risk that these babies will be born addicted to narcotics and suffer debilitating illnesses related to the mothers' drug usage. Because these laws have often targeted pregnant women who use crack cocaine, the children who are born addicted to this drug are sometimes referred to as "crack babies." South Carolina is one state that has taken an aggressive stance in criminalizing illegal drug usage during pregnancy.

In 1989, using its already-enacted child endangerment statute, South Carolina instituted a program designed to end the use of drugs during pregnancy by prosecuting such conduct as a felony. The state child-endangerment statute was not enacted to address this type of harm to a fetus, nor had it ever been interpreted to encompass such conduct. Thus, this program involved an entirely unprecedented application of the child endangerment statute. In order to maximize the discovery and future deterrence of this conduct, the state required notification when a newborn tested positive for drugs. To date, the state has criminally prosecuted as many as 40 women under this program. Two women, Cornelia Whitner and Malissa Crawley, were prosecuted under this statute and are now serving prison terms for using crack cocaine during their pregnancies in 1992. Upon conviction, they challenged their sentences, arguing that the application of the child endangerment statute to their conduct was unconstitutional because they did not have fair notice that the statute was applicable to their conduct.

One of the fundamental principles of the criminal law is that citizens must have fair notice as to what types of conduct will be considered criminal. The rationale is that individuals can adjust their behavior to meet the requirements of the law only if the law is knowable and certain. Whitney and Crawley argued that although the child endangerment statute was on the books at the time they used drugs during their pregnancies, there was no way they could have known that the statute would have criminalized their conduct because the statute refers to child endangerment and not fetus endangerment. Therefore, they argue that the statute, by definition, does not apply to them and that if it does, they did not have fair notice of its application.

In reviewing their appeals, the South Carolina Supreme Court concluded that once the fetus is viable and capable of living apart from the mother it is considered a "child" for purposes of the child endangerment statute although it is still inside the mother's womb. The court held that since it had recognized a viable fetus as a "child" for purposes of homicide and wrongful death statutes, it followed logically that a viable fetus should be recognized as a "child" for purposes of statutes related to child abuse and endangerment. The court reasoned that while abuse or neglect at any point during childhood can have a tremendous impact on a child, the abuse or neglect that can take place before birth can sometimes have even more devastating results. Thus, the word "child" in the statute should be read broadly to include a fetus at the point of viability. Furthermore, the court indicated that the criminal statute could be expanded to cover mothers who engage in other lawful conduct (such as consuming alcohol), if that conduct has the potential to impact the health and safety of the viable fetus.

Addressing the argument that the defendants did not have fair notice that their conduct was criminal, the court observed that it is "common knowledge" that the use of cocaine during pregnancy can harm the unborn child. According to the court that was sufficient and fair notice of "child" endangerment.

By expanding the child endangerment statute to cover this type of conduct, the court clarified one area of uncertainty, but perhaps simultaneously opened the door to a host of other uncertainties. For example, is it now unlawful and criminal for a woman to fail to seek prenatal care? Such failure certainly has the potential to impact the health and safety of the fetus. And what about a woman who ingests crack cocaine for the period of time prior to viability, arguably the most critical time in the unborn child's development? The statute as interpreted by the court does not seem to encompass this conduct, but it might.

If one of the goals of the criminal law is to punish those who act contrary to the law, then the law should be reasonably certain and knowable. To the degree that the language in criminal statutes is capable of being interpreted in ways that were perhaps not contemplated when the statute was enacted, there is a significant risk that morally "innocent" people will be unexpectedly confronted with the specter and stigma of a criminal prosecution. Thus, while broadly interpreting a criminal statute may help to address pressing social concerns in the short term, the added dimension of uncertainty will undoubtedly engender a degree of distrust and disrespect for the law over the long term.

Crime, Punishment and Death

It is perhaps an understatement to say that the death penalty is one of the most controversial areas of the criminal law. Statistics reveal that an overwhelming majority of Americans support the death penalty, and most would prefer that the process from conviction to execution proceed more swiftly than it does in our current system. In fact, Congress has responded to public concern regarding the lengthy appeals process in capital cases by enacting new laws that impose significant restrictions on the ability to file appeals in capital cases. Some speculate that these new guidelines could reduce the average length of time between conviction and execution from nine years to approximately four years. In addition to reduced access to the appellate process, fewer and fewer attorneys are willing to accept representation of defendants in capital cases. For some, this reluctance is motivated by personal or professional reasons. But for others, the reason is that they simply are not compensated in accordance with the tremendous amount of work required to present their clients' appeals competently and zealously in the various courts.

Of course, one of the reasons that the appeals process is so important in capital cases is that the consequences of error are so severe. The thought that even one innocent person might be executed forces even the staunchest supporters of the death penalty to concede that the appellate process is and should be a necessary component of the system. Nonetheless, it seems that the increasing pressure to hasten the process to execution is often accompanied by the implicit suggestion that some degree of risk is acceptable if swifter and more certain punishment will make the death penalty a more effective deterrent. Hidden in that type of cost/benefit analysis is perhaps a rationalization that we can never truly be certain of anyone's guilt and that the truly innocent will be filtered out of the system through the trial or appellate process long before the death penalty is imposed, much less implemented. But consider the case of Rolando Cruz, an innocent man who sat on death row for ten years for the rape and murder of a ten-year-old girl.

Shortly after his arrest, doubts began to surface as to Rolando Cruz's guilt. The police were unable to find any physical evidence or eyewitness testimony linking Cruz to the crime. Although Cruz originally told police that he had information related to the crime, it was later revealed that he didn't have any such information and that his statement had been a ruse to collect the reward money. At trial, the only piece of evidence produced against Cruz was a statement in which Cruz allegedly told police that he had a "dream" that allegedly contained critical details of the crime that only the killer would know. This "dream" statement turned up for the first time just a few days prior to trial and curiously had not been documented by anyone. Cruz vehemently denied making the statement. Despite the startling lack of solid evidence, Cruz was convicted and sentenced to death. After the initial conviction was overturned on appeal, Cruz was tried a second time and again found guilty and given the death penalty.

To add to the question of Cruz's innocence, between his first and second trials someone else confessed to the crime for which Cruz had been charged, convicted and sentenced. However, even after this confession and new DNA evidence linking the confessed killer to the crime, Cruz was tried yet a third time after the second conviction was overturned. During the third trial a key witness, a police officer, admitted that he had fabricated the evidence against Cruz. The case against Cruz was finally dismissed after ten years, and the lawyers and police officers who falsified the case against Cruz are themselves now facing indictment for their roles in repeatedly placing an innocent man on death row for ten years.

To some, the Cruz case might seem like an aberration, an example of the justice system spinning out of control because of the egos and ambitions of the personalities involved. Certainly this cannot be representative of the "typical" capital murder prosecution. In any event, in this case, the egregious conduct of the officials involved eventually surfaced and an innocent man was *not* put to death. All of these are accurate perspectives on the Cruz case and provide some measure of cautious optimism that the system indeed works. But there is also another more chilling perspective. The three primary factors—time, access to the courts, and attorneys—that enabled

Cruz to pursue his case three times are currently being reduced to a bare minimum by new legislation. The next Rolando Cruz will face tougher hurdles, more limited time and far fewer resources.

Overall, capital punishment probably raises more questions than it resolves. For example, it is often heralded as an effective deterrent to crime. That is, people will forego engaging in certain criminal activity for fear that they will receive the death penalty if convicted. Yet there is no accurate way to measure this claim. How does one measure something that does not occur, much less articulate a rationale for its non-occurrence? It is also frequently stated that the death penalty serves society's need for retribution. But that retributive ideal is sometimes lost amid the macabre and party-like atmosphere outside of some prisons on execution day.

Finally, there are disturbing racial disparities in death row populations that should at least give pause to reflect upon the role that America's history of racial intolerance might play in the dispensation of death penalty sentences. In one recent case, two black men received a half-million dollars each from the state of Florida because they were wrongly convicted of the murder and robbery of two gas station attendants. As in the Cruz case, there was no physical evidence linking either of them to the crime. However, they were coerced into making confessions. Several years later, when a white man confessed to the murders and passed a polygraph test indicating that he was being truthful in his confession, the sheriff ignored this evidence because he was satisfied that he had two black men already on death row for the murders. It was not until someone wrote a book about the case that a full investigation and eventual pardon occurred, and the wrongfully convicted men were released after spending almost a decade on death row. Now, twenty-three years later, they have each received a half-million dollars as recompense for the years lost to them because of patently racist attitudes. Like the Cruz case, this case might also be dismissed as an aberration, a flaw in the system. But also like the Cruz case, it took several years to discover this intentional flaw.

These cases might also be considered the "close calls." They represent the wrongful convictions, as opposed to the wrongful executions. It is unlikely that society will ever know the extent of the wrongful executions because often the passionate pursuit of justice on behalf of the death row inmate that may have existed prior to an execution is buried with the defendant. The criminal justice system moves on to other cases and causes célèbres, and in the end there is no genuine closure. But because the death penalty represents the convergence of so many profound and conflicting issues—life, death, guilt and innocence—perhaps real closure is not possible.

Maybe the best we can hope for is to try to limit the forces that converge to create the close calls.

FOR FURTHER CONSIDERATION

1. There is a well-known criminal law maxim that "ignorance of the law is no defense." What does it mean to "know" the law, and why do we have such a standard in the area of criminal law?
2. The criminal law seeks to punish those who are considered morally blameworthy. Are there instances when factors other than moral blameworthiness should be considered when deciding to prosecute or punish? For example, are there reasons that the father of four who robs a bank at gunpoint should not face prosecution or punishment at all? What if he stole the money because he was desperate and one of his children was near death from starvation? Should the law make an exception in this case? If so, who decides when exceptions are to be made?
3. What is the justification for allowing statutes outlawing fornication and adultery to remain on the books in many states when they are rarely enforced?
4. If the legislature decided to repeal the state murder statute, would that mean it would no longer be a crime to kill another person? What role, if any, would the common law play in this scenario?
5. The criminal justice system draws distinctions between juvenile offenders and adult offenders in terms of punishment. For example, in most jurisdictions, an adult who commits first-degree murder would be eligible for the death penalty, while a fifteen-year-old juvenile offender would be incarcerated until the age of 21 and then released with his criminal records sealed. What is the justification for this differential treatment? Should juveniles be eligible for the death penalty?
6. In many domestic violence cases, the victim (often the wife) does not want the defendant prosecuted after the incident and often refuses to testify. If the victim of a crime does not want the defendant prosecuted, should the government nevertheless proceed with the case? What goals of crime and punishment are promoted by such a prosecution?

2

Basic Concepts of Criminal Law

Actus non facit reum, nisi mens sit rea. [The act is not criminal unless the intent is criminal.]

—Legal maxim

Criminal statutes define conduct that falls below prescribed legal and moral standards and thereby causes identifiable social harm. Not every instance of unlawful conduct is punished, however, and not every social harm is redressed. Thus, before beginning a discussion of specific criminal statutes, it is necessary to explore some fundamental concepts that are critical to an understanding of the structure and application of the criminal law. This chapter will focus on four criminal law concepts—the voluntary act, the mental state, causation and social harm—that provide the foundation for most criminal statutes and assist society in selecting those individuals who are morally blameworthy and deserving of punishment.

THE VOLUNTARY ACT

To secure a conviction under a criminal statute, one element the government must prove is that the defendant performed a *voluntary act* that resulted in a social harm. The act must be voluntary because moral blameworthiness can be more accurately assessed when there is some degree of certainty that defendants have acted according to their own free will. Furthermore, if one of the goals of punishment is deterring unlawful conduct, then deterrence can be effective only to the extent that individuals make voluntary choices with respect to their conduct. Problems arise, however, when attempting to draw the line between voluntary and involuntary actions. Consider the following circumstances:

Sid, a chronic sleepwalker, arises one night in a sleepwalking state, drives ten miles to the home of a friend and viciously beats his friend to death with a baseball bat. After the incident, Sid returns home and sleeps soundly until he is awakened by police officers who come to arrest him the next morning. Sid is stunned by the arrest and claims that he has no recollection of the events of the previous night. At trial, Sid argues that, because he was in a sleepwalking state, he could not control his actions and therefore could not have acted voluntarily. Is Sid likely to be successful with this defense?

Sid's success will depend upon the jury's understanding and acceptance of sleepwalking and its impact on Sid's ability to consciously control his actions. If it can be demonstrated that Sid's sleepwalking state was such that he lacked conscious control of his actions, then under the law he did *not* act voluntarily, even though his actions resembled those of someone acting with conscious control. The result is that Sid would not be considered morally blameworthy for the death of his friend because he did not act according to his own free will. Moreover, from a punishment perspective, because Sid's conduct was not conscious and voluntary, it is unlikely that punishment or the threat of punishment can serve as an effective deterrent to Sid or others in Sid's situation. (An actual sleepwalking defense case is considered in the case study section of this chapter.)

How can we best determine if a person has acted voluntarily? It is fair to say that the majority of actions are performed by individuals while in a conscious state and with full awareness of their actions. These actions are, by definition, voluntary. Therefore, the best approach for determining involuntary behavior is to focus on those actions that occur either in an unconscious state or without the actor's prior awareness or control. Conduct performed during sudden seizures, blackouts or reflexes would likely fall into the category of involuntary conduct since such actions are not the result of the actor's prior awareness or control and may even be surprising to the actor.

Closer cases arise when an individual has had repeated sleepwalking, seizure or blackout episodes. Under such circumstances, a strong argument may be made that these individuals are on notice that they could suddenly lapse into an unconscious state during which they might be incapable of controlling their conduct. To the extent that they fail to take steps to control the condition that leads to the involuntary conduct, then these individuals should be considered morally blameworthy for any resulting conduct. Therefore, if it were determined that Sid the Sleepwalker was aware that he had a chronic (and violent) sleepwalking problem and yet failed to do anything to prevent this behavior, then he might be considered morally blameworthy for the death of his friend because he failed to take steps to correct the sleepwalking condition that led to the involuntary conduct.

For purposes of criminal law, the voluntary act can take many forms. It can be a physical act, such as pointing a gun or taking another person's property. It can also be a verbal act, such as an agreement between two parties to commit a crime or making a false statement under oath. The voluntary act can also be a failure to act when there is a legal duty to act, such as failing to provide food or other necessities of life to one's child. To impose liability for a failure to act, the law must first impose a duty upon the individual to affirmatively act under certain circumstances. The legal duty may arise by virtue of statute (parental duty to support a child) or special relationship (doctor/patient, lifeguard/swimmer). A legal duty arises in these relationships because of the inherent dependency of one person upon another for health, safety or protection. To further explore this notion of a legal duty, consider the following case:

A young woman is viciously and repeatedly attacked outside an apartment building. Thirty-eight people in the apartment building either watch the attack or hear the young woman's cries for help for more than half an hour, but choose not to help or become involved. The woman dies as a result of the attack. Can any of the onlookers be charged with homicide for failing to assist the woman?

In this instance, there would be no criminal liability for the onlookers because there is no legal duty to act. Courts and legislatures have not imposed a legal duty upon strangers to affirmatively assist victims of unlawful attacks. Since the onlookers are strangers to the victim, there is no special relationship between the parties that would legally require active interference by the onlookers. Thus, while there may be a moral duty to act, it is not sufficient to provide a basis for criminal responsibility. Although this may be a somewhat "uncomfortable" result, it is logical (and perhaps necessary) from a criminal prosecution standpoint. Without a specific legal duty to act, who would be criminally prosecuted from among the thirty-eight onlookers in the apartment building? In other words, can we accurately determine that the onlookers' failure to act renders them morally blameworthy such that a criminal sanction is necessary? What if their failure to act was the result of an inability to act, that is, they were in a state of shock or had no access to a telephone? What if they honestly believed the attack wasn't serious enough to warrant a call to the police? Finally, how can we know whether their failure to act caused her death? Is it possible that she would have died anyway, despite the onlookers' efforts to assist? The point is that without a specific legal duty to act, it is difficult to assess moral blameworthiness and criminal responsibility. The requirement of a legal duty to act ensures that we are able to identify specific individuals who may be liable for failing to act under certain circumstances. As for our onlookers who failed to act in the previous example, perhaps any "punishment" for their conduct is best left to institutions outside of the criminal justice system.

One noteworthy situation in which some states require strangers to affirmatively act to assist others is when a motorist injures another motorist who is injured as a result of an automobile accident. These statutes typically make it a misdemeanor offense to fail to render assistance to an injured person under such circumstances. To further encourage individuals to fulfill this obligation, many states have adopted "Good Samaritan" statutes, which provide that drivers shall be immune from civil liability for actions performed in good faith while exercising reasonable care.

THE MENTAL STATE

To obtain a criminal conviction, in addition to proving a voluntary act, the prosecutor must prove that the defendant acted with an "evil mind" or a bad *mental state* at the time of the offense. Proof of the defendant's mental state is necessary since the criminal law seeks to punish only those who are morally blameworthy. It is important to understand, however, that bad thoughts or evil intent alone are not sufficient to impose criminal liability. A person may fantasize about murdering his boss and may even reveal those fantasies to friends, but it is only when he begins to act upon those thoughts that the criminal law becomes relevant. Thus, the voluntary act and the mental state must both be present at the time the crime is committed. Consider the following example:

> After receiving a failing grade in chemistry class, Sam Student hated his college chemistry professor, Professor Bunson. In fact, Sam constantly fantasized about and planned numerous ways to permanently get rid of Professor Bunson. One day, as Sam is descending the stairs, he suddenly trips, falls forward and runs directly into Professor Bunson, who is coincidentally on the same stairway. The force of Sam's fall knocks Professor Bunson to the ground, where he strikes his head on the concrete and is killed instantly. After Sam gets up, he is shocked to see Professor Bunson lying motionless on the ground. His shock immediately turns to glee, how-

ever, when he realizes that Professor Bunson will never give another failing grade in chemistry. Sam walks away whistling happily. Is Sam guilty of homicide for the death of Professor Bunson?

Assuming that Sam's trip on the staircase was truly accidental and not the result of negligent or intentional conduct, then he should not be responsible for the death of Professor Bunson. Although it is true that Sam resented Professor Bunson and wanted to get rid of him, he was not acting on those thoughts at the time he tripped on the steps. In other words, Sam's evil intent did not combine with a voluntary act to cause the death of Professor Bunson. In fact, Sam's trip on the staircase appears to be entirely accidental. Sam is therefore not considered morally blameworthy for the death of Professor Bunson.

Not surprisingly, the mental state is one of the most difficult elements of a crime to prove. This is because it requires an inquiry into a person's thought processes, which can be easily disguised or misrepresented. Of course, the most direct method for determining a defendant's mental state at the time of the offense is to simply ask the defendant. However, in most instances, unless making a confession, the defendant is unlikely to be the most reliable source. Additionally, defendants may elect to exercise their constitutional right to remain silent, thus barring the government from asking questions related to mental state or any other aspect of the crime. The primary method then for proving the defendant's mental state is by the use of *circumstantial evidence*. If the prosecutor can prove that the defendant engaged in certain voluntary actions at the time of the crime, then it may be inferred that the defendant intended the natural and probable consequences of those actions. For example, a person who spreads gasoline throughout a building and then sets fire to the building probably intends to burn the building. Circumstantial evidence permits us to draw inferences as to the defendant's mental state based upon solely that person's conduct at the time of the offense.

THE MODEL PENAL CODE'S FOUR MENTAL STATES

The Model Penal Code (MPC), which serves as a model for state criminal codes, has established four mental states for purposes of evaluating a defendant's behavior at the time of the criminal offense. According to the MPC, defendants may be convicted only if they acted purposely, knowingly, recklessly or negligently with respect to each material element of an offense. Material elements of an offense include *conduct elements*, *result elements* and *circumstance elements*. The following language from a typical vehicular homicide statute will illustrate these elements: "A person shall be convicted of vehicular homicide if he causes the death of another while operating a motor vehicle in an unlawful manner." To be liable under this statute, a defendant must engage in a certain type of conduct, under certain circumstances, and cause a certain result. If we break the statute down into its elements, the conduct element of the statute would be "operating a motor vehicle" because this language describes the particular conduct that the defendant must undertake. The circumstance element would be "in an unlawful manner" because it defines the specific circumstances necessary for conviction under this statute. Finally, the result element would be "causing the death of another" because it describes the specific result necessary for a criminal conviction.

The MPC requires that the government prove at least one of the MPC mental states with respect to each material element of the offense. If the government wanted to prove that the defendant acted "knowingly" under the vehicular homicide statute, it would have to prove that the defendant: "[knowingly] caused the death of another while [knowingly] operating a motor vehicle in a [knowingly] unlawful manner."

Since the language shown is a bit awkward, statutes are generally not written in this fashion. Instead, what is more likely to appear in a statute book is the following: "A person may be convicted of vehicular homicide if he knowingly causes the death of another while operating a motor vehicle in an unlawful manner." Although this version contains only one reference to the mental state (knowingly), it is understood that the MPC format requires proof of that mental state for each material element (i.e., conduct, circumstances and result) for a conviction. The next sections will separately examine each of the MPC mental states.

Purposely

Under the MPC, a defendant acts *purposely* if it is his "conscious object" to engage in certain conduct set forth in the statute (the conduct element) or cause a certain result set forth in the statute (the result element). Here, the term "conscious object" means to act intentionally with a specific target or goal in mind.

A defendant may also act purposely if he acts with awareness that certain circumstances exist as set forth in the statute (the circumstance element). To illustrate these concepts, assume the following:

While driving, Vic Vengeful sees his worst enemy, Hal, standing with a crowd of people. Vic is overcome by his feelings of hatred for Hal and decides to run Hal over while driving at a high rate of speed. To accomplish this, Vic steps on the accelerator, drives onto the sidewalk and directly into the crowd toward Hal. Upon impact, Hal is instantly killed and so are two other people who are standing next to Hal.

In this scenario, Vic could be charged with purposely causing the death of Hal because it was his "conscious object" to cause Hal's death by striking him with his car. In other words, Vic specifically intended to accomplish that objective (Hal's death) and intentionally engaged in conduct to accomplish that result.

What about the two bystanders who were killed? Could Vic be charged with purposely causing their deaths? Although Vic did, in fact, cause their deaths, it would be difficult to prove that he did so purposely since it was not his "conscious object" to cause their deaths. That is, he did not set out to cause their deaths, as his only intent was to kill his worst enemy, Hal. To assess Vic's conduct in relation to the deaths of the bystanders, let's explore the next MPC mental state, "knowingly."

Knowingly

Under the MPC, a person acts knowingly if he is aware that his conduct is of a particular nature or aware that it is practically certain that his conduct will cause a particular result. Returning to the circumstances of Vic driving into Hal and the bystanders, it is likely that Vic knowingly killed the bystanders because he knew Hal was standing in a crowd. Further, he had to know that by driving his vehicle into Hal at a high rate of speed while Hal was standing in close proximity to others, it was practically certain that others would be killed. So, while Vic did not intentionally set out to kill the bystanders, given the nature of his conduct and his knowledge concerning the likely consequences of his conduct, it is likely that he knowingly caused their deaths.

As a practical matter, the difference between purposely causing a death and knowingly causing a death is literally only a matter of degree. In the former instance, a defendant will likely be charged with first-degree murder, while the latter will probably yield a second-degree murder charge.

Recklessly

A person acts *recklessly* when he engages in conscious risk taking that causes a social harm. According to the MPC, the risk of harm or death must be "substantial and unjustifiable," and the defendant's choice to proceed in light of the risk must constitute a "gross deviation" from the standard of conduct that a law-abiding person would observe under the circumstances. To illustrate:

Sid Shooter's next-door neighbors constantly have loud parties in their home. On several occasions, Sid has angrily complained about the noise, but to no avail. One day, during a particularly loud party, Sid, in a fit of rage, decides to show his neighbors that he means business. Sid takes his rifle, walks into his neighbors' front yard and fires a single warning shot into the front window. At the time of the shot, although Sid hears noises coming from the house, he does not see anyone in front of the window and does not intend to harm or kill anyone. If one of the occupants of the home is killed by the shot, can Sid be charged with murder?

Under these circumstances, Sid acted recklessly because shooting into an occupied home gives rise to a substantial risk that the occupants might be harmed or killed. Additionally, there is rarely, if ever, any justification for a person to engage in this type of life-threatening conduct. Therefore, it is reasonable to conclude that Sid's conduct is far removed from the standard of conduct that a law-abiding person would observe under the circumstances. Because Sid chose to engage in this highly risky behavior despite the great potential for harm, his behavior manifested an *extreme reckless disregard* for the value of human life.

Negligently

Negligent conduct under the MPC is unintentional risk taking. Liability for negligent conduct is based upon the defendant's failure to perceive a substantial and unjustifiable risk that a reasonable person would have perceived under the circumstances. As in the context of reckless conduct, an initial determination must be made as to whether the risk is substantial and unjustifiable. If so, it must then be determined whether a reasonable person would have perceived the risk under the circumstances and presumably avoided liability by not engaging in the conduct. The defendant's conduct is thus compared to the reasonable person under the circumstances. Consider this example:

Terry Talker is using her portable cellular telephone while driving on the interstate. During the call, she unexpectedly drops the telephone and it falls to the floor of the vehicle near her feet. As Terry scrambles to find the telephone, she loses control of the vehicle, crosses the median, and strikes an oncoming vehicle, killing the driver of that vehicle.

In evaluating Terry's conduct, the failure to focus one's full attention on the road while driving on the interstate certainly creates a substantial and unjustifiable risk of injury to the driver and others on the road. But, we must further consider how a reasonable person would have behaved under similar circumstances. Given the nature of the risk in this case, it is perhaps fair to say that a reasonable person would have remained focused on the road or pulled over to the side of the road before attempting to retrieve the telephone. Therefore, Terry's failure to perceive the substantial and unjustifiable risk of injury rises to the level of *criminal negligence* insofar as it falls below the conduct of a reasonable person under the circumstances.

Non-MPC Mental States

In addition to the four recognized mental states in the MPC, two other terms that are carry-overs from the common law appear with some frequency in modern criminal codes. These terms are intentionally and willfully. *Intentionally* is typically equated with the MPC mental state of "purposely" because to act intentionally, a person must act with a specific goal or objective in mind. The term *willfully* has had numerous meanings throughout the common law and generally means to act with a bad or evil motive. In certain contexts (e.g., tax fraud), "willfully" has been defined more specifically to mean the "voluntary and intentional violation of a known legal duty." To secure a conviction under this standard, the government must prove that the defendant was aware of and understood a specific legal obligation and yet failed to comply with its requirements.

STRICT LIABILITY

Strict liability is a troublesome concept in criminal law because it allows for a criminal conviction without proof of the defendant's mental state. If one of the purposes of criminal law is to punish those who are morally blameworthy, then how can the law allow punishment without specific proof that the defendant acted in a morally blameworthy manner? One rationale for strict liability offenses is that they allow the government to regulate conduct in areas where the public interest in such regulation outweighs the need to prove that the defendant acted with bad motive or intent. In the aftermath of the Industrial Revolution, the government sought to regulate economic and social conditions through the creation of a special class of economic crimes. By criminalizing inappropriate or unsafe business practices, the government demonstrated its willingness to shoulder the burdens of economic expansion. What this meant was that rather than forcing consumers to bring private civil actions for damages suffered as a result of business misconduct, the government prosecuted the responsible parties. To maximize the deterrent effect of these economics-based criminal offenses, many statutes imposed a standard of strict liability. This meant that the government did not have to prove that the defendant acted with any bad intent or mental state. Instead, it was sufficient for purposes of a conviction simply to show that the defendant engaged in the prohibited conduct. To illustrate:

Food Company has a warehouse for storing food prior to shipment to its retail outlets. Upon inspection, it is determined that the food in the warehouse is being exposed to contamination by rodents and other unsanitary conditions. The CEO of Food Company is charged under a state criminal statute that makes it unlawful to "store or hold food under unsanitary conditions where it may become unsafe to use as food." The maximum penalty for this offense is the payment of a $500 fine.

Because the statute does not require that the defendant act with any bad intent or mental state, the CEO may be convicted if it is proven that, as CEO of Food Company, he was responsible for and had the power to prevent or correct the contamination violation. There is no requirement that he have prior knowledge of or have participated in the actual violation. He is liable because he is deemed to have engaged in the prohibited conduct by virtue of his responsible position as CEO.

To offset the potential harshness associated with finding criminal liability without a specific finding of bad motive or intent, strict liability crimes usually provide for less severe penalties than crimes requiring proof of a mental state. Thus, the penalty for strict liability offenses is usually limited to the payment of a fine.

Another fairly common example of a strict liability offense is speeding. After being stopped, many motorists attempt to explain why they did or did not intend to speed (e.g., late for an appointment, just following the flow of traffic) only to be met with a blank stare and usually a ticket from the officer. The reason for the blank stare and the ticket is that speeding is a strict liability offense. Therefore, as long as there is proof that the motorist engaged in the conduct of exceeding the speed limit, that is sufficient for a conviction. Why is speeding a strict liability offense? The answer is twofold and related, in part, to the historical rationale for strict liability offenses. First, if the government were required to prove through the trial process that every motorist stopped for speeding did, in fact, intend to speed, there would be a tremendous backlog of minor traffic cases in the court system. Second, and perhaps more important, the government has determined that it is in the best interest of the public health and safety to punish those who violate speed limit laws in the most efficient and effective manner possible. The need to protect society from speeders outweighs any potential benefits that might accrue to individuals by requiring the government to prove the mental state in each and every speeding case. Again, in this instance, eliminating the need to prove intent is offset by a penalty structure that is usually limited to the payment of fines.

CAUSATION

As explained before, in order to impose criminal liability there must be a finding that the defendant performed a voluntary act with the necessary mental state. However, consider the following:

Sally Shooter has recently been fired from her job and decides to get even with her boss. She purchases a gun and plans to kill her boss as he arrives for work early one morning. Sally strategically hides outside the building and sees her boss approaching from across the street. As Sally raises the gun and prepares to shoot, her boss sees her and begins running to avoid Sally's shot. Unfortunately, her boss runs into the path of an oncoming vehicle and is instantly killed. Sally is pleasantly surprised by this turn of events and walks away feeling that her boss "got what he deserved." Can Sally be convicted for murdering her boss?

This fact pattern illustrates the issue of *causation*. To impose criminal liability, it must be determined that, in addition to acting voluntarily with a bad mental state, the defendant both directly and legally caused the harmful result. In the case of Sally Shooter, she can be convicted of murder if she both directly and legally caused the death of her boss. This section will explore the meaning and interaction of direct and legal causes.

There can be many *direct causes* of a harmful result. One method for determining whether a particular factor is a direct cause is to ask the question, "But for the occurrence of this particular factor, would the harmful result have happened when it did and how it did?" If the answer to this question is "no," then we can identify that factor as a direct cause of the harmful result. This analysis is often referred to as the "but for" analysis of causation. Applying the "but for" analysis to Sally Shooter's situation, we can identify the following direct causes with respect to the death of Sally's boss.

a. But for Sally pointing her weapon at her boss and frightening him, would he have run abruptly into the street and been hit by a car? The answer is probably "no." Thus, Sally's act of pointing the gun at her boss is a direct cause of his death.

b. But for the fact that Sally's boss abruptly ran into the busy street when he did, would he have been hit by a vehicle at that time? Again, the answer is probably "no." Therefore, the boss's own act of running into the busy street is also a direct cause of his death.

c. But for the vehicle driver operating his vehicle at the time that Sally's boss ran into the street, would Sally's boss have been struck by the vehicle and killed? The answer is probably "no." The vehicle driver is therefore also a direct cause of Sally's boss's death.

Once the direct causes have been identified, the next step is to identify the legal cause or *proximate cause*. In criminal law, we identify the legal cause by asking, "Which of the factors identified as direct causes is morally blameworthy and therefore deserving of punishment for causing the harmful result?" In most instances, the answer to this question will determine who should face criminal prosecution. Again, referring to the facts of Sally Shooter, three direct causes have been identified. The question is now: Which direct cause is morally blameworthy for the boss's death? Let's examine each direct cause in turn.

a. Is Sally's conduct morally blameworthy? Sally hated her boss, planned to murder him and began to carry out her plan. It is likely that she would have succeeded if her boss hadn't spotted her and run into traffic. Thus, Sally's conduct set in motion a chain of events that resulted in her boss's death even though the death did not occur exactly as Sally had planned. Sally is morally blameworthy for placing her boss in a position such that he lost his life while trying to avoid her felonious conduct.

b. Is Sally's boss morally blameworthy for his own death? Obviously, the boss cannot be subject to criminal prosecution since he is dead. If we identify the boss as the morally blameworthy factor, then what we are really concluding is that his conduct was sufficiently blameworthy to supersede any of the other direct causes and relieve them of any blameworthiness. In this case, it might be reasonably expected that an individual confronted by another person pointing a deadly weapon would decide to flee in order to avoid harm. Unfortunately, Sally's boss fled into oncoming traffic. However, this miscalculation should not be sufficient to identify him as the morally blameworthy party so as to relieve the other direct cause(s) of criminal liability. In other words, the boss's conduct of running was a reasonable and foreseeable result of Sally's felonious conduct.

c. Is the driver of the vehicle morally blameworthy for the death of Sally's boss? While the circumstances are tragic, it is likely that the driver was genuinely surprised by the fact that Sally's boss abruptly ran into traffic. Almost certainly, the driver was not acting based upon any evil motive or intent and was probably unable to avoid the fatal collision. Thus, it would be extremely difficult to argue that the driver of the vehicle is somehow morally blameworthy for the death.

A careful examination of the three direct causes leads to the conclusion that Sally's intentional conduct began a sequence of events that led to the death of her boss, even though she had not planned for the death to occur as it did. Further, neither of the two remaining direct causes is of sufficient magnitude to relieve Sally of moral blameworthiness.

As illustrated above, the causation determination is a two-step analysis: (1) The direct cause(s) of the harmful result must be identified by asking the "but for" question. (2) Choosing from among the direct causes, the legal or proximate cause must be determined by asking who or what is morally blameworthy. When performing this analysis, two additional factors must also be considered.

First, a person may intend to cause harm in one manner and, in attempting to do so, may start a sequence of events that eventually causes harm, although not in the intended manner. Although this occurred in the example with Sally's boss, in some instances the resulting harm may be completely unexpected. For example, assume that when Sally's boss sees her pointing a weapon at him, instead of running to avoid Sally's shot, he decides to take his own life by ingesting a cyanide pill that he carries with him daily. The primary concern under these circumstances would be whether the unintended harm (the boss's death by cyanide poisoning) is so unexpected and so remote that it is morally unjust to hold Sally responsible for the unintended outcome. In other words, is the boss's intentional conduct in taking his life sufficiently unforeseeable that it supersedes Sally's intentional conduct and moral blameworthiness?

Second, occasionally a person may set out to cause harm to one victim but instead causes harm to an innocent bystander. Assume, for example, that Sally had aimed at her boss but missed, instead shooting and killing an innocent bystander. In this situation, Sally would nevertheless be criminally responsible for the resulting harm because she performed a voluntary act with the necessary mental state and caused a harmful result to the innocent bystander. Generally speaking, that is all that is required for criminal liability under most statutes. Thus, the fact that the wrong victim was harmed is irrelevant in terms of imposing criminal liability. This is sometimes referred to as the "transferred intent" doctrine because, for purposes of criminal prosecution, we can transfer Sally's intent to kill her boss to the innocent bystander.

SOCIAL HARM

The final essential ingredient for criminal responsibility is the identifiable *social harm.* The defendant's conduct must produce a specific unlawful result, that is, cause a death or other injury, a loss of property, and the like. It is referred to as a social harm because society, through its legal system, has determined that when conduct falls below a certain standard and produces a harmful result, every member of society shares that harm. Criminal cases are therefore entitled "People v. Smith" or "State v. Jones" in recognition of the fact that society must now redress the harm or other injury. The defendant's conduct in causing the harmful result must also be unjustified. Consider the following example:

Herb Homeowner is awakened in the middle of the night by the sound of breaking glass. Alarmed by this noise, Herb grabs his revolver, which he keeps at his bedside, and proceeds downstairs to investigate. As he approaches the kitchen, Herb is suddenly confronted by a gun-wielding intruder. The intruder points his weapon in Herb's direction as if preparing to shoot. Herb then raises his own weapon and shoots first, killing the intruder. Is Herb guilty of murder?

It is clear that Herb performed a voluntary act with at least the intent to harm the intruder. It is also clear that Herb's conduct caused the intruder's death. What is not so clear is whether Herb's conduct has produced an unjustified social harm. If society has determined that homeowners may protect themselves from violent intruders by using appropriate force, then Herb's conduct does not fall below any societal standards. Clearly the death of the intruder is a harm, but it is not the type of harm that society has chosen to redress. In fact, it is likely that society encourages Herb's behavior under the circumstances and would consider his conduct self-defense.

CASE STUDIES

Sleepwalking and the Voluntary Act

This chapter introduced a hypothetical that discussed criminal liability for violent acts committed while the defendant is in a sleepwalking state. Although such cases are quite rare, when they occur they spotlight the troublesome concept of what is meant by acting voluntarily for purposes of criminal law. Is it simply the ability to move one's arms and legs? Or is it the ability to move one's body with the conscious knowledge of one's conduct and its consequences? The first degree-murder case of Scott Falatar brings these issues into sharp focus.

On January 16, 1997, Scott Falater brutally stabbed his wife 44 times while she screamed for help. After the attack, he went in and out of the house a couple of times, put on a pair of gloves, dragged his wife into the backyard pool and held her head underwater to drown her. Alerted by the wife's screams, a neighbor watched in horror as Falater drowned his wife. When police arrived, Falater said that he had been asleep and had no knowledge of his wife's death. Additionally, he could offer no explanation for the blood and scratches on his body. In light of the physical evidence and the eyewitness, Falater was arrested and charged with first-degree murder. Falater now insists that he cannot remember killing his wife because he was in a sleepwalking state. This failure to remember forms the essential basis of Falater's affirmative defense to the charge of first-degree murder. That is, he does not deny killing his wife; he denies that he was acting consciously and voluntarily while doing so.

Demonstrating that Falater acted consciously and voluntarily will be a critical component of the prosecution's case. To prove his guilt beyond a reasonable doubt, the government must show that Falater was moving consciously and deliberately under his own control and not under the influence of third parties or other external forces. At trial, this proof will likely be supported by the testimony of the neighbor who saw Falater walking around and apparently acting deliberately as he drowned his wife. Furthermore, there is at least some evidence that Falater attempted to cover up his crime by hiding his clothes and the knife. At minimum, the effort to cover up the crime suggests that Falater had some awareness that his conduct was unlawful and sought to conceal his behavior and avoid the consequences that would follow if the crime were discovered.

With this kind of compelling evidence, the Falater case seems at first blush to be a prosecutor's dream, because there is unequivocal evidence that Falater directly caused his wife's death *and* there is direct eyewitness testimony. However, for purposes of the criminal law, mere actions are not enough, even when supported by direct eyewitness testimony. To satisfy the criminal law requirement of moral blameworthiness, there must be proof beyond a reasonable doubt that Falater was acting under his own conscious control.

From the defense perspective, to prevail on his sleepwalking defense, Falater will first have to overcome a tremendous amount of skepticism concerning the notion of sleepwalking. Many people regard sleepwalking as a joke and do not believe that people can perform complex activities such as walking, driving and/or talking without being in conscious control of their behavior. Thus, in order to refute the prosecution's proof that he was acting consciously and deliberately, Falater will have to convince jurors that it is truly possible to be completely unaware of one's conduct and yet move around as if fully conscious. Falater's defense will almost certainly be assisted by the testimony of a sleep disorder expert, who will attempt to explain the nature of sleepwalking and its effect on one's ability to act voluntarily. The role of the expert witness in this case will not be to tell jurors that Falater was in fact sleepwalking the night he killed his wife. That is a question the jury must resolve during the deliberation process. Instead, the expert's role is to serve as a resource for explaining the scientific evidence related to sleepwalking and how it might have affected Falater's behavior. In that regard, the expert will likely explain that a sleepwalking person is in a state between actual sleep and wakefulness and has basic physical control over his body, but not *conscious* control. Therefore, although the sleepwalker may appear to act purposely, the level of consciousness necessary for moral blameworthiness is missing. Again, this testimony will not prove that Falater was sleepwalking the night he killed his wife. It merely helps to explain the conduct of a sleepwalking person. The jury must draw its own conclusions as to whether this is what occurred on the night in question.

Although a few successful defenses to crimes have been presented using a sleepwalking defense, in those cases there has been a history of sleep disorders or sleepwalking exhibited by the defendant or his family members. These cases present compelling issues for purposes of examining one of the fundamental concepts of crime and punishment: the voluntary act. In the end, the jury considering the sleepwalking defense will have the extraordinarily difficult task of considering all of the evidence and attempting to draw the line between voluntary and involuntary behavior in a controversial area where the line between consciousness and unconsciousness is blurred.

Victimless Crimes and Social Harm

As explained in this chapter, another fundamental component of a criminal statute is that it must redress an identifiable social harm. The notion of social harm is based upon the common law belief that when a person's conduct falls below prescribed legal and moral standards, not only does the victim suffer, but society as a whole has also been harmed. The offender has breached the general agreement that citizens will conform their conduct to the moral dictates of the criminal law. Society, then, through the office of the government prosecutor, must express its legal and moral condemnation of the conduct and redress this harm by bringing the offender to justice. In most statutes, the social harm is quite clear. For example, with theft crimes, society suffers a harm when an offender interferes with an owner's private property interests without the owner's consent. Similarly, in sexual assault cases, the physical and emotional harm visited upon victims is a trauma that reverberates throughout society. In other statutes, however, the identifiable social harm is not so clear or is at least debatable.

In 1982, Michael Hardwick was arrested and charged with engaging in an act of sodomy with another male in the bedroom of Hardwick's home. At the time, Georgia's sodomy statute provided that the offense of sodomy occurs when a person submits to any sexual act involving the sex organs of one person and the mouth or anus of another. The potential punishment for this offense was not less than one and not more than 20 years in jail. Although the sodomy case against Hardwick was ultimately not prosecuted, he filed suit against the state challenging the constitutionality of Georgia's sodomy statute. Hardwick alleged, among other things, that there was no rational basis for such a law because there was no identifiable social harm other than the presumed belief of a majority of voters in Georgia that homosexuality is immoral and unacceptable. Hardwick's case was eventually presented to the U.S. Supreme Court.

In their opinion, a majority of the Supreme Court justices concluded that the Georgia legislative decision to outlaw sodomy is a moral choice. The Court reasoned that all statutes represent moral choices and the morality choices of the majority should not be invalidated by the Court simply because a few (such as Hardwick) disagree. Despite the fact that the language of the sodomy statute was clearly broad enough to encompass both heterosexual and homosexual conduct, the Court focused its opinion on the statute as applied to homosexual behavior. Specifically, the Court observed that recognizing a right to engage in homosexual sodomy would "cast aside millennia of moral teaching." Additionally, according to the Court, condemnation of such practices is "firmly rooted in the Judeo-Christian moral ethics and standards."

The question that continues to be debated in the aftermath of the Court's opinion is whether the historical moral foundation for the sodomy statute as articulated by the Court constitutes a sufficient social harm to criminalize the conduct. In the Hardwick case, the state of Georgia, in an effort to offer a more concrete statement of the social harm inflicted by sodomy, argued that the statute seeks to prevent conduct that could lead to such adverse consequences as spreading communicable diseases or fostering other criminal activity. However, the state's failure to prosecute Hardwick in this case and the fact that the state had not enforced the sodomy statute for at least a decade before the Hardwick case severely undercut this claim.

On the issue of enforcement, it is noteworthy that in states that do actively prosecute offenders under sodomy statutes, these prosecutions are, for the most part, brought in cases of homosexual conduct. This practice of selective prosecution seems to suggest that the social harm is not simply related to the acts outlined in the sodomy statute, but to the specific parties engaging in the conduct identified in the statute. More specifically, the social harm arises from a moral condemnation of the lifestyle choices of the parties who engage in the conduct. This conclusion does not end the inquiry, however, and raises again the question of whether this moral condemnation is an objective and identifiable social harm that requires criminalization of the conduct.

As the Court noted in the Hardwick case, laws represent moral choices. This statement is particularly accurate in the area of criminal law, where society, through the legislative process, expresses its moral outrage and exercises its authority to punish and stigmatize those who fall below certain moral standards. Because of the potential for severe and lasting effects upon those who are prosecuted, criminal laws should have objective and identifiable social harms beyond mere reference to the historical immorality of the conduct. After all, not every immoral act produces a social harm that must be criminalized. Thus, to characterize the social harm of sodomy in terms of morality is the equivalent of saying that sodomy is immoral because it is immoral. That is, we assume that criminal laws in general encompass conduct that is considered immoral. The requirement of an identifiable social harm tells us why it is immoral and what specific impact that immorality has on society in terms of social harm. Therefore, the social harm cannot and should not be a mere restatement that the conduct is immoral.

Of course, this is not to suggest that individuals cannot make personal moral assessments of certain conduct or that society cannot openly express its moral condemnation of certain behaviors or lifestyle choices. However, the point at which this assessment and expression becomes troublesome is when it takes the form of criminal laws that are general in nature but selectively enforced without objective and identifiable social harms. Perhaps the most revealing aspect of sodomy statutes is that most are rarely enforced against anyone. It is likely that this represents an implicit compromise between totally repealing such laws (which, some argue, would send the message that society condones the conduct) and actively enforcing them when there is no objective and identifiable social harm.

In November 1998, the Georgia Supreme Court struck down the sodomy statute under which Hardwick had been charged. In doing so, the court held that private, consensual sexual activity between adults deserves the utmost protection from governmental interference. Thus, the court for the first time recognized that consensual sexual activity between all adults deserves protection and that distinctions should not be made based upon whether sexual activity between certain adults is considered morally objectionable.

Causation and Expert Testimony

The element of causation is crucial in every criminal case because it is the critical link that ties the defendant directly to the unlawful conduct. The causal connection is even more important in homicide cases, when the stakes are usually quite high for the defendant. Once the prosecutor proves that a death occurred and that it occurred by wrongful conduct, then he or she must prove that the death and wrongful conduct are directly attributable to the defendant. Again, because of the gravity of the consequences for the defendant, this causal link must be clear and direct. Moreover, as explained in this chapter, the defendant's conduct must be of sufficient magnitude to overcome any other direct causes that might have resulted in the victim's death.

At common law, when medical science was not nearly as advanced as it is today, the "year-and-a-day" rule was developed to help determine criminal responsibility. This rule was an artificial mechanism for linking a wrongful death to the defendant's behavior. Pursuant to the year-and-a-day rule, a defendant could be charged with criminal homicide for the death of a victim only if the death occurred within a year and a day of the infliction of the fatal wound. If the death occurred beyond a year and a day, the defendant could not be prosecuted because there was too much uncertainty and the causal connection between the defendant's conduct and the death was deemed broken.

With the advances in medical science, the year-and-a-day rule has been abolished in most jurisdictions. This means that a defendant may be prosecuted for a victim's death without regard to the length of time between the defendant's conduct and the victim's demise. Of course, there must still be proof that the defendant's conduct caused the victim's death. As a practical matter, the more time that elapses between the wrongful conduct and the death, the greater the likelihood that the defendant can mount a strong defense to the causation element of the crime, even without the assistance of the year-and-a-day rule.

Causation can also play a pivotal role in cases when there has not been a significant amount of time between the defendant's conduct and the victim's death. For example, one of the key factors in the Louise Woodward case was who or what caused little Matthew Eappen's death. On February 4, 1997, Ms. Woodward made an emergency call to report that eight-month-old Matthew Eappen had been injured. At the time of the call, Woodward, a native of England, was alone with the child, caring for him at the home of her employers, Eappen's parents. When police arrived, the baby had a two-and-a-half-inch skull fracture, hemorrhaging and brain damage. Matthew Eappen died four days later. Because of the nature of the child's injuries and the fact that she was home alone with him at the time of the injuries, Woodward was initially charged with assault. These charges were elevated to first-degree murder when the baby died.

Since causation is a fundamental component of any criminal case, the prosecutor in the Woodward case had the burden of proving that there was a wrongful death and that Louise Woodward caused that death. In other words, the baby's death must be directly linked to her unlawful conduct. It is not enough for purposes of the criminal law to simply prove that the baby was left alone in her care and subsequently died. The causal link must be demonstrated beyond a reasonable doubt.

The prosecution's theory of the case revolved around the "shaken-baby syndrome." They sought to prove that while the child was in Woodward's care, he was violently shaken for a period of time while his head was being simultaneously struck against a blunt surface. The defense team on the other hand agreed that the baby died of severe head injuries. However, they further contended that the child died as a result of a three-week-old head injury that suddenly began to "rebleed" on the night of February 4th, thereby causing his death. This dispute centered on the critical issue of causation. Did Louise Woodward cause the baby's death by violently shaking him and striking his head against a surface? Or was the baby's death caused by an earlier injury (apparently inflicted by unknown persons) that erupted again the night of his death?

As is typical in cases of this nature, both sides presented expert medical testimony. The prosecution's case focused on the nature of shaken baby syndrome in attempting to demonstrate that Matthew's death was caused by violence. They presented testimony (and the autopsy showed) that there were no signs of a preexisting head injury. The prosecution also demonstrated that the severity of the head injuries on the night of Matthew's death precluded any extended period of lucidity during which he might have appeared normal for several weeks prior to a sudden death. In other words, after the infliction of an injury as severe as Matthew's, most children experience an immediate onset of symptoms such as lethargy, seizures and hemorrhaging.

In contrast, the defense argued that Matthew had suffered a mild skull fracture several weeks before his death. They further alleged that this fracture caused no noticeable symptoms in the child until a blood vessel burst several weeks later on the night of his death. The defense also highlighted the fact that the child did not have any obvious marks on his scalp or injuries to his neck or vertebra, which might indicate that he had been shaken or that his head had been struck. Notably, the defense did not offer any evidence as to how Matthew's alleged earlier injury might have occurred. However, it is important to understand that for purposes of the criminal law, they did not have to offer any such evidence.

In a criminal trial, the prosecution has the burden of proving each material element of the offense beyond a reasonable doubt. As discussed in this chapter, causation is considered a material element of the offense of murder (and practically every other criminal offense). The prosecution in the Woodward case chose to proceed on the theory that Louise Woodward caused Matthew's death on the night of February 4th, by inflicting a severe and fatal head injury. Therefore, their proof as to Woodward's conduct and causation was necessarily focused on the events of that night.

Because the defendant in a criminal case has no burden of proof, Woodward did not have to prove or disapprove anything. It is not uncommon, however, for criminal defendants to pursue a defense strategy designed to increase the likelihood of reasonable doubt in the minds of the jurors. The defense team's strategy in this case was to simply deny that Woodward caused the severe injury on the night of February 4th. In support of that theory, they argued that the child's death occurred as a result of an injury inflicted several weeks earlier. Again, they did not have to prove who inflicted the earlier injury, only that there was a preexisting injury that could have erupted to cause the child's death on February 4th. If the jury believed that the prior injury existed and could have caused Matthew's death, then that fact would cast strong doubt on the prosecution's theory that Woodward caused the death by violently shaking the child on the night of February 4th. Moreover, if the jury believed that the preexisting injury caused Matthew's death, then they were obligated to acquit Louise Woodward, *no matter how that prior injury occurred.* Again, the prosecution's theory in the case was that Louise Woodward caused the death on February 4th. They did not seek to establish that she caused an injury at any other time prior to the night of Matthew's death.

At the conclusion of the trial, the jury convicted Louise Woodward of second-degree murder, which indicated that they accepted the prosecution's theory that she inflicted the severe head injuries on the night of February 4th. Thus, it appears that after weighing the expert testimony in the case related to causation, the jurors were more inclined to believe the prosecution's version of what transpired in the Eappen household on the night of Matthew's death. Ten days after the verdict, in a surprising turn of events, the judge in this case reduced the jury's verdict to involuntary manslaughter and sentenced Louise Woodward to the time she had already served, 279 days in jail. This aspect of the case will be discussed in a case study in the next chapter.

FOR FURTHER CONSIDERATION

1. Would a person who commits a crime while under the influence of a hypnotic trance be considered a voluntary actor? What factors might influence the decision as to whether this is voluntary conduct?
2. As discussed in the chapter, the criminal law does not impose liability for failure to act unless there is a legal duty to act. Should there be exceptions to this rule? For example, should a man who calmly watches a toddler walk into a busy intersection and get struck by a vehicle be prosecuted for the child's death if he does nothing to save the child? Is the threat of criminal prosecution likely to compel action under these circumstances? Is this the best use of the criminal law, or are there other alternatives to address "callous indifference?"
3. One area of the criminal law in which it is a crime merely to communicate bad thoughts is threatening the President of the United States. A person may be prosecuted for such a threat without any showing that he performed a voluntary act in furtherance of those threats, and even if the defendant considered the threat a joke. Why does the criminal law include this exception? Is it because U.S. presidents are particularly sensitive individuals? What goals are promoted by such a criminal statute?
4. Do strict liability crimes that purport to protect the public health and safety, yet punish offenders with minimal fines, really have any deterrent effect? Consider again the CEO of Food Company in the section on strict liability. Is he likely to be deterred by the payment of a $500 fine? What about a $500,000 fine? Are there other penalties that are more likely to deter such conduct, such as jail or probation? Could the law impose such penalties for strict liability offenses?

5. How strong must the causal connection be between the defendant's conduct and the victim's death? For example, should a husband who brutally assaults his wife be responsible for her death if she commits suicide three years after the assault because of physical ailments and depression related to the assault? At what point can a wrongdoer be certain that his initial conduct will not be linked to the victim's death? Would it make a difference if the wife left a suicide note saying that her suicide was a *direct result* of her husband's brutal assault?

3

Unlawful Killings

Murder most foul, as in the best it is.

—Shakespeare

The term *homicide* encompasses every type of unlawful killing and is generally divided into two specific categories of criminal conduct: murder and manslaughter. These categories of criminal conduct will be explored in this chapter.

MURDER

At common law, murder was considered one of the most heinous offenses and, as such, was punishable by death. *Murder* is broadly defined as an "unlawful killing with malice aforethought." Historically, this meant that the unlawful killing was performed with an evil, wicked motive or intent or performed as a deliberate, cruel act without provocation. However, as the law gradually evolved, the term *malice aforethought* shifted away from its common law meaning and came to embrace four mental states that would transform an unlawful killing into murder. The four mental states are *intent to kill, intent to do serious bodily harm, extreme reckless disregard* and *felony murder*. Thus, an unlawful killing is performed with "malice aforethought" (often referred to as simply "malice" in most statutes) if the defendant causes a death while acting with one of these four mental states.

The following examples will help illustrate each of the four mental states that comprise "malice aforethought."

Intent to Kill

Vic Vengeful, after a bitter argument with Hal, becomes so enraged that he decides to kill Hal. After several weeks of planning the perfect crime, Vic purchases a revolver and a disguise. One day, as Hal is leaving his home, Vic confronts him and shoots him to death in his driveway.

In this example, it is clear that Vic caused Hal's death with the intent to kill. Vic wanted to kill Hal, planned to do so and acted in a manner that clearly indicated that he intended to cause Hal's death. Vic can be convicted of intentional murder.

Generally those who commit murder with intent to kill are considered very dangerous because they act with a conscious purpose to cause the death of another. Typically (although not always), a person who acts with the intent to kill also engages in *premeditation and deliberation*. What this means is that the person thinks about the idea of killing (premeditation) and also considers the consequences of committing the murder (deliberation). If, after this period of premeditation and deliberation, the person goes forward with the intent to kill, then first-degree murder has been committed according to the criminal statutes in most jurisdictions. Additionally, in those jurisdictions that have the death penalty, this defendant would be highly likely to receive such a punishment. The premeditated, deliberate murderer is usually subjected to the harshest punishment available under the law in the jurisdiction. The rationale for this is that a person who thinks about and considers the potential consequences of committing a murder prior to actually committing it is, in theory, the most dangerous type of criminal and therefore deserving of the most severe punishment available.

In cases of premeditated and deliberate murder, the government, in addition to proving the voluntary act and the mental state (intent to kill), must also prove that the defendant premeditated and deliberated. It is important to understand that premeditation and deliberation are not mental states for the crime of murder, but are instead aggravating factors surrounding the mental state of intent to kill. Premeditation and deliberation can take place over a short period of time (e.g., one or two minutes) or a longer period of time (e.g., one year). However, the closer in time these factors occur to the actual commission of the crime, the more difficult it becomes for the government to prove that the defendant actually had the time to think about committing the crime and to consider the consequences.

How does the prosecutor prove that the defendant engaged in premeditation and deliberation? Considering the example, when Vic purchases a weapon and a disguise prior to committing the crime, this can be considered *planning activity* for the commission of the crime. Planning activity prior to the crime is strong circumstantial evidence that the defendant is thinking about committing the crime and considering the consequences. Circumstantial evidence is evidence from which we may draw inferences as to the defendant's intent. Certainly, if prior to committing a murder the defendant purchases the means to commit the crime, then it is more likely than not that the defendant is thinking about committing the crime and also considering the consequences.

Other circumstantial evidence of premeditation and deliberation is the *manner in which the crime is committed.* In the example, Vic purchases a disguise and waits outside Hal's home to commit the murder. The manner in which the crime is committed in this example suggests that Vic stalked Hal, learned his schedule and waited for him to leave his home. Additionally, Vic took precautions to hide his identity to prevent witnesses from being able to identify him. These activities strongly suggest that Vic thought about the crime as well as the consequences of engaging in this criminal conduct.

Another indication of premeditation and deliberation is the nature of any *previous relationship between the defendant and the victim.* In the example, Vic and Hal had a bitter argument prior to the murder. Such evidence strongly suggests that Vic might be motivated to think about killing Hal and engage in conduct to carry out that plan. Thus, the government can build a circumstantial evidence case for premeditation and deliberation by showing any planning activity and focusing on the manner in which the crime was committed as well as on any prior relationship between the defendant and the victim.

A few words about *motive*: Although motive is not an element of any crime, most prosecutors will attempt to offer some proof of the defendant's motive or reason for committing the crime. Why would the government offer proof on an element that is not a required part of the criminal case? While the government does not have to offer such proof, the practical reality is that most juries want to know *why* the defendant acted as he or she did. It is perhaps basic human nature to want to believe that people do not commit horrible crimes without some reason for doing so. Therefore, if the government can provide some framework—the motive—then it becomes easier to put the other pieces of the puzzle together (i.e., voluntary act, mental state, causation and social harm).

Intent to Do Serious Bodily Harm

While driving, Vic sees his sworn enemy, Hal, crossing a busy intersection. At that moment, Vic decides to drive his car into Hal to disable and hospitalize Hal for a while and cause Hal to incur enormous hospital bills in the process. Vic drives his vehicle into Hal while going approximately 10 mph. Upon impact, Hal falls to the ground, strikes his head on a concrete curb and is killed instantly.

Although Vic did not intend to kill Hal, Vic's actions did, in fact, cause Hal's death. Vic acted with *intent to do serious bodily harm*, which set in motion a chain of events that led to Hal's death. In this instance, Vic is responsible for the ultimate consequences of his actions and is morally blameworthy for Hal's murder.

To be convicted of murder in instances when the defendant intends to do serious bodily harm, the defendant's conduct must be of a life-threatening nature such that death is a natural and foreseeable consequence of the defendant's conduct, even though he does not intend to kill. The rationale for classifying the defendant's conduct as murder is that a person who intentionally engages in life-threatening conduct should be morally blameworthy for the natural and foreseeable consequences of that conduct.

What are natural and foreseeable consequences? Generally, if the defendant's intentional life-threatening conduct could set into motion a chain of events that make it highly likely that a death will occur as a result of that conduct, then the death is considered natural and foreseeable. In the last example, Vic struck Hal with his vehicle with the intent to do serious bodily harm. Given the nature of the life threatening conduct (striking Hal's with a car), there was a very high likelihood that Hal injuries would be so severe that his death might result even though Vic did not intend that result. Therefore, Vic is morally blameworthy for Hal's death.

Extreme Reckless Disregard

A defendant can be charged with murder even though he did not intend to kill or do serious bodily harm to the victim. Instead, liability may be imposed if the defendant intentionally engages in conduct that creates an extremely high risk that death will occur. For example:

As target practice, Vic decides to shoot out a light bulb through the open window of an adjacent office building. Because it is a workday, Vic knows that the building is occupied, but he is fairly confident that his aim will be accurate. Vic shoots and hits the light bulb as planned. Unfortunately however, the bullet continues to travel, ricochets off a steel post and strikes an office worker, fatally injuring her.

Although Vic did not intend to kill or do serious bodily harm to anyone, his actions did, in fact, cause the death of the office worker. Because Vic knew that the office building was occupied and knew that shooting a deadly weapon into an area occupied by people could result in a serious injury, Vic consciously took a chance that someone might be injured or killed. Vic acted in an extremely reckless manner and with *extreme reckless disregard* for the value of human life. Vic is therefore responsible for the death of the office worker.

Murder committed while the defendant is acting with extreme reckless disregard for the value of human life is sometimes referred to as "universal malice" or "depraved heart" murder. These terms indicate that the defendant consciously engages in extremely risky, life-threatening conduct, although not intending to harm any particular person. To assess whether the defendant is engaging in conscious risk taking, it is important to determine what the defendant knows about the circumstances at the time of his conduct. In the example, Vic knew that the building was occupied because it was an office building on a workday. Vic also knew that shooting a weapon within close proximity to other human beings created a grave risk that someone might be injured or killed. Vic is therefore morally blameworthy for the natural and foreseeable consequences of his conscious risk-taking conduct.

Felony Murder

Although a person may not intend to kill or do serious bodily harm or engage in conscious risk taking, he may nevertheless be charged with murder if he intentionally causes a death during the course of and in furtherance of a felony. Consider the following example:

Vic decides to burn one of the office buildings he owns in order to collect the insurance proceeds. Vic plans to start the fire via a remote timer on a Sunday evening when the building is completely unoccupied. Vic burns the building as planned. The next morning, the police discover not only evidence of Vic's arson but also the body of a homeless man who had broken into the building to sleep for the night.

Although Vic did not intend to kill or seriously injure anyone and took precautions to make sure that the building would be unoccupied, Vic nevertheless caused the death of the homeless person. Furthermore, Vic caused the death during the course of committing the felony of arson. While the death was unintentional, the arson was not. Because the arson was committed intentionally, the law of felony murder allows this intent to be transferred to the unintentional death, thereby raising it to the level of murder. The rationale for transferring the felonious intent is that people will be deterred from engaging in life-endangering felonies if there is a strong likelihood that they will face murder charges should a death result from their felonious conduct.

The law of felony murder has undergone considerable change over the last two decades. Because felony murder imposes liability (often for first-degree murder) for a death that is caused *unintentionally,* there was a growing concern in many jurisdictions that, in some instances, the results of applying the felony murder doctrine were unduly harsh. The following examples will illustrate this point:

1. Rick Robber walks into State Bank and demands money from the teller. At the same time, an elderly woman pedestrian walking past State Bank peers into the bank through the glass doors and witnesses Rick pointing a gun at the teller. Suddenly realizing that the bank is being robbed, the elderly woman screams, clutches her chest and falls to the sidewalk. The woman later dies, and it is determined that she suffered a heart attack as a result of witnessing the bank robbery. Can Rick be charged with murder based upon a theory of felony murder?
2. Fred Fraud concocts a scheme to solicit donations on behalf of a nonexistent charity. To further his scheme, Fred drafts and prepares to mail letters to specifically targeted gullible individuals. As Fred is driving to the post office to mail the letters, a child darts out in front of his vehicle. Unfortunately, Fred is unable to brake in time and strikes and kills the child. Assuming that Fred's scheme to solicit donations through the mail is the felony of mail fraud, can Fred be charged with felony murder for the unintentional death of the child?

These two examples illustrate some of the inherent difficulties with the felony murder doctrine. In the first example, it is true that Rick was committing a felony (robbery). It is also true that an unintentional death occurred while the felony was being committed. However, should the felony murder doctrine be so broad as to encompass the unintentional (and perhaps unexpected) death of the elderly pedestrian who happened to walk past the bank at the precise moment of the robbery? Many jurisdictions, in an effort to narrow the boundaries of the felony murder doctrine, would conclude that

Rick is not responsible for the death of the elderly woman because it was not a natural and foreseeable result of his felonious conduct. In other words, the elderly woman's death was not the type of result that might be expected to follow from Rick's conduct and, therefore, he should not be morally blameworthy for her death. Thus, one limitation on the scope of the felony murder doctrine imposes liability only for those unintentional deaths that are natural and foreseeable consequences of the defendant's felonious conduct.

The second example presents a similar issue with respect to the potential scope of the felony murder doctrine. Once again, it is true that Fred was engaged in a felony (mail fraud). It is also true that the unintentional death of a child occurred. However, is this the type of felonious conduct that might be expected to result in a death? In other words, is the act of mailing fraudulent letters the kind of life-endangering felony from which an unintentional death might be expected to occur? Again, in an effort to narrow the scope of the felony murder doctrine, most courts would determine that Fred could not be charged with felony murder for the death of the child because he was not engaged in an inherently dangerous felony at the time of the death. Since his conduct was not life endangering, the death would not be considered a natural and foreseeable consequence of Fred's actions. In fact, from the example, it appears that the death was completely accidental and therefore Fred would not be morally blameworthy for the child's death.

MANSLAUGHTER

The crime of *manslaughter*, as distinguished from murder, involves causing the unlawful death of another without malice aforethought. This means that the defendant unlawfully caused a death but did not possess any of the four mental states required for malice aforethought. The two subcategories of manslaughter—voluntary and involuntary—will be discussed in the following sections.

VOLUNTARY MANSLAUGHTER

Historically, the crime of voluntary manslaughter was known as a "heat of passion" crime. The traditional example of a "heat of passion" killing involved a husband who arrived home early to discover his wife in a "compromising position" with another man and became so enraged that he killed one or both of them. The resulting crime(s) were considered manslaughter and not murder because the husband's "passions" were so inflamed by the circumstances that he acted in a morally blameworthy manner before he had sufficient time to cool off and consider the consequences of his actions.

Thus, although criminally responsible for the deaths, the husband who acted in the heat of passion was considered less blameworthy than someone whose actions derived from malice or "cold blood." This is because society recognizes that human beings have certain frailties that make it particularly difficult to act in a morally responsible manner under certain circumstances. In recognition of these frailties, the criminal law has established a compromise: A defendant whose actions result from "heat of passion" is criminally responsible for any resulting death. However, criminal liability will be based upon theories of voluntary manslaughter rather than murder, which means that the defendant, if convicted, will incur a less severe penalty.

When examining the facts surrounding cases of voluntary manslaughter, many of them closely resemble cases of intentional murder, that is, it looks as if the defendant intended to kill and acted upon that intent. For example, if we consider again the husband who discovers his wife in a "compromising position" and immediately decides to kill her, these circumstances closely resemble intentional murder since the husband clearly intends to kill his wife. What is it then that takes this conduct out of the realm of intentional murder and places it into the category of voluntary manslaughter? To be classified as voluntary manslaughter, the defendant must be "adequately provoked" and not have an opportunity to calm down prior to causing the death. Furthermore, the defendant's conduct must comport with that of a reasonable person under the circumstances. Thus, to determine if conduct meets the criteria for voluntary manslaughter, four questions must be considered:

1. Was the defendant provoked?
2. Would a reasonable person have been provoked under the circumstances?
3. Did the defendant actually "cool off" or calm down prior to the killing?
4. Would a reasonable person have cooled off under the circumstances?

If the defendant was not actually provoked or had, in fact, cooled off prior to causing the death, then there is no need to consider what a reasonable person would have done under the circumstances because the defendant himself does not meet the criteria for "heat of passion." However, if it is determined that the defendant was provoked and did not cool off prior to causing the death, then the conduct of the reasonable person under the circumstances must be considered. When applying the reasonable person standard, the judge or jury is asked to consider what would have constituted reasonable conduct given all of the surrounding circumstances.

Applying the four-step analysis to the husband in the example, if it is first determined that the husband was actually provoked by discovering his wife's infidelity, then the second consideration will be: Would a reasonable person who discovered his spouse under similar circumstances have been provoked? If a reasonable person would not have been provoked, then the defendant's conduct is considered unreasonable under the circumstances and the defendant will not meet the criteria for voluntary manslaughter. There is no need to consider the issue of "cooling off." However, if a reasonable person would have been provoked, then the defendant's conduct will be considered reasonable under the circumstances and we can proceed to the third step in the analysis and consider the issue of "cooling off."

If the defendant has actually cooled off prior to causing the death, then the crime is not voluntary manslaughter. A person acting with a "cool mind" has ample opportunity to consider the moral and legal consequences of his actions. However, if it is determined that the defendant has *not* actually cooled off prior to causing the death, then the final step in the analysis is whether a reasonable person would have cooled off under the circumstances. If a reasonable person would not have cooled off, then the defendant's conduct is considered reasonable and the defendant fully meets the requirements for voluntary manslaughter. If a reasonable person would have cooled off, however, then the defendant's conduct is considered unreasonable and falls outside the boundaries of voluntary manslaughter.

Adequate Provocation

Since one of the main criteria for determining whether a defendant meets the standard for voluntary manslaughter is whether there was adequate (reasonable) provocation, it is important to identify the types of circumstances that might constitute adequate provocation. The following list, while not exhaustive, provides some guidance as to the kinds of circumstances likely to be considered adequate provocation.

1. Discovering an unfaithful spouse in a "compromising position." While the common law right to claim "heat of passion" was limited to husbands discovering wives in such circumstances, today it applies equally to wives as well. Additionally, in some jurisdictions, "heat of passion" might be available for the discovery of unfaithful conduct in nonmarital relationships.
2. Witnessing violence against a third party, usually a relative.
3. Being the victim of an unprovoked and violent battery.

4. Hearing about certain conduct that would constitute adequate provocation if actually viewed. For example, if the defendant hears about the violent battery of his mother, this might constitute adequate provocation.

Two circumstances that typically do not rise to the level of adequate provocation are hearing mere words (no matter how obscene or derogatory) and witnessing damage to property. The rationale for excluding mere words as adequate provocation is twofold. First, allowing a person to exact "punishment" on another for uttering mere words could potentially interfere with the victim's constitutionally protected right to free speech. Second, it would be difficult, if not impossible, to determine exactly which words constitute adequate provocation in any given situation. While some words might be universally considered offensive, the meaning and impact of words change over time; even if a list could be compiled, it would have to be continually modified as society's understanding and acceptance of terms changed.

The rationale for not allowing damage to property to serve as adequate provocation for voluntary manslaughter is simply that human life is to be valued over and above material possessions, no matter how valuable and cherished. Additionally, there are other mechanisms in place, both criminal and civil, for addressing the violation of property rights.

Cooling Off

As previously explained, a person who has been adequately provoked must not have cooled off in order to fit the criteria for voluntary manslaughter. The term "cooling off" generally means that the person has had sufficient time to recover from the disturbance that ignited the passion. As it is difficult to determine what constitutes sufficient time to cool off, each situation must be evaluated on its own facts. When considering whether a defendant has cooled off, it is necessary to examine all of the surrounding circumstances that provide evidence of the defendant's mental state, as well as the amount of time that has elapsed since the incident that inflamed the passion. For example, did the defendant appear outwardly calm? Was he performing everyday activities in a seemingly normal fashion? Did he physically remove himself from the situation that inflamed the passion? Did he verbally indicate that he had calmed down? Were there any factors that could have reignited the passion? None of these factors, alone or in combination, provides conclusive evidence that the defendant has calmed down. In fact, the opposite could be true since many of the factors previously discussed could also indicate that the defendant is "simmering," waiting for an opportunity to act on his passions. Nonetheless, these factors do provide circumstantial evidence from which we can begin to draw reasonable inferences with respect to the defendant's mental state.

Voluntary Manslaughter and Causation

Causation is a particularly important issue in voluntary manslaughter cases because an unlawful killing may be reduced from murder to voluntary manslaughter if it is determined that the defendant's conduct was caused or provoked by certain behavior. The circumstances must therefore be carefully analyzed to establish whether the "provocation" actually *caused* the violent reaction by the defendant. The following example illustrates the application of causation in the context of voluntary manslaughter.

Tim Temper is angry with his business partner, Jack, and decides to kill him. After acquiring a weapon and planning the perfect crime, Tim drives over to Jack's house. On the way, Tim unexpectedly spots his wife and Jack in a passionate embrace in a remote coffeeshop. Shocked and angered by this apparent betrayal, Tim barges into the coffeeshop and kills Jack. Is this a case of voluntary manslaughter?

If we examine the factors necessary for voluntary manslaughter, there is clearly a question as to whether Tim's act of killing Jack was provoked by viewing the passionate embrace or whether viewing the embrace simply hastened the implementation of Tim's previous plan to murder Jack in cold blood. Although viewing one's spouse in a passionate embrace with one's business partner would likely constitute adequate provocation, there is a question as to whether it actually provoked or caused the murder in this instance.

Voluntary Manslaughter as a Defense

Because voluntary manslaughter allows conduct that closely resembles intentional murder to be reduced to a lesser offense based upon adequate provocation, it is often used as a defense to a charge of intentional murder. A defendant using voluntary manslaughter as a defense in a criminal trial essentially admits the wrongful act—the unlawful killing. However, the defendant argues that rather than being motivated by malice aforethought (the necessary element for murder), he was adequately provoked by the circumstances surrounding the crime, that is, he acted without malice aforethought. If, after examining the necessary requirements for adequate provocation and cooling off, the judge or jury believes this defense, then the defendant will be convicted of and punished for the lesser offense of voluntary manslaughter.

INVOLUNTARY MANSLAUGHTER

Involuntary manslaughter is an unintentional death that results from the commission of an unlawful act not amounting to a felony or from the commission of a lawful act in a criminally negligent fashion.

Unlawful Act Not Amounting to a Felony

One theory of involuntary manslaughter attributes moral blameworthiness to a defendant if a death results while the defendant is committing an unlawful act not amounting to a felony. The defendant's unlawful act typically violates a misdemeanor statute that is designed to protect human life. Consider the following example:

Barry Burner has just completed the annual task of raking dead leaves from his lawn. Instead of taking the time to place the leaves in bags this year, Barry decides to gather the leaves in a field adjacent to his home and quickly burn them. The field is within the city limits. There is a misdemeanor statute in the jurisdiction that prohibits burning within the city limits. Barry starts the fire and take precautions to contain it. Despite his precautions, an unexpected strong wind blows and the fire spreads through the field and to a nearby home (not Barry's). The home is quickly engulfed by the blaze, and the elderly owner of the home is trapped inside and dies as a result of smoke inhalation.

In this case, Barry's conduct violates a misdemeanor statute that prohibits setting fires within city limits. Because of the higher concentration of people and property within city limits, uncontrolled fires create a risk that injury or death will result. Therefore, it is likely that the legislature enacted the misdemeanor statute as a means to protect human life. Although Barry did not intend to cause a death, his violation of the statute did, in fact, cause a death. Barry is morally blameworthy for the natural and foreseeable consequences of his actions, although those consequences were not intended. Because liability is imposed upon a defendant for an unintentional death that results from engaging in unlawful conduct not amounting to a felony (misdemeanors), this category of involuntary manslaughter is considered analogous to felony murder. In fact, this form of involuntary manslaughter is sometimes called "misdemeanor manslaughter."

A Lawful Act Done in a Criminally Negligent Manner

A defendant may also be liable for an unintentional death caused while he is acting in a lawful, but criminally negligent, manner. To illustrate, let's change the facts of the Barry Burner example.

Barry Burner has just completed the annual task of raking dead leaves from his lawn. Because he is aware of the misdemeanor statute prohibiting burning within the city limits, Barry takes the leaves to a field outside of the city limits (although there are several farmhouses nearby). The day Barry chooses to burn the leaves is particularly windy, but since Barry needs to get the burning done as quickly as possible, he decides to go ahead with his plans. Barry also decides to use an accelerant to ensure that the fire burns rapidly. Due to the strong winds and the accelerant, the fire burns the leaves quickly and continues to spread uncontrollably. Unfortunately, it ultimately spreads to a remote farmhouse and causes the death of the occupant inside.

In this case, Barry has not violated any law by burning the leaves. However, Barry's conduct, while lawful, may be considered criminally negligent under the circumstances. It is likely that a reasonable person under the circumstances would not have burned the leaves on such a windy day and certainly would not have used an accelerant. Although Barry did not intend to cause a death, by engaging in such negligent conduct he manifested a wanton and reckless disregard for the value of human life and is responsible for the natural and foreseeable consequences of his actions.

Involuntary Manslaughter and Causation

In cases of involuntary manslaughter, the defendant's unlawful or negligent conduct must be the cause of the unintentional death. One area where this issue has become somewhat controversial is the context of driving while intoxicated. Assume the following set of facts:

Sandy Sipper is leaving her company's annual holiday party and is intoxicated. She nevertheless decides to drive home. Because Sandy realizes that she is intoxicated, she carefully controls her vehicle and observes all of the posted speed limits so as not to attract attention to herself. As she is driving through her neighborhood, a child suddenly darts into the street to retrieve a ball. Sandy is unable to stop her car in time and strikes the child, causing his death. It is later determined that, under the circumstances, no one (intoxicated or not) would have been able to avoid striking the child. Assuming that it is a misdemeanor violation to drive while intoxicated, is Sandy guilty of involuntary manslaughter for unintentionally causing a death while committing the unlawful act of driving while intoxicated?

One response to this question is "no," because although Sandy was driving while intoxicated, her act of driving in this condition did not cause the death of the child since no one would have been able to avoid striking the child under the circumstances. Because there is no *causal connection* between Sandy's violation of the misdemeanor statute and the unintentional death, Sandy is not guilty of involuntary manslaughter.

Another theory, however, would impose liability upon Sandy for any consequences that result from her decision to drive while intoxicated, whether those results are caused by her intoxication or not. Essentially, this is a theory of *strict liability*. Because driving while intoxicated creates such a grave risk that someone will be injured or killed, anyone who engages in such conduct will be responsible for any harmful results. This is a prime example of using the criminal law as a strong deterrent to protect against reckless conduct that poses a great risk to society as a whole.

CASE STUDIES

Murder and Assisted Suicide

As discussed earlier in this chapter, one of the mental states for the crime of murder is intent to kill. Additionally, if the intent to kill is accompanied by premeditation and deliberation, the crime is typically charged as first-degree murder, making the defendant eligible for the death penalty in many jurisdictions. In some instances, however, conduct that appears to fall within the parameters of premeditated and deliberate murder may, for a variety of reasons, be excluded.

In 1991, Marjorie Wantz and Sherry Miller were both suffering from medical conditions that resulted in debilitating pain. Although their illnesses were serious, neither woman was terminally ill. Nevertheless, both women sought the assistance of Dr. Jack Kevorkian to assist them in terminating their lives. Kevorkian, a retired pathologist, had become famous for attending and assisting in the suicides of numerous terminally ill individuals. In fact, Kevorkian had invented a machine specifically designed for the purpose of helping individuals commit suicide. The "suicide machine," as it was called, was connected to patients desiring to die by inserting needles into their veins and attaching strings to their fingers in order to enable them to control the flow of drugs into their systems. Under the patient's control, the machine would eventually release a deadly combination of barbiturates and potassium chloride. Both Wantz and Miller terminated their lives with the assistance of Dr. Kevorkian.

Dr. Kevorkian was subsequently charged with two counts of murder for the deaths of Wantz and Miller. For the crime of murder, a person must unlawfully cause the death of another with malice aforethought. As discussed in this chapter, malice aforethought is a term used to describe one of four mental states necessary for the crime of murder: intent to kill, intent to do serious bodily harm, extreme reckless disregard and felony murder. In addition to the mental state, the defendant must also cause the death, that is, the death must be a direct and natural result of the defendant's actions.

Although at common law it was considered murder to assist another with a suicide, modern statutes have rejected that analysis and define the crime of assisting suicide as a separate offense with lesser penalties than murder. In spite of this statutory distinction, there is nevertheless a fine line between causing the death of another for purposes of murder and assisting a person to complete the act of suicide. Typically, if a person merely provides the means to commit suicide, but does not actively participate, then the crime is classified as assisting suicide. *Active participation* may take the form of conduct ranging from prodding a person who is considering suicide to actively pulling the trigger at the request of the suicidal person. Again, however, if a person merely provides the means to complete the act and does nothing else, then that conduct is excluded from the murder statute. In light of the "active participation" criterion, drawing the fine distinction between murder and assisting suicide often results in a complex factual inquiry because the jury must assess the defendant's level of participation in the suicidal act. This is particularly difficult in cases like those involving Kevorkian because often the only witnesses to the act are the persons committing suicide (who are deceased at the time of the defendant's trial) and the person assisting the suicide, who is now on trial and likely to make self-serving representations.

For example, in the suicides of Miller and Wantz, it was determined that Kevorkian inserted the needle in Wantz's arm in order to release the chemicals into her bloodstream. He also placed a mask tightly around Miller's face when it was determined that she could not be properly connected to the suicide machine. Are these actions sufficient to constitute "active participation" by Kevorkian? Or was Kevorkian merely providing the means for Wantz and Miller to commit suicide? The court in the Kevorkian case determined that the murder statute did not encompass Kevorkian's conduct in these cases since he did no more than provide the physical means for Miller and Wantz to take their lives. Thus, he did not actively participate in causing their deaths. Since the state could not charge Kevorkian with murder in these cases, he was subsequently charged with the deaths under the state's common law ban on assisted suicide. During the trial, the state attempted to prove that Kevorkian provided the means for the two women to commit suicide with the intent that the means be used to commit suicide. Kevorkian's primary defense was that he only intended to relieve pain and suffering for the women and the deaths were an unfortunate "secondary result." After a jury trial, which Kevorkian attended sporadically, he was acquitted.

To date, Dr. Kevorkian has not been convicted for any of the suicides he has assisted despite being tried several times. Many believe that the most likely reason for the failure to convict Kevorkian under the assisted suicide statutes is juror sympathy. Often, in assisted suicide cases, the relatives of the deceased person testify that the decedent desired death and carefully planned and carried it out with the family's support. Moreover, there are usually videotapes of the deceased individuals taped prior to their deaths during which they express their wishes to terminate their lives because of their tremendous suffering. Against this backdrop, it is exceedingly difficult for jurors then to assign moral blameworthiness to the person who merely seems to have assisted these patients to end their lives with a degree of dignity.

Of course, the primary concern with the rationale and outcomes in these cases is the potential for future abuse. Critics of assisted suicide argue that vulnerable populations such as the elderly, the mentally ill or the poor might be attracted to such radical and extreme solutions in lieu of seeking other practical or therapeutic alternatives. Thus, the practice of assisted suicide could eventually be widely used by and against certain "undesirable" and "burdensome" populations. For this reason, opponents of assisted suicide contend that defining this conduct as murder and thereby increasing the potential for murder charges and convictions in these cases would necessarily enhance deterrence and prevent this potential abuse.

Murder and Voluntary Manslaughter

The distinguishing factor between murder and manslaughter is the concept of malice aforethought. Murder is an unlawful killing with malice aforethought, while manslaughter is defined as an unlawful killing without malice aforethought. As discussed earlier in the chapter, there are two species of manslaughter: voluntary and involuntary. Voluntary manslaughter involves intentional conduct and, in many instances, closely resembles the conduct necessary for intentional murder. That is, the defendant intentionally commits an unlawful killing. However, in cases of voluntary manslaughter, depending upon the factual circumstances, the defendant will not be guilty of the greater crime of murder because the criminal law recognizes that human beings may occasionally be driven to act "in the heat of passion." As explored in this chapter, these special circumstances are fairly limited and the defendant's conduct must be reasonable under the circumstances. Because of the fine line between intentional murder and voluntary manslaughter, juries deciding these cases are usually presented with difficult choices and some very novel defense theories.

On August 20, 1989, Lyle and Erik Menendez brutally shot their parents to death in the family's mansion in Beverly Hills. After their arrest, the brothers were charged with first-degree premeditated and deliberate murder. During the trial, the prosecution alleged and proved that the brothers carefully planned and carried out the murders of their parents. The plan included the creation and use of false identification to purchase guns two days prior to the killings. Although motive is not a necessary element of proof in a criminal case, the prosecution also established a motive to put the case in a rational framework for the jurors. The motive, according to the prosecution, was quite simple: greed. The brothers thought their parents were going to disinherit them and were desperate to maintain their upscale standard of living. To bolster their proof on the motive of greed, the prosecution showed that after the killings the brothers went on an extravagant spending spree and purchased, among other things, a $70,000 Porsche and $15,000 in jewelry and money clips.

In the face of compelling evidence of premeditated and deliberate first-degree murder, the Menendez brothers chose to present an affirmative defense during the trial. Thus, they did not deny killing their parents. They did, however, claim that the killings were justified. Specifically, the brothers claimed that the murders were committed in self-defense after they had been victimized by years of physical, emotional and sexual abuse by their parents. This affirmative defense called upon jurors to understand that, on the night of the killings, the brothers were in a state of extreme fear and killed their parents in order to prevent future harm to themselves.

At the conclusion of the trial, the judge ruled that based upon the facts, complete acquittal was not an option in the case. For acquittal to be an option, the brothers would have had to present a compelling case for self-defense. For example, if at the time of the killings, the brothers were acting reasonably to protect themselves from imminent deadly force by their parents, then they would have had a valid claim for self-defense. However, there was no evidence in the case to establish that at the time of the killings their parents presented even the slightest threat, much less a deadly threat. Therefore, the jury had four options to choose from for purposes of conviction: first-degree murder, second-degree murder, voluntary manslaughter, and, surprisingly, involuntary manslaughter.

In the first trial, the separate juries each deadlocked on the appropriate conviction. The brothers' affirmative defense had apparently hit the mark with some jurors, who were only prepared to convict on voluntary manslaughter. After a second trial, however, the Menendez brothers were both convicted of first-degree murder.

This case illustrates how the same factual circumstances can be subjected to vastly different interpretations. In this case, the prosecution presented the facts as premeditated, deliberate and cold-blooded murder. The defense, while not denying that the brothers killed their parents, described those same facts as a self-defense killing done to prevent further abuse. The distinction between these two versions had serious consequences in terms of the potential punishment. A conviction for first-degree murder would yield a penalty of fifteen years to life (or the death penalty in certain instances). In contrast, a voluntary manslaughter conviction would yield a maximum of three, six, or eleven years in prison, depending upon the circumstances. Given the vastly different penalties, it is obvious that defendants will have a strong incentive to persuade the jury that the circumstances warrant at most a conviction for voluntary manslaughter.

Not surprisingly, cases such as these ultimately turn upon credibility. Which version of the facts is more believable? Which witnesses are more credible? In the Menendez case, the prosecution's version of the events was bolstered by a confession the brothers made to their psychiatrist. In addition, the brothers' alleged fear that they had to defend themselves with the use of deadly force that night because they believed their parents were going to kill them was unsupported by any reliable evidence. In the end, the second jury in the Menendez cases likely concluded that the brothers' tales of abuse and fear were a cleverly crafted attempt to mitigate the punishment for a crime that was premeditated, deliberate and wholly unjustified. However, not all defenses raised in these kinds of cases are unsuccessful.

Two decades ago in San Francisco, former city supervisor Dan White climbed through a window in the San Francisco City Hall building, confronted Mayor George Moscone and killed him after firing several shots at pointblank range. After reloading his weapon, White then went down the hall to confront his political nemesis, Harvey Milk, and brutally murdered him as well. White's motive for the killings was his frustration at not being reinstated to his position as a San Francisco city supervisor, a position from which he had recently resigned.

White was charged with first-degree murder for both killings, and the cases seemed destined for a quick conviction on those charges, particularly since White had provided a confession shortly after the crimes. At trial, however, White offered one of the most unique defenses in the history of criminal law. His defense, now known as the "Twinkie defense," was that he acted while under the influence of excessive amounts of sugar, which combined with his depression and frustration over personal and professional problems and caused him to explode in a murderous rage. White claimed that prior to the murders he was consuming tremendous amounts of sugar every day, sometimes eating as many as five candy bars at one time. By raising this defense, White was offering an affirmative defense. In other words, he was not denying that he killed Mayor Moscone and Harvey Milk. Instead, he was asking to be convicted of a lesser offense—voluntary manslaughter—because of his sugar-induced diminished capacity at the time of the killings.

After considering all of the evidence, the jury convicted White of voluntary manslaughter, and he received the maximum sentence of approximately eight years in prison (of which he served only five). After the verdict, the city of San Francisco was in an uproar at what appeared to be a miscarriage of justice, given the overwhelming evidence of premeditation and deliberation in this case. One explanation that has been proffered for the jury's apparent acceptance of White's bizarre and unprecedented defense is related to the controversial political context of the case. One of the victims, Harvey Milk, was the first openly homosexual city supervisor in San Francisco's history. Prior to his death, Milk had successfully campaigned against and defeated an initiative that would have resulted in gay and lesbian teachers being fired from their positions in public schools because of their sexual orientation. Jurors in the White trial were undoubtedly aware of Harvey Milk's background and his controversial stances. Many observers suspect that the verdict in the White case was, in part, a backlash to this controversy. If that is the case, then this case is much more than an illustration of how voluntary manslaughter may successfully be used as an affirmative defense to a charge of first-degree murder. It is about politics, culture and bias, three unspoken factors that very likely influenced and bolstered the credibility of Dan White.

Murder and Involuntary Manslaughter

As discussed in the previous chapter, the jury in the Louise Woodward case concluded that she caused the death of Matthew Eappen and convicted her of second-degree murder. The prosecution charged first- and second-degree murder in the case and throughout the trial sought to prove that Woodward caused Matthew's death with intent to kill or with intent to inflict serious bodily harm. The defense argued very simply that Woodward did not cause the death and was not guilty of the crime of murder. In light of this denial, the defense chose to submit the case to the jury using an "all or nothing" strategy. That is, either the jury believed the prosecutor's version of the facts and convicted of first- or second-degree murder or they believed the defendant's version and voted for complete acquittal. This was considered risky because the defense chose not to have the jury consider lesser offenses such as voluntary or involuntary manslaughter. In many cases, these additional choices can provide options for a compromise verdict if jurors are split on particular issues surrounding the case. However, Woodward's defense strategy was not to present these additional choices to the jury and hope for complete exoneration based upon what they considered strong evidence that she did not cause the death.

The defense strategy failed, and Louise Woodward was convicted of second-degree murder and sentenced to life with the possibility of parole after fifteen years. It was clear from the verdict that the jury believed Woodward caused the death and chose one of the two verdict options available to them—second-degree murder. Shortly after the trial, in a post-sentencing hearing, the defense asked the judge to set aside the second-degree murder conviction because it was unsupported by the evidence. In addition, the defense urged the judge to replace the murder conviction with a manslaughter conviction despite the fact that the defense strategy throughout the trial had been focused on precluding that option from the jury's consideration. The defense conceded that they had made a tactical error and that Louise Woodward should be convicted of manslaughter since her behavior would fit "comfortably" within the definition of manslaughter.

Less than two weeks later, in a stunning reversal of the jury verdict, the judge reduced the second-degree murder conviction to involuntary manslaughter and sentenced Woodward to time served, a mere 279 days. The judge concluded that it was time for the case to reach a "compassionate conclusion" and released Woodward from jail. With the reduction to involuntary manslaughter, the judge essentially determined that, rather than acting with malice, Louise Woodward injured the child while acting out of "confusion, inexperience, frustration, immaturity, and some anger." In other words, Woodward may have behaved in a grossly negligent fashion that resulted in the child's death, but she did not act with the intent to kill or seriously injure the child. Importantly, the judge agreed with the jury's conclusion that Woodward did in fact cause the death of Matthew Eappen. That aspect of the jury's verdict was unchanged; Woodward is still criminally responsible for the death. However, what the judge's ruling did alter was the conclusion as to Woodward's mental state as she engaged in the conduct that caused the death. If her rough handling of the child was the result of confusion, frustration and some anger, then, according to the court, she could not have acted with the malice necessary for first- or second-degree murder. Instead, her conduct more appropriately fit the category of involuntary manslaughter, which is an unintentional death that results from grossly negligent conduct.

Interestingly, many observers of the trial agreed that Woodward's conduct on the night of Matthew's death probably fit the category of gross (criminal) negligence sufficient for an involuntary manslaughter conviction. Many also concluded that the second-degree murder conviction was a result of the jury's limited choices in terms of a verdict. Because of the defense team's "all or nothing" strategy, jurors were left with few alternatives once they concluded that Woodward did in fact cause the death of Matthew Eappen. What alarmed most observers, however, was the sentence that the judge imposed once the crime was reduced to involuntary manslaughter. Although a manslaughter conviction could have yielded anywhere from zero to 20 years, the judge chose to sentence Woodward to the approximately ten months she had already served in jail prior to and during the trial. Because Woodward was determined to be the cause of the child's death, many believed that a longer sentence should have been imposed to reflect the wrongful nature of her conduct. Accordingly, many observers identified this aspect of the case as the true miscarriage of justice. Nonetheless, the judge's decision was subsequently upheld, and Louise Woodward was free to return to her native England. The parents of Matthew Eappen have since filed a civil lawsuit against Woodward for the wrongful death of their son.

FOR FURTHER CONSIDERATION

1. It is often said that a person who premeditates and deliberates before carrying out a murder is the most dangerous type of criminal. But is the premeditated murderer more dangerous than, for example, a person who sees an elderly person crossing an intersection and, on a whim, decides to run over that person with his car? Which type of murderer is more likely to be deterred before committing the crime?
2. Why can't evidence of planning activity *after* the murder (such as leaving the country) be used to establish premeditation and deliberation?

3. Can or should a wife be prosecuted for first-degree premeditated and deliberate murder if she removes the life support from her terminally ill husband after agonizing over the decision for several days?
4. Felony murder is considered first-degree murder in most jurisdictions, particularly if the felony is one that is considered inherently dangerous. Is it fair to punish someone who unintentionally causes a death while committing a felony in the same manner as one who kills intentionally? If the rationale for felony murder is to deter dangerous felonies, are there other ways for the criminal law to accomplish this goal?
5. If certain words are universally considered offensive, why shouldn't these words serve as the basis for adequate provocation?

4

Sexual Assault and Related Offenses

It takes two to speak the truth—one to speak, and another to hear.
—Thoreau

Criminal *sexual assault* covers a broad range of *sexual conduct* that occurs by force and without the victim's consent. The unlawful sexual conduct can be divided into two categories:

1. Sexual intercourse, which is the most serious of the categories, includes nonconsensual vaginal and anal intercourse as well as oral-genital contact. For this offense, there is typically a requirement that some type of bodily penetration occur, no matter how slight. When these acts are combined with force and lack of consent, this conduct is commonly referred to as rape.
2. Sexual contact, a lesser offense, includes nonconsensual sexual touching of the victim in certain areas (e.g., genitals, breasts, thighs) for the purpose of sexual arousal or gratification. Unlike sexual intercourse, there is no requirement that any type of bodily penetration occur, and the touching may occur over or under the victim's clothing.

To be classified as criminal sexual assault, the sexual conduct must occur by force and without the consent of the victim. Because the issues of force and consent are often analyzed in the context of rape (as opposed to sexual contact), they will be explored in that context in this chapter. Additionally, as the following discussion demonstrates, the issues of force and consent are often interrelated in that if lack of consent is demonstrated, then it is likely that some type of force was used to accomplish the unlawful act.

FORCE

In rape cases, force can take the form of actual physical force, threat of force, or taking advantage of circumstances that render the victim helpless or somehow unprotected. A threat of force must usually be a threat of serious bodily injury and, therefore, does not include threats that involve the deprivation of property, such as loss of employment. Force may also include instances when the victim is in a helpless or unprotected state such that the rape can occur without actual or threatened force. To illustrate:

Sarah Sleeper has been unable to sleep for several nights. To alleviate her insomnia, she decides to take more than the prescribed dosage of her prescription sleeping pills and falls into a deep sleep. That night, an intruder breaks into Sarah's home with the intent to commit a rape. The intruder enters Sarah's bedroom and is surprised to discover that he does not have to use any type of force to commit the attack since Sarah never awakens from her deep sleep. Would this be considered rape?

Although the intruder did not use force or threaten force, he took advantage of the fact that Sarah was in a semiconscious state. In the criminal law, this is known as using *constructive* force. This means that although actual or threatened force was not used, the use of force will be implied under the circumstances to protect victims who are, for whatever reason, rendered helpless and unable to protect themselves. Thus, the intruder's conduct would be considered a "forcible" rape committed without the victim's consent.

Other situations that might render a victim helpless and unprotected include intoxication or drug-induced states (whether voluntary or involuntary), comatose states, sudden unconsciousness and, as discussed later, when victimized by fraudulent misrepresentations.

WITHOUT CONSENT

In addition to the element of force, the sexual conduct must occur without the consent of the victim. To determine whether there is lack of consent, the victim's conduct must be examined. Since the primary focus of criminal law is punishment of those who are morally blameworthy, criminal cases almost always examine the conduct of the *defendant* in order to assess criminal liability. Therefore, one obvious question that arises in rape cases is, Why is there such a concern with the victim's conduct? The answer to this question involves the nature of the underlying conduct. Because the underlying conduct, sexual intercourse, is lawful if engaged in by consenting adults, the question for purposes of criminal liability becomes: When does inherently lawful conduct cross the line to become unlawful conduct? Examining the element of force alone to answer this question would not yield an entirely reliable result because, theoretically, the parties could consent to the use of force in sexual conduct. Thus, we need to examine both force and whether there is a lack of consent in order to determine when lawful sexual conduct crosses the boundary and becomes rape or other unlawful sexual conduct.

Historically, lack of consent was measured by whether the victim resisted. Although at common law the victim was required to "resist to the utmost" (usually this meant physically resisting the attacker), today the law recognizes verbal resistance as well as circumstances when there may be a complete lack of resistance. This expanded definition of resistance acknowledges that victims of sexual assault should not be required to physically defend themselves in order to establish that a rape occurred, particularly when such physical resistance might result in greater harm to the victim. Consider the following:

Wendy Walker is out for her daily walk in a neighborhood park. Wendy is suddenly grabbed from behind, and her attacker, holding a knife to her throat, tells her not to make a sound or she will be killed. Wendy is terrified and afraid for her life. As a result, Wendy does not resist her attacker and is sexually assaulted. Since Wendy did not resist her attacker, does that mean that she consented to the assault?

Although Wendy did not resist the attack and therefore did not openly manifest her lack of consent, her behavior was motivated by a desire to save her life. If the failure to resist is caused by fear that resistance will cause greater physical harm or loss of life, then the victim is not required to resist in order to demonstrate lack of consent. In some instances, however, it might be necessary to demonstrate that the victim's fear was such that it would have caused a reasonable person to forego resistance. In this example, because the attacker displayed a deadly weapon and threatened serious bodily injury, it would certainly be considered reasonable for the victim to forego resistance.

Lack of consent may also be present if the victim's consent is induced by fraud. For example:

Polly Patient went to her doctor complaining of stomach pains. After a brief examination, Polly's doctor informs her that she has a rare stomach virus that can only be cured by a mix of medication and sexual intercourse with him. In fact, the doctor's statement is not true, and taking the medication alone can cure Polly's ailment. Because Polly trusts her doctor's advice, she begins to engage in a series of sexual encounters with him, believing that she will be cured. Can Polly's doctor be guilty of rape even though Polly has apparently consented to sexual intercourse?

While it appears that Polly consented to sexual intercourse with her doctor, her consent was induced by fraud. Polly was not given sufficiently complete and accurate information to make an informed and valid consent concerning her treatment plan and sexual intercourse with her doctor. Moreover, it appears that Polly's doctor took advantage of his position of trust and authority to fraudulently obtain Polly's consent. Under these circumstances, victims like Polly are perhaps particularly susceptible to fraudulent representations because of the preexisting relationship of trust they have established with the perpetrator of the fraud. However, should every instance of fraud operate to invalidate the victim's consent? Consider this example:

Frank Fraud works for a local used-car dealership. Frank decides to tell his single women customers that he can provide discounts on automobiles if they engage in sexual intercourse with him. (As it turns out, Frank has no authority to provide discounts to customers.) Several of Frank's women customers agree to his proposition, only to discover later that he cannot provide the discount. Has Frank raped these customers?

Frank's case is similar to that of Polly's doctor in the sense that they both used fraudulent statements to induce their victims to consent to sexual intercourse. However, the cases are arguably different because of the nature of the relationship used to perpetrate the fraud. If there is a relationship of trust and confidence between the parties, the victim is more likely to accept the representations as made in good faith. In contrast, if the relationship resembles more of an "agreement" between strangers such as the Frank Fraud discount, then it raises a question as to the victim's own gullibility and responsibility for the outcome of a failed agreement.

Finally, it should be noted that in instances when the victim is induced by fraud to consent to sexual intercourse, although it appears that no force is used, in fact the force is "constructive." As discussed earlier in this chapter, the criminal law will imply the use of force in situations when victims are rendered helpless or unable to protect themselves for whatever reason, even if that reason is based upon what turns out to be misplaced trust in a preexisting relationship.

DATE RAPE

One of the most conceptually difficult and controversial categories of sexual assault is date or acquaintance rape. In these instances, the parties either have a preexisting dating relationship or have recently become acquainted prior to the rape incident. This preexisting relationship or acquaintanceship adds yet another layer of complexity to the determination as to when consensual interaction crosses the boundary into illegal conduct. To illustrate:

Shelly Student and her friends go to Florida for spring break. While there, she and her friends attend many of the beach parties and meet lots of new people. Shelly notices Max at several of these parties and thinks he is very handsome. After introducing herself to Max and chatting for a while, Shelly agrees to accompany Max to his hotel room so they can become further acquainted without the distraction of loud music and other people. Once inside Max's hotel room, Shelly and Max consume several beers while relaxing on the couch. As they are talking, Shelly notices that Max is beginning to touch her and is making explicit sexual references to her body. Shelly then becomes noticeably uncomfortable, but she says nothing in hopes that Max will notice her discomfort and resume their friendly discussion. Instead, Max begins kissing Shelly and encouraging her to "loosen up." Shelly tries to pull away, but Max tightens his grip on her and assures her that everything is going to be fine if she just relaxes. The more Shelly pulls away, the tighter Max presses her down on the couch. Shelly begins crying and pleads with Max to stop, but to no avail. At this point, Shelly becomes afraid and no longer resists Max's efforts. Afterwards, Max thanks Shelly for a "good time" and asks if he can see her again the next night. Shelly says nothing and leaves the room calmly. For several weeks, Shelly does not mention the events of that night to anyone because she is ashamed and afraid of what people might think of her. Did Max rape Shelly?

One of the most troublesome evidentiary aspects of date/acquaintance rape cases is that the parties involved are highly likely to have diametrically opposed recollections of the events. For example, Max will likely recall the encounter with Shelly as a casual date. He will recall that Shelly introduced herself to him, willingly came to his hotel room and consumed alcohol. He will likely insist that Shelly "knew what was coming" since she agreed to come to his room. He will also probably acknowledge that while Shelly initially seemed a little "uptight," as things got going, she "relaxed and enjoyed it."

From Shelly's perspective, she will acknowledge that she willingly accompanied Max to his hotel room in order to talk and become further acquainted with him. She will also agree that they consumed alcohol while in the room. However, Shelly will recall that she became uncomfortable when Max began touching her and making explicit sexual references. She will also recall that her discomfort was noticeable, yet Max continued his aggressive conduct despite her obvious discomfort. She will recall that Max began using physical force to restrain her and refused to acknowledge her pleas to stop. She will then explain that she did not immediately report the incident because of shame and fear of what others might think of her; after all, she was drinking alone with him in his hotel room shortly after meeting him.

Since the victim and the defendant are often the only witnesses to the events surrounding the date/acquaintance rape, the judge or jury must sort out all of the factual evidence presented and ultimately assess the credibility of the two individuals involved. In the end, the verdict will depend upon who presents the most credible version of events, considering all of the factual circumstances. Although blaming the victim and/or forcing her to discuss her sexual history in open court can be a disturbing facet of any rape prosecution, it is particularly acute in cases of date/acquaintance rape. Because the prior relationship between the parties overshadows the issues of force and lack of consent, from an evidentiary perspective, it may appear that more force and more resistance are necessary to establish that consensual behavior has crossed the boundary into unlawful sexual conduct. Additionally, when refuting the evidence against him in a date/acquaintance rape case, the defendant may be able to introduce evidence of prior consensual sexual conduct with the victim. This will inevitably compel the victim to suffer the embarrassment associated with publicly revealing the intimate details of her sexual history with the defendant.

One practical consideration in these types of "close" cases when the evidence is sharply conflicting and the costs for the victim are unusually high is whether the criminal trial process is the most appropriate forum for resolving these issues. In other words, given the enormous potential for public humiliation of the victim and the uncertainty of the outcome at trial, would a private forum be more effective in terms of resolving the issues and reducing the victim's potential exposure to further victimization? This private option for resolution assumes that in some instances, particularly if the parties had a dating relationship, the victim may not desire a public criminal prosecution of the defendant and the public humiliation often associated with that process. Instead, she may simply want to confront the defendant, force him to admit his guilt and accept responsibility for his behavior. In this private setting, it may be possible for the victim to regain the sense of power and control that she lost as a result of the defendant's unlawful conduct. Moreover, knowledge that a private resolution option is available may encourage more victims of date/acquaintance rape to come forward because it removes the potential for further humiliation that undoubtedly deters many victims from reporting these offenses. Obviously, a private resolution of the issues should only be considered an option for the victim and should not be considered if the victim desires a resolution through the criminal trial process.

MARITAL RAPE

The issue of rape between spouses adds yet another layer of complexity to the topic of criminal sexual assault. Not only do the victim and defendant in a marital rape case have a preexisting relationship, but that relationship is sanctioned by the state, with an expectation that there will be consensual sex between the spouses. Given these expectations, it becomes even more difficult to determine when consensual sexual behavior crosses the boundary into unlawful conduct. This difficulty is further complicated by the fact that, traditionally, the government has been extremely reluctant to interfere unnecessarily with the privacy and sanctity of the marital relationship. Therefore, "misconduct" that occurs within the confines of the marital relationship is often resolved informally or, in more extreme cases, through the formal processes of domestic relations courts.

Nevertheless, sexual assault can and does occur within the marital relationship. To make the factual determination a little less difficult in these circumstances, marital or spousal rape statutes usually provide that there must be some evidence of force (e.g., physical injury to the victim) and/or evidence that the spouses have been living separate and apart for a specified period of time. Clearly, if there is evidence of physical injury to the victim, then that fact makes the issues of force and lack of consent easier to demonstrate. Physical injury associated with a sexual assault also strongly indicates that the marital relationship has reached a point where formal intervention in some form is necessary despite the government's traditional hands-off approach.

Similarly, requiring the spouses to have lived separate and apart for a specified period of time provides some evidence that the marital relationship has broken down and that the traditional expectations that accompany the relationship are no longer present. In other words, living separate and apart is an indication that the parties may have withdrawn the consent to sexual relations that is implicit in the marital relationship.

One unique feature of marital rape statutes is the penalty structure. Because of the government's overriding concern with preserving the marital/family relationship if at all possible, penalties in marital rape cases sometimes allow for counseling (both family and individual) in lieu of criminal prosecution if the victim and defendant consent to this form of "punishment." If the defendant/spouse completes the counseling requirements, then the criminal charges are dismissed. Of course, these statutes also provide for traditional criminal prosecution if the victim and/or defendant refuse to consent to the counseling program or if the defendant fails to successfully complete the program requirements.

STATUTORY RAPE

Historically, *statutory rape* laws were enacted to protect the chastity and morality of young women. These statutes made it a crime for a man to have sexual intercourse with a young woman under a certain age (usually eighteen), even if the young woman consented to the act. (Today, of course, statutory rape provisions protect minors of both genders.) Further, it did not matter whether the man actually believed that the young woman was above the specified age of consent, because statutory rape was/is a strict liability offense. This means that as long as the sexual conduct occurred between the victim and the defendant, the defendant could be convicted of statutory rape without regard to his mistaken belief. To illustrate:

Craig Clubber approaches an attractive young woman at a nightclub one evening and begins a conversation. When the conversation turns to the topic of age, the young woman tells Craig that she is nineteen, and Craig believes her based upon her physical appearance and the fact that the nightclub has a strict policy of not admitting anyone under the age of eighteen. As the conversation progresses, Craig invites the woman back to his apartment and she agrees to accompany him. Once inside the apartment, the two have consensual sex. One week later, Craig discovers to his shock and dismay that the young woman is actually a fifteen-year-old high school student and that he is being charged with statutory rape. Can Craig argue that he honestly believed the young woman was nineteen? Can Craig also argue that the young woman completely consented to intercourse even though she was only fifteen?

In most jurisdictions in the United States, Craig would not be able to argue that he was deceived or reasonably believed that the young woman was nineteen. This argument would fail because the law of statutory rape is not concerned with Craig's mental state or his beliefs. Since statutory rape provisions are intended to promote the broader social policy of protecting the chastity and morality of minors, the law is only concerned that the sexual conduct occurred. The protection of minors under these circumstances is deemed to outweigh any protections that might accrue to the defendant by permitting an inquiry into the defendant's mental state or beliefs at the time of the act. Furthermore, even if the young woman consents to the sexual conduct, the law does not recognize her consent as valid since it is presumed that she is not of sufficient age to understand the consequences of entering into a sexual relationship. Therefore, if it is determined that Craig had sexual intercourse with the fifteen-year-old woman, then he can be convicted of statutory rape without regard to whether the woman consented and/or whether Craig honestly believed she was nineteen.

In a small number of jurisdictions, however, Craig would be able to argue that he reasonably believed the young woman was nineteen. The judge or jury would then be required to examine all of the circumstances surrounding the sexual conduct to determine if it was in fact reasonable for Craig to have such a belief. For example, the trier of fact would consider how the young woman was dressed and behaved, what she told Craig concerning her age, and the fact that she was in a nightclub that had a strict policy against admitting anyone under the age of eighteen. After examining all of these factors, the trier of fact would then determine if it was reasonable under the circumstances for Craig to believe that the young woman was nineteen. If his belief was reasonable, then Craig would not be guilty of statutory rape, even though the young woman was only fifteen.

One rationale for permitting a defendant to present an argument based upon his reasonable belief concerning the victim's age is simply that times have changed. Young people are becoming sexually aware and sexually active at earlier ages. Moreover, modern trends in fashion and makeup often make it difficult to determine the exact age of many young people based solely upon outward physical appearance. Therefore, in some instances today, it is much easier for an unsuspecting male or female to be deceived by a young woman's or man's behavior and outward physical appearance. To relieve the potential for unfairness in these situations, a defendant charged with statutory rape will be allowed to present arguments as to what he or she reasonably believed based upon the facts presented to him or her at the time of the sexual conduct. Again, however, few jurisdictions allow arguments based upon the defendant's reasonable belief, and most continue to adhere to a strict liability standard, which promotes the broader social policy of protecting minors. Defendants in these cases will therefore shoulder the burden and suffer the consequences of their mistaken beliefs.

It should also be noted that, in addition to statutory rape provisions, many sexual assault statutes contain provisions that proscribe sexual conduct between specific categories of individuals. The categories generally encompass relationships wherein an adult is entrusted with the care, custody or control of a minor or is in a position of trust or authority vis-à-vis the minor. Such relationships would include, for example, teacher/student, foster parent/child, and babysitter/child relationships. Like statutory rape provisions, these statutes are usually strict liability in nature because they are designed to protect minors from the abuse of trust and manipulation that can result if sexual conduct is introduced into these relationships, even if the minor consents.

RAPE SHIELD STATUTES

In an effort to prevent some of the embarrassment and humiliation to victims that can result from the criminal trial process in rape cases, almost every jurisdiction has enacted a rape shield statute. Rape shield statutes generally prohibit the introduction of evidence related to the victim's past sexual behavior unless that evidence fits within one of the very limited exception categories. Overall, rape shield statutes have been successful in keeping the focus of rape trials on the defendant's conduct rather than the victim's sexual history and reputation.

One of the limited exceptions in rape shield statutes that permits the introduction of evidence related to the victim's sexual history arises when the proposed evidence is relevant and is offered as an alternative explanation for the physical evidence in the case. For example, the defendant may seek to offer evidence that the victim engaged in sexual intercourse with another person during the relevant time period of the alleged sexual assault in order to offer an alternative explanation for the presence of semen collected from the victim. Evidence of the victim's sexual history may also be offered to establish prior, recent consensual sexual encounters between the defendant and the victim. Finally, evidence of the victim's sexual history may be offered to demonstrate that the victim might have a motive to fabricate a rape charge against the defendant. For instance, if the defendant claims that the victim is making a false allegation of rape because the defendant terminated their dating relationship, then the defendant may be permitted to offer evidence that the victim has previously made false allegations of rape after the termination of other dating relationships. Because most of the evidence related to the victim's sexual history is of a highly sensitive nature, the judge will review it in a private hearing to determine whether it is relevant and whether it complies with the provisions of the rape shield statute *before* it will be admitted in open court.

SEX OFFENDER LEGISLATION

One of the more recently controversial areas of crime and punishment involves the treatment of repeat sex offenders. Repeat sex offenders are those who have committed several sex-related offenses and, by their conduct, indicate an inability to control deviant sexual impulses. Many of these repeat sex offenders specifically target and commit offenses against minors and are generally categorized as pedophiles. In an attempt to combat the problem of repeat sex offenses, particularly those that target children, many states have enacted criminal and civil legislation designed to remove these offenders from society at the earliest possible moment and for the longest possible time. Despite the effectiveness of this legislation, however, some of the statutes have met with constitutional challenges because they fail to provide appropriate procedural and substantive protections to those suspected or convicted of committing sex offenses. For example, several states have passed sexual predator laws that allow convicted sex offenders to be civilly committed to an institution *after* they have served their term of imprisonment. Those challenging such legislation argue that a period of civil commitment following the prison sentence inflicts an additional, unwarranted and potentially limitless punishment on a defendant who has already served the statutory penalty for his crime.

While state legislatures have been busy enacting statutes to address the grave concern of removing these offenders from society, a more complex constitutional issue has developed regarding repeat sex offenders who are released into society after serving a term of punishment for their offenses. Controversial legislation, popularly known as "Megan's law," seeks to protect society from the likelihood that sex offenders will commit further crimes upon their release from prison. These laws typically require convicted sex offenders to periodically register with local law enforcement for a specified number of years after their release. Additionally, in some jurisdictions, law enforcement may be permitted to release the names and addresses of convicted sex offenders to the communities where they reside upon release from prison. The primary rationale for this legislation is that sex offenders, who have a very high rate of recidivism, will be deterred from committing further offenses if they are carefully monitored by law enforcement and, in some instances, the community at large. Nevertheless, the registration requirement and the release of this information to the community have raised a number of constitutional and practical concerns.

On the constitutional front, there is a concern that release of the offender's personal information to the community infringes upon the fundamental privacy interests of convicted sex offenders, who have properly served time for their offenses and should not be made to suffer the further indignity of having society continually reminded of their past criminal behavior. A further constitutional concern is that the periodic registration requirement and monitoring by law enforcement imposes an additional punishment and stigma above and beyond the statutory punishment designated for the offense. Finally, the potential for vigilante justice is a realistic practical concern as communities are made aware of released sex offenders in their midst and may be tempted to take the law into their own hands on the slightest suspicion. In light of these concerns, the need for sex offender legislation to protect society from harms inflicted by repeat sex offenders must inevitably be balanced against the legitimate privacy interests of convicted offenders who have served time for criminal conduct and ultimately seek to return to society.

CASE STUDIES

Victims, Defendants and Date Rape

Rape is one of the most controversial and widely debated topics in the criminal law. As such, it presents some of the most complex issues of proof in the context of a criminal trial. During a rape trial, the prosecutor must prove beyond a reasonable doubt that the defendant engaged in sexual intercourse with the victim by force and without the victim's consent. In some cases, the defendant denies that the sexual conduct ever occurred. The prosecutor will usually respond to this denial by presenting DNA evidence or other physical evidence linking the defendant to the victim. In other cases however, the defendant will admit that sexual intercourse occurred but will argue that it occurred without force and with the consent of the victim. This type of defense automatically shifts the focus of the factual inquiry to the victim's conduct at the time of the offense. Thus, the crime of rape is unusual in the sense that it is one of the few crimes that requires some proof of the victim's conduct during the commission of the crime as a necessary component of establishing the defendant's guilt.

In some instances, an examination of the victim's conduct can take the form of merely inquiring into what occurred during the incident in question. But, in other cases, the factual examination could result in a wide-ranging exploration of the victim's past sexual history as the defendant attempts to establish that the victim consented to sexual intercourse during the incident in question. This intensely personal focus on the victim's conduct and sexual history often creates an atmosphere in which it appears that the victim is on trial rather than the defendant. As discussed in this chapter, rape shield statutes can help prevent broad-based and irrelevant attacks on the victim's credibility and limit the possibility that the victim will be further humiliated and victimized by the criminal trial process. However, rape shield statutes cannot protect victims from all inquiries and revelations concerning their sexual histories. Thus, the defendant who is arguing that the victim consented to sexual intercourse is entitled to present relevant evidence to support the defense. Such evidence, often presented through the defendant's own testimony, almost always directly contradicts the victim's explanation of what occurred during the incident in question. Therefore, the typical rape trial becomes a question of credibility. Who is more credible—the victim or the defendant? Which version of events is more believable? This contest of credibility becomes even more acute in date or acquaintance rape cases, when there is a preexisting relationship or friendship between the parties. That is, from a credibility standpoint, it becomes even more difficult to draw the line between when the preexisting consensual relationship ended and the nonconsensual sexual assault began.

Only two people know what happened on the lawn of the Kennedy compound in Palm Beach, Florida, on March 30, 1991, and they had two completely different accounts of the evening. Earlier that evening, after talking and dancing with William Kennedy Smith for a couple of hours at a Palm Beach nightspot, Patty Bowman agreed to give Smith a ride home when he told her that he didn't have transportation. Once at the Kennedy home, Smith and Bowman kissed and took a walk on the beach. Bowman then says that Smith asked her if she wanted to swim and she declined the invitation. She then recalls that Smith removed his clothes, tackled her, pinned her down, cursed at her and raped her despite her frantic struggles and screams. Smith, on the other hand, denied that an assault occurred and said that the two had consensual sex on the beach after a night of partying together at the nightclub. After a police investigation, Smith was charged with sexual battery (rape) and battery.

The pretrial and trial proceedings in the Smith case highlighted several controversial issues related to rape cases in general and date/acquaintance rape cases in particular. For example, one of the first issues debated prior to the trial was the release and publication of the victim's name. In Florida, it is a crime to publish or broadcast the names of rape victims. Yet, numerous print and broadcast media repeatedly identified Patty Bowman as the victim in the Smith case, each arguing that her name was already widely known from a supermarket tabloid publication. The practice of giving anonymity to rape victims is based in part on the fact that the crime of rape is a uniquely personal and humiliating offense that often leaves victims feeling ashamed, utterly powerless and afraid that they will be blamed for what happened to them. In fact, the sense of shame and fear may be so intense that many rape victims would rather let the crime go unreported than face the potentially intrusive questioning and stigma associated with being a victim of rape. Therefore, to alleviate the sense of shame and powerlessness and to give victims some sense of control over who has access to this highly personal information, rape victims names are kept confidential. Additionally, if any portion of the trial is televised, the victim's visual image is not displayed. In the Smith case, after several media outlets discovered Bowman's name and reported it, Patty Bowman commented that she might not have come forward and reported the incident if she had known her name would be released to the media.

There is, however, another side to the issue of maintaining the confidentiality of victims' names in rape cases. Those who support the release of victims' names contend that keeping the names secret helps to perpetuate the stereotype that rape victims are somehow to blame and that their reputations may be permanently damaged simply by bringing accusations of rape. Accordingly, release of the names would send the message that rape victims are just like other crime victims and help to alleviate some of the stereotyping and stigma associated with rape prosecutions.

A second and equally controversial issue concerning witness testimony also developed prior to trial in the Smith case. Before the trial, at least three other women came forward and alleged that William Kennedy Smith had raped or assaulted them in the past. Because date rape cases are so difficult to prove and hinge almost entirely on issues of credibility, this type of evidence would undoubtedly have added some measure of credibility to the prosecution's case because it could tend to show that the defendant had a particular method of operation when committing these offenses. However, in Florida (and most jurisdictions), evidence of the defendant's prior bad acts is not admissible unless the acts bear a striking similarity to the conduct in the crime currently being prosecuted. This rule protects defendants from being convicted and punished simply because the trier of fact believes they are bad people with a history of bad conduct. In the Smith case, although there were some similarities in the three women's stories (e.g., being overpowered and assaulted by Smith), the alleged attacks took place under markedly different circumstances than the encounter with Bowman. Thus, the judge ruled that the evidence of prior bad acts was inadmissible. This meant that Bowman's testimony would essentially stand alone against Smith's in the contest of credibility.

Prior to trial, not only was Bowman's identity revealed, but it was also reported that she was a 30-year-old single parent with a history of late-night partying and drug use. In contrast, the defendant, William Kennedy Smith, was a Georgetown medical student and scion of the politically powerful Kennedy family. During the trial, Bowman's testimonial account of the events of March 30 was described as emotional and somewhat convincing. Her recall of the events, however, was hampered by numerous memory lapses that quite possibly damaged her credibility with jurors. In sharp contrast, Smith's testimony was crisp and consistent, never varying from his assertion that he and Bowman engaged in consensual sex despite a sometimes blistering cross-examination by the prosecutor in the case. In the end, it took the jury 77 minutes to acquit Smith of the charges.

In these types of cases, the question that inevitably arises is what more, if anything, could have been done to aid the prosecutor's case in this battle of credibility? Because the victim apparently lost some ground because of her inability to recall certain events during her testimony, perhaps the testimony of a rape trauma expert might have helped jurors to understand the traumatic circumstances surrounding rape, which might have helped explain Bowman's apparent memory lapses. It is important to understand that the testimony of rape trauma experts does not establish that the rape occurred, but merely helps to explain how and why the behavior of rape victims might vary from what might otherwise be expected. For example, some rape victims might wait for several weeks before reporting the assault. A rape trauma expert could explain that such conduct might indicate that the victim was in a state of shock as a result of the trauma of the event. Again, this does not mean that a rape occurred, only that it could have occurred even though the victim did not report it for several weeks. The jury must ultimately determine what occurred based upon all of the evidence and testimony.

Another factor that might have lent some credibility to the victim's testimony in this case was the testimony of other assault victims. The need for corroboration has long been a troublesome issue in the context of rape because it suggests that a victim's testimony is simply not enough on its own and that there must be some other evidence to support it. Although corroboration in rape cases was a formal evidentiary requirement in many jurisdictions, it has since been removed, at least as a formal requirement. The fact remains, however, that rape victims still face an uphill battle at trial, particularly in date rape cases when the victim may have engaged in certain consensual conduct that might be considered a "prelude" to sex. In these instances, it is not uncommon to hear statements such as, "What was she doing there at that time anyway?" or "What else did she expect when she accompanied him to his home after knowing him for such a short time?" While such questions may reflect a crude attempt to blame the victim for what occurred, they may also reflect a genuine attempt to balance the defendant's culpability with concerns about the victim's personal responsibility—a uniquely difficult task for uniquely defined criminal conduct.

Rape and the Marriage "Penalty"

As discussed in this chapter, marital rape cases are among the most difficult to prove in criminal law. Because of the marital status of the parties and the presumption of consent to sexual relations, the material elements of force and lack of consent are exceedingly difficult to demonstrate. Essentially, the prosecutor must prove that the spouse alleging rape manifested a clear intent to revoke the consent to sexual relations that is inherent in the marital relationship. This evidence may be demonstrated by the fact that the parties have lived separate and apart for a period of time or that there was actual physical force involved. The trial of John Wayne Bobbitt illustrates the issue of marital sexual assault in one of the most factually bizarre cases in the history of criminal law.

The Bobbitt case, like so many other rape cases, involved two sharply contrasting versions of what occurred on the night in question. According to John's wife, Lorena, John Bobbitt liked forced sex; on the night of June 23rd he pushed her, ripped off her clothes and forced her to have sex. After the assault, in a state of extreme anger, Lorena severed her husband's penis and left home with it, ultimately throwing it out of her car window into a field. Based upon the extraordinary events of that evening, Lorena was charged with malicious wounding, and John was charged with marital sexual assault, which is a slightly different crime than marital rape. At the time, the Virginia marital rape statute required that the spouses live separate and apart or that the victim show serious physical injury. Since the Bobbitts were still living together and Lorena showed no signs of serious physical injury, John could not be charged with marital rape. He was instead charged with the lesser offense of marital sexual assault, which carried a maximum penalty of 20 years in prison (marital rape carried a maximum penalty of life in prison).

The Bobbitt case, although quite unique in some respects, was typical in the sense that the resolution of the issues came down to a question of credibility. Who presented the most believable version of the events of the night in question? The prosecution argued that Lorena had suffered a history of being emotionally and sexually abused by her husband throughout the marriage, which culminated in her defensive attack on him on the night of June 23rd. On the witness stand, however, John Bobbitt denied raping his wife at any time in their marriage, and specifically on the night of June 23rd. His defense attorney argued instead that Lorena was a jealous, frustrated wife, who struck out in anger at her husband that evening.

After four hours of deliberation, the jurors acquitted John Bobbitt of marital sexual assault. Although convictions are extremely difficult in marital rape cases, the prosecution's work was probably made more difficult in the Bobbitt case by the inconsistencies in Lorena's story concerning what occurred and why she acted as she did on the night of June 23rd. Moreover, despite the fact that there are statutes that criminalize sexual assault in the marital context, many people are still of the opinion that rape simply cannot occur within the confines of the marital relationship. That is, once consent has been given in the marital relationship, that consent is valid for all purposes and under all circumstances. Also implicit in this belief is the notion that spouses should not air their marital "dirty laundry" in public, and certainly not in a criminal trial.

Prosecution and conviction in marital rape cases may also be hindered by the government's traditional reluctance to get involved in the marital relationship, at least with respect to bringing criminal charges against spouses for conduct that occurs during the marriage. When domestic problems arise, states typically prefer to channel these disputes to domestic relations courts, which will seek to preserve the marital relationship if it all possible, particularly if children are involved. Against the historical backdrop of the government's hands-off attitude in the area of marital privacy, marital rape statutes represent something of a compromise in the sense that states now have statutory weapons to intervene and bring criminal charges to protect spouses when rape occurs in the marital relationship. However, to lessen the impact of the criminal trial process, the penalty structure in some marital rape statutes allows for less severe sentences, and some even provide that the defendant may undergo counseling as part of the "punishment," with an eye toward reconciliation of the marital relationship. Sadly, in many cases, when the marriage has reached a point where the state must intervene to bring criminal charges for rape, the likelihood of a lasting reconciliation may be dim. Given this reality, in some states there has been a call for harsher penalties for marital rape, in recognition of the fact that this unlawful conduct is no different than other kinds of violent sexual assaults and should be punished accordingly.

The Bobbitt case illustrated the prosecution of a marital sexual assault case in a most unusual factual setting. Despite its bizarre facts, however, it helped to place the national spotlight on the need for legal protection within the marital relationship. The case also raised the public's conscious about the complexities associated with the prosecution of sexual assault laws in the context of the marital relationship.

Relevant Evidence, Defendant's Rights and Rape Shield Statutes

To combat the potential for further humiliation and trauma to victims in rape prosecutions, many states have enacted rape shield statutes. These laws are designed to exclude evidence of the victim's past sexual history unless that evidence fits within one of a few carefully crafted exceptions. Line-drawing difficulties arise, however, when attempting to determine whether certain evidence offered by the defendant falls within one of those exceptions. Depending upon where the lines are drawn, the defendant may be effectively precluded from presenting evidence in his defense.

Sportscaster Marv Albert was charged with forcible sodomy and assault in connection with an incident in which he was alleged to have repeatedly bitten the victim and forced her to perform oral sex in a hotel. As part of his defense, Albert sought to present evidence that the victim had a history of mental problems and that she had engaged in threatening behavior when a previous relationship with another individual ended. The judge in the Albert case decided that much of this defense evidence was inadmissible under Virginia rules of evidence and the Virginia rape shield statute. According to the court, none of the evidence of prior bad conduct by the victim was relevant and, if admitted, would serve to unfairly taint the victim's reputation and credibility. In other words, the defense could offer no credible basis to demonstrate that the victim's previous behavior with other people in unrelated circumstances was in any way linked to the conduct that occurred on the night of the alleged forcible assault by Albert.

The Albert ruling, based in part upon the rape shield statute, was one example of the dramatic impact of rape shield statutes on modern rape trials. Prior to the enactment of rape shield statutes, juries could actually consider the victim's character for immoral behavior as a strike against her credibility in a rape prosecution. Rape shield statutes were enacted to serve as a gatekeeping mechanism to prevent the introduction of testimony that merely tended to show that the victim may have committed bad acts in the past. Again, under rape shield statutes, defendants must demonstrate that the evidence offered is *relevant and somehow linked to the case being prosecuted.*

Faced with the exclusion of his defense evidence and confronted with mounting evidence of his own tawdry sexual history, Albert pleaded guilty to a misdemeanor assault charge. After his plea, questions immediately arose as to whether the application of the rape shield statute in this case prevented Albert from adequately presenting a defense to the charges against him as guaranteed by the Sixth Amendment to the Constitution. This question squarely raises the issue of whether the concern for protecting victims of sexual assault has resulted in a criminal justice system that has gone overboard and begun to sacrifice the defendant's constitutional rights. Since most rape shield statutes are written to allow for the introduction of very limited and relevant evidence, courts have interpreted the statutes very narrowly. The statutes are an attempt to strike a balance between the defendant's rights and the victim's privacy by allowing the introduction of relevant evidence relating to the victim's sexual history. While the defendant has a constitutional right to present evidence in his defense, that right is not absolute. The defendant's task in a sexual assault trial then is to clear the hurdle of establishing the relevancy of the evidence to the issues at trial, rather than simply seeking to introduce evidence that the victim was a bad person. Although this standard presents some difficult line-drawing decisions, it represents the best effort to protect the defendant's right to a fair trial while simultaneously protecting the victim's right to privacy.

Abuse of Power and Statutory Rape

As explained in this chapter, certain sexual conduct between adults and minors is classified as statutory rape without regard to the defendant's belief as to the victim's age and/or whether the victim consents to the conduct. Historically, statutory rape laws were enacted to protect the chastity of young women, although today the statutes are applied equally to protect young men. Despite the modern gender-neutral interpretation and application of statutory rape laws, the historical purpose behind the statutes and their gender-specific application continues to influence both public opinion and judicial outcomes in certain cases. The case of Mary Kay Letourneau illustrates the perils and gender-specific issues surrounding such relationships, particularly when they occur between teacher and student and when the victim is a young man.

Although married at the time, Mary Kay Letourneau, a teacher, began a sexual relationship with a thirteen-year-old student. The relationship included sending passionate notes to the child and culminated with her giving birth to the student's child. After her arrest and prosecution for statutory rape, the judge sentenced her to six months in jail and three years of sex offender treatment. As part of her probation, Letourneau was strictly prohibited from contacting the young man. Shortly after her release from jail, however, Letourneau was discovered in the company of the young man again and was sent back to prison to complete a seven-and-a half-year-sentence. (At the time of her incarceration, it was also discovered that Letourneau was pregnant with another child, apparently also fathered by the student.) Throughout this ordeal, the boy claimed that he was not a victim, but a willing participant in a consensual sexual relationship with his teacher. Of course, the law of statutory rape does not acknowledge his willing participation, and because of his age he is deemed incapable of consenting or willingly participating in such a relationship.

One of the fundamental issues raised by this case is the potential for abuse of power and trust in teacher/student relationships. In these relationships, teachers are often powerful authority figures and/or mentors in students' lives. Students, on the other hand, who are taught to respect and obey teachers as authority figures, are typically very trusting, dependent and quite vulnerable in the context of teacher/student interaction. Given this inherent imbalance of power, problems arise when teachers cross the boundary and take advantage of students' trust and vulnerability for purposes of their own sexual gratification. Such conduct violates the teacher/student relationship in ways that can have long-lasting and devastating effects on the students involved, even when the students believe they are willingly participating in these relationships. The reality is that while some students claim to be willing participants, most young people in these situations feel simultaneously flattered and confused by the attention from a trusted teacher, without realizing that they are involved in an abusive situation. Moreover, in some instances, even when the student/victim comes to the realization that something is wrong, he or she may feel ashamed and blameworthy for the conduct and may not fully comprehend the abusive and manipulative nature of the circumstances for many years. Statutory rape laws exist for the express purpose of protecting minors who cannot mentally or emotionally act as willing participants in such sexual relationships. Additionally, because certain adult/minor relationships may be particularly susceptible to this type of unlawful conduct, many statutes carve out special categories that specifically address sexual abuse in relationships of trust and authority.

Despite the fact that the statutory rape laws are now gender neutral and no longer designed solely to protect young women, the tendency to view the statutes as primarily protecting women prevails. The Mary Kay Letourneau case highlighted the lingering effects of gender bias in statutory rape crimes. After her conviction, Letourneau was sentenced to community-based treatment and six months in jail because the judge in her case concluded that Letourneau would benefit from such a sentencing alternative. Of course, the gender-related question that arises from Letourneau's punishment is whether a man who had been convicted of the statutory rape of a thirteen-year-old girl would have been given a similar sentencing alternative. Because the scenario of male as perpetrator and female as victim fits neatly within the historical rationale for the statute, the punishment would probably have been more severe. When a young man is the victim of an adult woman, however, there is a tendency to view the conduct not as a crime, but as the fulfillment of a young boy's sexual fantasy. In other words, the crime of statutory rape is viewed as an initiation into male adulthood, rather than as a felony offense. This perception may then have an impact on the criminal trial and punishment of the female perpetrator. Realistically, of course, the crime of statutory rape exploits children (male or female) who are ill-prepared to engage in sexual relationships with adults. The harm to children is no less significant simply because the perpetrator is female. Thus, the prosecution and punishment of this crime must reflect that the conduct is serious sexual abuse and demonstrate that the law will be enforced to protect all children without regard to gender.

FOR FURTHER CONSIDERATION

1. Consider the case of a rape victim who is afraid of becoming pregnant or contracting a sexually transmitted disease and begs her attacker to put on a condom before the assault. Would she be deemed to have consented to the assault? Why or why not?
2. Do you think victims of date/acquaintance rape would prefer to resolve these issues in a private setting to avoid the harshness of a criminal prosecution? What motivates victims to come forward in these cases? What are the costs and benefits of a criminal prosecution to the victim? Identify some ways to resolve these issues that might minimize the costs to victims while still accommodating the desire for a just result.
3. Should more jurisdictions permit defendants charged with statutory rape to offer evidence as to their reasonable beliefs concerning the victim's age? Does public policy now favor such a change despite the historical rationale for statutory rape provisions?

4. Would statutory rape include a situation when the defendant has consensual sexual intercourse with a 21-year-old female who, because of a mental handicap, has the mental age of a twelve-year-old?
5. Does a community have a "right to know" if a convicted sex offender is living in their midst? If so, why? Would the same reasoning apply if the individual were a convicted burglar or arsonist?

5

Preparatory Criminal Conduct

Crime like virtue has its degrees.

—Racine

To provide efficient and effective law enforcement and ensure the safety of citizens, police officers must be able to detect and prevent criminal activity at the earliest possible moment. Criminal conduct is rarely a spur-of-the-moment idea. Often, those who engage in criminal activity have contemplated and planned their actions to varying degrees. During the planning stage, those considering criminal activity may also encourage others to join them or provide some other form of assistance. Although it is not a crime to have "bad thoughts" or merely discuss criminal activity with others, when conduct goes beyond mere thoughts or discussion, under certain circumstances it may rise to the level of punishable criminal conduct. This chapter will explore the preparatory stages of criminal activity and examine when preparation to commit a crime becomes a crime itself.

SOLICITATION OF A CRIME

Occasionally, individuals planning criminal activity do not intend to personally commit the unlawful act. Instead, they intend to solicit and encourage others to carry out the criminal conduct. A person who solicits, urges or encourages another to commit an unlawful act has gone beyond the stage of simply having bad thoughts and into the realm of acting upon those thoughts. The act of soliciting another to commit a crime, although still part of the preparatory or planning stage of criminal activity, rises to the level of criminal conduct. To illustrate:

Debbie Dim decides to have her husband killed so that she can use his life insurance proceeds to travel around the world. Debbie knows that it would be "too obvious" if she committed the crime herself, so she seeks the services of a hit man recommended by one of her friends. Although Debbie doesn't know it, the "hit man" is really an undercover police officer. Debbie arranges a meeting with the assassin, who (unknown to Debbie) is wearing a recording device to tape their entire conversation. During the conversation, Debbie reveals her desire to have her husband murdered within the next week and offers the assassin $5,000 plus a percentage of the expected life insurance proceeds once the job is done. The assassin takes the money and tells Debbie that he will get back to her. Is Debbie guilty of a crime?

Although Debbie did not personally plan to murder her husband, she intended that his murder take place and took affirmative steps to solicit a third party to carry out the criminal conduct. Considering all of the surrounding circumstances, it is reasonable to conclude that Debbie has gone beyond merely thinking or wishing that her husband were dead and has engaged in specific conduct that provides concrete evidence of the seriousness of her intent. Debbie would therefore be guilty of soliciting the murder of her husband.

Two questions that often arise in the area of criminal solicitation are: Why does the criminal law punish individuals for soliciting others to commit crimes? Isn't solicitation really just another form of expressing "bad thoughts," which is not punishable under the criminal law? The rationale for punishing the crime of solicitation is threefold. First, as in the example, if there is evidence of intent and sufficient conduct in furtherance of that intent, then those who solicit others to engage in criminal conduct have exhibited a level of dangerousness sufficient to pose a genuine threat to society. Second, if one of the goals of criminal law is deterrence, then punishment of those who solicit others to commit crimes as soon as they have reached a level of dangerousness sufficient to society will deter others from planning, preparing or soliciting others to engage in criminal conduct. Lastly, law-abiding citizens should not have to fear being subjected to the continual solicitations and urgings of those who would like to engage in criminal conduct.

As a prerequisite for the crime of solicitation, the person being solicited (the "solicitee") must understand that she or he is being asked to engage in criminal conduct and ultimately refuse to go along with the plan. Typically, the solicitee is the only witness to the transaction; if she or he does not interpret the request of the solicitor as an urging to engage in criminal conduct, then there is little chance that the solicitor's conduct will be reported to authorities. Similarly, the solicitee must ultimately refuse to engage in the criminal conduct because, again, there is little chance that the solicitee will report the conduct to authorities if he accepts the solicitation and agrees to carry out the plan. In fact, if there is an agreement by the solicitee to carry out the criminal conduct, then the crime is no longer solicitation and becomes instead the crime of conspiracy (addressed in the next section).

Since it is not a crime to have bad thoughts or merely to discuss those thoughts with others, one difficulty associated with the crime of solicitation is proving the solicitor's intent to encourage another person to engage in criminal conduct. Consider the following example:

Sam and Eric meet regularly for drinks on Friday evenings. One Friday, Sam confides to Eric that he and his wife are having serious marital difficulties. Sam then says aloud that he would pay a large sum of money to anyone who would make his wife "disappear." Sam emphasizes his statement by repeating it several times while looking very seriously at Eric. Although Eric does not say anything in response to Sam's statements at the time, Sam's serious demeanor nevertheless frightens him. The next day, Eric reports his concerns to the police and tells them that he suspects Sam is trying to get someone to murder his (Sam's) wife. When the police arrive at Sam's home that day, they find Sam and his family enjoying a backyard barbecue. The police question Sam about his statements to Eric, and Sam is shocked that Eric even took the statements seriously. Sam acknowledges that while he may have been angry with his wife when he made the statements, he would never consider killing her or anyone else. Is Sam guilty of solicitation based upon his conversation with Eric?

This example illustrates the problem of defining the point at which bad thoughts become serious enough to hold a person criminally responsible for those thoughts. In this example, Sam was having bad thoughts concerning his wife, which he conveyed to his friend Eric. Again, it is not a crime to have bad thoughts or even to speak about those thoughts with others. The rationale for this is that even though people may have bad thoughts and even discuss those thoughts, there is always the possibility that they simply may not be serious enough to act upon the thoughts. If, however, there is some evidence of acting on bad thoughts, then those actions provide some indication of the intent to actually move forward with the criminal conduct. In the case of Sam and Eric, there is insufficient evidence of Sam's desire to act upon his thoughts. He did nothing but make the statements several times, which may not be enough evidence of his intent to carry out any crime against his wife.

The difficulty of drawing the definitional line between a person who is merely expressing bad thoughts and one who actually intends to have another commit a crime has led many states to impose a statutory requirement that there be some corroborating evidence of criminal intent in cases of solicitation. This means that when considering all of the surrounding circumstances, there must be clear and convincing evidence of the solicitor's criminal intent. In the case of Sam and Eric, corroborating evidence of intent might be present if, for example, Sam had specifically asked Eric to commit the offense or to assist in identifying someone to commit the offense. Perhaps even stronger corroborating evidence of intent would be present if, at the time of the statements, Sam had given Eric a weapon or money to assist in committing the criminal offense. Each of these additional factors would provide circumstantial evidence of some action beyond mere bad thoughts and enable a more clear assessment of the solicitor's actual intent.

The "Innocent Instrumentality"

Sometimes a person contemplating criminal activity procures the assistance of another through deception. If the person actually committing the crime is, for whatever reason, unaware that he or she is engaging in criminal conduct, then that person is considered an innocent instrumentality of the solicitation. Not being aware that he or she is engaging in criminal conduct, the innocent instrumentality does not possess the necessary mental state for criminal liability. The solicitor is, however, criminally liable for the conduct of the innocent instrumentality. To illustrate:

Jan and Kim work in the same office. One day Jan tells Kim that their boss has decided to give her (Jan) several cartons of office products from the office storage closet. Jan tells Kim that she doesn't have time to get the boxes and asks Kim to get them from the storage closet and place them in her (Jan's) car. Kim, who is glad to do a favor for a friend, retrieves the products from the storage closet and places them in Jan's car. Unbeknownst to Kim, the boss did not authorize the removal of the office products, and Jan is using Kim to steal the products. Are Jan and Kim both guilty of larceny?

If Kim did not know that Jan was stealing the office products and believed that Jan was authorized to take them, then Kim cannot be guilty of larceny. Although she committed a voluntary act, Kim did not have the intent to steal because she was not aware that the removal of the office products was not authorized. Instead, Jan used Kim as an *innocent instrumentality* to commit the crime. This means that Jan had the intent to steal, but used another innocent person to carry out the voluntary act. Jan is nevertheless morally blameworthy and criminally liable for the theft of the office products.

Of course, in such instances, it is necessary to examine all of the surrounding circumstances of the crime to determine if indeed the "innocent instrumentality" believed that she was not engaging in criminal conduct. For example, if Kim knew that the company (and the boss) had a strict policy against allowing employees to take office products or if the amount of the office products strongly suggested that they could not be gifts, then there is some circumstantial evidence that Kim perhaps knew that taking the office products was not authorized. Kim may then become a co-conspirator and an accomplice to the crime with Jan because Kim has the necessary mental state, that is, knowledge that she is performing an unlawful taking and the intent to go forward with the unlawful conduct.

CONSPIRACY

The crime of *conspiracy* requires an agreement between two or more parties to commit an unlawful act and the commission of an *overt act* in furtherance of the agreement. Like the crime of solicitation, the conduct examined in conspiracy cases takes place before the actual commission of the criminal offense. Once again, the critical question involves determining when the preparatory conduct has gone beyond merely having bad thoughts and into the realm of acting upon those thoughts. In the area of conspiracy, the requirement of an overt act in addition to the conspiratorial agreement provides some circumstantial evidence that the parties have reached a sufficient level of dangerousness (i.e., gone beyond mere bad thoughts) to warrant punishment for their conduct.

One reason for punishing conspiratorial agreements is the concern that when people come together and agree to engage in criminal conduct, there is a greater likelihood that their goals and objectives will be accomplished. They are more likely to be overcome by a "mob mentality" from which they can derive the necessary moral support to carry out their criminal activities. The three major issues that arise when examining the crime of conspiracy involve defining the parties to the conspiracy, measuring the scope of the conspiratorial agreement and determining when the conspiracy terminates. These issues will be addressed in this section.

The Conspiratorial Agreement and the Parties to the Conspiracy

A conspiratorial agreement can be written, verbal or implied by conduct. Because a conspiracy involves an agreement between parties, in some instances simply identifying the parties who have actually agreed to engage in the unlawful conduct will reveal the parties to the agreement. When the conspiratorial agreement is implied by conduct, however, it becomes more difficult to determine the participants in the conspiracy. For example:

Bonnie and Clyde are husband and wife and business partners in the ownership of a used-car dealership. Because profits are declining, Clyde devises a plan to insure that the dealership remains competitive. Specifically, Clyde asks his chief mechanic, Floyd, to turn back the odometers on several used vehicles so they can sell the cars for more than their actual values. Bonnie is not present during this discussion and is not aware of Clyde's plan. Over the next several months, Bonnie sees Floyd using a special tool on the odometers of certain used cars. She further notices that these cars are selling for several hundred dollars more than their apparent worth and that, coincidentally, profits at the dealership have increased dramatically. Although Bonnie suspects that something unsavory may be occurring, she decides to do nothing and continues to enjoy the increased profits. Has Bonnie become a part of the conspiratorial agreement between Clyde and Floyd?

Although Bonnie was not present during the original conspiratorial agreement between Clyde and Floyd, she can nevertheless become part of the agreement and a member of the conspiracy. If Bonnie has knowledge of the unlawful activity and accepts the benefits of increased profits from the crime while failing to do anything to prevent it, then she can become a co-conspirator. Bonnie's knowledge of the criminal activity can be demonstrated circumstantially by the fact that she is in the used-car business and very likely has some knowledge of standards for evaluating and selling used cars. Additionally, Bonnie observed Floyd tampering with the automobiles and yet did nothing to question or prevent the apparent illegality. Instead, as a partner in the business, Bonnie reaped the profits from the unlawful activity. Considering all of the circumstantial evidence, Bonnie has become a party to the conspiratorial agreement even though she was not present during the initial agreement between Clyde and Floyd. It should be emphasized, however, that mere knowledge of illegal conduct is not enough. To become part of an ongoing conspiracy, a third party must both have knowledge and manifest some conduct that indicates a desire to further the objectives of the conspiracy. Bonnie meets the "knowledge plus" requirement by accepting the profits derived from Clyde and Floyd's unlawful scheme.

Not surprisingly, family relationships can create difficulties when prosecuting a conspiracy based upon implied conduct and circumstantial evidence. Consider this example:

One Saturday morning, Jack asks his wife, Jill, to drive him to the local bank. As they arrive at the entrance of the bank, Jack instructs Jill to wait outside with the engine running while he goes in to make a withdrawal. When Jack returns to the car, he tells Jill to quickly drive home. Several hours after Jack and Jill arrive home, the police arrive and arrest them both for conspiracy to commit bank robbery and bank robbery. Jill is shocked by the arrest and claims that she had nothing to do with planning or executing the bank robbery. Will Jill be successful with this argument?

Because of the nature of family/marital relationships, there are innumerable activities that may resemble conspiratorial conduct, but may in fact be nothing more than the normal cooperative activities that take place among family members. Family members should not be deemed involved in criminal activities simply because they have engaged in certain familial conduct. Because of the marital relationship, in the Jack and Jill example, it is critical to examine Jill's knowledge of the surrounding circumstances, rather than relying solely upon her conduct as a measure of whether there was a conspiratorial agreement. Relevant considerations in this example would be whether it was "normal" for Jill to drive Jack to the bank and wait outside with the engine running. If this conduct was peculiar, perhaps it should have alerted Jill that something was amiss. Additional circumstantial evidence might include whether Jack appeared nervous at any time during the trip to the bank and/or made any statements that might have revealed his intent to engage in unlawful conduct. Each of these circumstantial factors will be a helpful, although by no means conclusive, measure of whether Jill was an innocent family bystander or part of a conspiratorial agreement to commit bank robbery.

The Unlawful Act Requirement

As discussed earlier, a conspiracy involves an agreement between two or more persons to commit an unlawful act. In most instances, the unlawful act that serves as the objective of the conspiracy must be a crime. However, a small number of jurisdictions permit a charge of criminal conspiracy when the objective of the conspiracy would not be criminal if one person engaged in that conduct. For example, some statutes make it a crime for two or more persons to conspire to damage a person's reputation or business or commit acts that injure the public health or morals. If done by one person, such conduct would not be criminal, although it might raise questions of civil liability. But if two people agree to damage another's reputation, then they may be charged with the crime of conspiracy. One fundamental problem that arises when basing a charge of conspiracy on conduct that is not inherently criminal is fair notice to citizens as to the potential for criminal liability. More specifically, if the unlawful act is not criminal when committed by one person, is it fair to subject individuals to the stigma and punishment associated with criminal conduct simply because two people agreed to engage in that same conduct? This potential for unfairness has led many jurisdictions to limit liability for conspiracy to instances when the unlawful act is itself a crime.

Overt Act

The overt act element of a conspiracy is not very difficult to prove. In fact, at common law, proof of an overt act wasn't even required. Many jurisdictions later included the overt act requirement because it provides some circumstantial evidence of the conspirators' intent to proceed with the objectives of the conspiracy. In other words, the overt act demonstrates that the conspirators have moved beyond the stage of mere bad thoughts. Therefore, any act in furtherance of the objectives of the conspiracy will be sufficient to meet the overt act requirement. For example, if two parties agree to commit an armed bank robbery, an overt act in furtherance of that unlawful objective might be acquiring the weapon that will be used to commit the crime. Acquiring the weapon provides some circumstantial evidence of their intent to proceed with the criminal objective of robbing the bank.

The Scope of the Conspiratorial Agreement

Conspiracy is a specific intent offense. This means that the defendants must consciously set out to engage in specific unlawful conduct. The scope of the conspiratorial agreement is measured by what the parties specifically intend to accomplish as their overall objective as well as any other unlawful activities that are necessary to carry out their criminal objectives. Defining the scope of a conspiratorial agreement may be demonstrated by the following example:

Riff and Raff agree to construct a bomb and set it to detonate at night in an unoccupied building. Riff and Raff are unaware that security guards occasionally patrol the interior of the building during the evening hours. On the night the bomb explodes, two security guards are patrolling inside the building and are killed as a result of the explosion. Can Riff and Raff be charged with conspiracy to commit murder?

Although Riff and Raff expressly agreed to construct a bomb and detonate it inside the building, they did not agree to kill anyone. In fact, they thought the building was unoccupied. It was not their objective or specific intent to kill anyone inside or outside of the building. That is, the scope of their conspiratorial agreement did not encompass killing anyone and involved only the destruction of property. Therefore, they cannot be charged with conspiracy to commit murder. Riff and Raff can, however, be charged with the crime of murder for the deaths of the security guards using a theory of extreme reckless disregard or one of felony murder. (Recall that these categories of murder do not require that the defendant actually intend to kill anyone.) Riff and Raff can also be charged with conspiracy to bomb the building since that was the actual objective of their conspiratorial agreement.

The scope of a conspiratorial agreement can change over time and may encompass additional "sub-agreements" necessary to achieving the overall objective. In the previous example, if Riff and Raff agreed to steal the necessary materials to construct the bomb in order to further the overall objective of destroying the building, then the agreement to steal the materials would be considered a sub-agreement of the overall conspiratorial agreement to destroy the building. Since the sub-agreement to commit the theft is considered part of the larger conspiratorial agreement, it would probably not be considered a separate conspiracy. This example illustrates that the scope of a conspiratorial agreement may consist of several sub-agreements that are necessary to carry out the criminal objective. The sub-agreements are not typically considered or charged as separate conspiracies because they are an essential part of the overall criminal objective.

Withdrawal from a Conspiracy

Even though a conspirator has explicitly or implicitly agreed with another to commit an unlawful act, he can nevertheless withdraw from the conspiratorial agreement and avoid some criminal liability if the withdrawal is done in a timely and effective manner. Again, consider the facts of the earlier Riff/Raff example and further assume that:

Although Riff originally agreed to detonate the bomb with Raff and assisted Raff in obtaining the bombing materials and constructing the bomb, Riff begins to have second thoughts about committing the crime of destroying the building. Riff conveys these thoughts to Raff, but Raff insists that they follow through with their plan.

On the evening they have scheduled to detonate the bomb, Riff mysteriously disappears. Raff nevertheless decides to go forward with the plans and places the bomb inside the building where it ultimately detonates. Will Riff be criminally responsible for conspiring to destroy the building? Or, has Riff effectively removed himself from the conspiracy? (*Note*: At this point, we are not considering whether Riff can be responsible for actually bombing the building. That question will be considered in the next section.)

To withdraw from a conspiratorial agreement, a conspirator must convey his desire to withdraw to all of his confederates. He must provide effective notice that he no longer supports the criminal objectives and voluntarily remove himself completely from the criminal association. Additionally, some jurisdictions require that the conspirator give notification to law enforcement authorities as further evidence of his intent to impede the successful commission of the unlawful objective.

In the Riff and Raff example, Riff conveyed the fact that he was having "second thoughts" about committing the bombing and disappeared on the day scheduled to commit the crime. While this conduct might be sufficient to constitute withdrawal, usually a conspirator's withdrawal statements must be more specific and unequivocal. In other words, there must be stronger circumstantial evidence of the conspirator's intent to withdraw. In any event, in most jurisdictions, even an effective withdrawal from the conspiratorial agreement does not relieve the conspirator of liability for the conspiracy. Instead, it relieves the withdrawing conspirator from criminal liability for actual crimes that are committed in furtherance of the conspiracy after the conspirator's withdrawal.

In addition to withdrawal, some jurisdictions permit abandonment or renunciation of the conspiracy. To abandon a conspiracy, a conspirator must do more than simply withdraw from it. He must completely and voluntarily abandon the goals of the conspiracy and take affirmative steps to impede the success of the conspiracy. Abandonment, if effective, relieves the abandoning conspirator from liability for the conspiracy itself. In the example, Riff's conduct would not rise to the level of abandoning the conspiracy.

Conspiratorial Liability

As explained earlier, the crime of conspiracy is punished because of the special danger presented by group activity that has a criminal objective. In fact, conspiracy is considered such a dangerous offense that even when conspirators proceed beyond the agreement stage and actually commit the crime as planned, the conspirators can still be charged with the crime of conspiracy and the criminal offense they commit. In the example of Riff and Raff, assuming they carry out the crime of bombing the building, they can be charged with conspiring to destroy the building and the crime of using an explosive to destroy a building (the substantive offense). By allowing the simultaneous charges based upon the conspiracy and the actual crime, the government can seek additional criminal penalties against the conspirators. Furthermore, it is hoped that the threat of conviction and punishment for both conspiracy and the actual crime will deter individuals from initially joining together for the purpose of engaging in unlawful conduct.

Another aspect of conspiratorial liability that is specifically designed to deter group criminal activity is vicarious liability. Vicarious liability means that a conspirator will be responsible for the criminal conduct of his coconspirators if those crimes are committed in furtherance of the conspiratorial agreement. Returning one last time to the Riff and Raff example, assume again that Riff and Raff agree to steal bombing materials and detonate a bomb to destroy an unoccupied building. However, only Raff actually steals the bombing materials, constructs the bomb and places it in the building. Riff would nevertheless be vicariously liable for the theft of the bombing materials and the destruction of the building because these offenses were committed in furtherance of the conspiratorial agreement, even though Riff did not personally commit these offenses. The key to vicarious liability is that the crimes must be committed in furtherance of the conspiratorial agreement. (Of course, Riff would also be liable for the overall conspiracy to destroy the building.) As discussed earlier, if Riff gives effective and timely notice of his withdrawal from the conspiracy, he may be able to avoid liability for the actual crimes committed in furtherance of the conspiracy after his withdrawal.

CRIMINAL ATTEMPTS

The crime of *criminal attempt* is punished to protect society by intervening, apprehending and prosecuting individuals at the earliest opportunity before a crime is completed. If criminal activity has not been stopped at either the solicitation or conspiracy stage, the law of criminal attempts provides one more opportunity to prevent the criminal conduct and the resulting harm to society.

To prove a criminal attempt, the government must demonstrate that the defendant has the intent to commit a specific offense and takes a "substantial step" toward completing that offense. By proving these elements, the government demonstrates that, although the crime was not ultimately completed, the defendant intended to commit the crime and took sufficient steps in furtherance of that criminal intent. The mental state (intent to commit an offense) plus the voluntary act (substantial step) provide significant evidence of the defendant's dangerousness to society. Further, although foiling the actual commission of the crime prevents a greater harm to society, there is nevertheless a harm to society with a criminal attempt because the defendant comes dangerously close to completing his criminal objective. The criminal law imposes liability for attempts in order to deter others from carrying their criminal activity to this dangerous point.

Intent to Commit the Offense

To be liable for a criminal attempt, the defendant must have the intent to commit a specific offense. For example, to be charged with attempted murder, the defendant must intend to kill the victim. Similarly, if the crime charged is attempted robbery, the defendant must have the intent to take property from the victim with the use of force. In most instances, circumstantial evidence will be used to prove the defendant's intent. Circumstantial evidence allows the judge or jury to draw inferences as to which crime the defendant specifically intended to commit. In cases of attempt, the circumstantial evidence of intent is usually developed by examining what steps the defendant took to begin carrying out the offense. Consider the following example:

Coach Clever is tremendously upset when his team loses the local high school football championship. The coach is so upset, in fact, that he decides to kill Coach Haskell, the coach of the opposing team. To further his plan, Clever purchases a high-powered assault rifle with a special telescope to help him zero in on his target. He then purchases a disguise, maps the quickest route to Haskell's home, withdraws money from his bank account, and secures a passport and plane tickets out of the country. On the morning that Clever plans to commit the murder, he sits in his car outside Haskell's home wearing the disguise with the loaded weapon, waiting for Haskell to emerge from his residence. Coach Clever also has his passport, money and plane tickets with him so as to make a quick and clean getaway after the killing. A neighbor, who observes Clever sitting in his vehicle, becomes suspicious and phones the police. Upon arriving at the scene, the police discover Clever in a disguise with the loaded weapon. After verifying Clever's identity, the police arrest him for an attempted murder. Did Coach Clever have the intent to commit the crime of murder?

Examining all of the surrounding circumstances, there is compelling evidence of Clever's intent to kill Haskell. First, Coach Clever was extremely bitter about the loss of the football championship, which provided a motive for the murder. Although motive is not an element of the crime and is not necessary to prove, it does provide a framework for understanding Clever's behavior in this case. Second, Coach Clever purchased a high-powered assault weapon specially equipped with a telescope to increase its accuracy when pointed at a target. Almost certainly, this type of weapon is capable of inflicting fatal injuries if used for that purpose. Third, Clever carefully planned his escape, which, at minimum, suggests that he fully intended to carry out the unlawful killing and immediately flee the jurisdiction. Taken together, there is strong circumstantial evidence that Clever had the specific intent to kill Haskell as opposed to merely frightening him or inflicting a nonfatal injury.

For the crime of attempt, however, it is not sufficient simply to prove that Clever had the specific intent to kill Haskell. There must also be evidence that Clever took a "substantial step" toward acting on his intent to kill.

Substantial Step

Evaluating whether the defendant has taken a substantial step toward the commission of a crime requires examining the defendant's voluntary actions in furtherance of the criminal activity. The substantial step requirement ensures that the defendant is exhibiting a level of dangerousness to society sufficient to warrant punishment. Because the elements of each crime differ, the conduct required for a "substantial step" will change according to the elements of the crime. There are, however, several questions the judge or jury might consider when determining whether the defendant has taken a substantial step. One consideration is whether the defendant was within "dangerous proximity" of completing the crime. Dangerous proximity can mean close in time, geography or preparation to committing the crime. Another consideration might be the level of apprehension created by the criminal conduct. Theoretically, if the crime is of a very serious nature and involves a high level of danger, then there is a greater likelihood that the defendant will stop and reconsider before completing his criminal activities.

In the example of Coach Clever, it is likely that he took a substantial step toward completing the crime of murder at the time of his arrest. As to "dangerous proximity," Clever was right outside Haskell's home with a loaded weapon, disguise, money and a passport and plane tickets. He intended to commit the crime as soon as Haskell emerged from his home. Clever was dangerously close in time, geography and level of preparation to committing the murder. It is not necessary that the defendant have taken the last possible step toward completing the crime in order to find that a substantial step has occurred. For example, in this case, the substantial step requirement can likely be met without finding that Clever actually pointed the weapon or shot at Haskell. The point of the crime of attempt is to allow law enforcement to interrupt the crime *before* there is any significant harm. Yet, at the point of interruption, there must be sufficient evidence of the defendant's intent. Therefore, when the defendant's conduct has reached a sufficient level so as to provide clear evidence of his intent, then he has taken a substantial step, although he may not have taken the last possible step toward committing the crime.

Examining the level of apprehension factor in this case will also yield the conclusion that the defendant has taken a substantial step. Although the crime of murder is serious and likely to create a high degree of apprehension, it seems unlikely that Clever was going to retreat from his conduct given his level of preparation and his apparent hatred for Haskell. Considering all of these factors, Coach Clever has probably taken a substantial step toward committing the crime of murder. Combining this evidence with Clever's specific intent to kill will likely produce a guilty verdict for the attempted murder of Coach Haskell.

ACCESSORY OR AIDING AND ABETTING LIABILITY

A person can be liable for the criminal conduct of another if he provides assistance before or during the commission of the crime. This type of criminal liability is referred to as *accessory* or *aiding and abetting* liability. If a person intends that a crime be committed and does something to encourage, promote or facilitate the commission of the crime, then according to the criminal law he is just as guilty as the person who actually commits the offense. A person who provides assistance to another is considered dangerous because, although he may not actually commit the offense, he has the necessary criminal intent and engages in some conduct that furthers the criminal activity. The criminal law punishes those who provide encouragement or assistance to others engaged in criminal conduct in an attempt to thwart the progress of criminal activity that depends upon the encouragement or assistance of others.

An accessory may be criminally liable for providing physical or verbal assistance or encouragement to another and may be liable without regard to whether he is present during the commission of the offense. Consider the following example:

Martha Mad is angry when she discovers that an intoxicated driver has seriously injured her mother in an automobile accident. After visiting her ailing mother in the hospital, Martha becomes even angrier and decides to seek revenge against the driver. One day, after leaving the hospital, Martha stops by her close friend Alan Aider's home. She discusses her situation with Alan and expresses her strong desire to kill the intoxicated driver. Martha then boldly asks Alan for a gun and specifically requests that he show her how to aim it to hit her target from a distance with one shot. Alan provides the weapon to Martha and takes her to his backyard for a two-hour target practice session. Martha is a fast learner and leaves Alan's home with the weapon. Later that day, Martha kills the driver of the vehicle in cold blood. Can Alan be guilty of the driver's murder too?

Since Alan provided the weapon to Martha with full knowledge of her plans and intent to use it, there is circumstantial evidence that he also had the intent that the crime be committed. Further, based upon his actions of providing the weapon and the training, Alan encouraged and facilitated Martha's criminal agenda. Although he was not present at the crime scene, Alan provided critical assistance to Martha's criminal conduct and is therefore liable for that conduct. As a result, Alan can also be charged with the murder of the driver. It is important to understand that there is no separate criminal offense of aiding and abetting. Instead, aiding and abetting is a legal theory used to impose criminal liability upon those who provide encouragement or assistance to others who commit criminal offenses. Accordingly, those who provide assistance to others before or during the commission of the crime will be charged with the *same offense* as the person who committed the crime.

Knowledge of the Criminal Conduct

Before a person may be criminally responsible for the conduct of another person, he must have knowledge of the anticipated criminal conduct. Knowledge is usually based upon information provided by the person committing the offense. In the previous example, Alan had knowledge of Martha's criminal activity by virtue of the information she provided. Knowledge of criminal activity may also be derived from being present at the scene of the crime. However, mere presence at the scene is not enough to impose criminal liability for the conduct of another. There must also be proof that the accessory had *knowledge of the criminal conduct*. For example:

Chip and Dale go to the mall one Sunday afternoon. As Chip waits in the car, Dale goes into the store ostensibly to make a purchase. Chip is not aware that Dale intends to steal several articles of clothing while in the store. Dale steals the clothes and calmly returns to the car, and Chip drives away. A security guard, who saw Dale steal the merchandise and get into Chip's car, records Chip's license plate number. Later that day, the police arrest Dale and a surprised Chip for the theft. Is Chip liable for Dale's conduct simply by being present outside the store while Dale committed the theft?

Even though Chip technically provided assistance to Dale in the form of a ride to and from the scene of the crime, he did so without knowledge of Dale's criminal activities. Without knowledge of Dale's criminal conduct, Chip cannot have the necessary intent that the crime be committed or the intent to promote or facilitate Dale's commission of the crime. Knowledge of the criminal conduct is therefore an essential ingredient for assessing liability for the conduct of another.

Before or During the Commission of the Crime

Liability for aiding and abetting the criminal conduct of another arises only if the assistance is knowingly provided *before or during* the commission of the crime. Thus, for every crime, liability for aiding and abetting will rest upon an initial determination as to when the crime is complete. Any assistance provided after the completion of the crime will be considered assistance after the fact and evaluated under a different criminal law standard. To change the facts of the Chip and Dale example, if Chip had knowledge of Dale's intent to steal once inside the store and served as the "getaway" driver, then he provided assistance during the crime, since the theft from the department store would not be complete until they reach a place of temporary safety away from the scene of the crime.

Aiding and Abetting versus Conspiracy

Based upon the definition of conspiracy discussed earlier in this chapter, it would seem that anyone who provides assistance to another before or during the commission of a crime would also be considered a co-conspirator. Indeed, that is often the case. It is possible, however, to encourage or assist in the criminal conduct of another without a prior conspiratorial agreement. Let's change the facts of the Chip and Dale example again.

Assume that Dale goes to the mall by himself to steal merchandise from a department store. A security guard observes Dale as he is leaving the store with the stolen merchandise and begins to chase Dale. Coincidentally, as Dale is running from the store, his friend Chip is driving past. Chip immediately recognizes that his friend has committed another department store heist and motions for Dale to get into the car. Dale jumps in with the merchandise and Chip speeds away. Dale thanks Chip profusely for helping him get away with the "goods."

In this instance, Chip had no prior knowledge of Dale's plan to steal merchandise from the department store and therefore could not be part of a conspiratorial agreement to commit theft. However, because Chip provided assistance to Dale as he was fleeing the scene of the crime, Chip can be liable for the actual theft because he aided and abetted Dale's conduct during the commission of the offense. In this example, the crime of theft would not be complete until Chip and Dale reached a place of temporary safety away from the scene of the crime.

Accessory after the Fact

If the criminal conduct is complete, any assistance provided at that point is considered assistance after the fact, and the person providing assistance is guilty as an *accessory after the fact*. Often, accessories after the fact provide assistance in concealing the crime or the fruits of the crime and intentionally hinder law enforcement efforts to investigate criminal conduct. In most jurisdictions, accessories after the fact, if convicted, are guilty of separate misdemeanor offenses and are not liable for the conduct of the person who actually committed the criminal offense. The actions of an accessory after the fact are not considered as serious or dangerous as the person who commits or facilitates the commission of the crime. Instead, an accessory after the fact is considered a threat to efficient and effective law enforcement. By taking affirmative steps to conceal crimes from authorities or hinder official criminal investigations, accessories after the fact are essentially committing a crime against the public authority.

To be liable as an accessory after the fact, the defendant must have knowledge of the completed criminal activity and do something to conceal or hinder law enforcement investigation of the crime. Mere knowledge of completed criminal activities is not enough because there is no legal obligation to report criminal conduct. But when a person has knowledge of criminal activities and takes affirmative steps to conceal them, then that person has committed a crime against the public by interfering with the efficient and effective investigation of criminal conduct.

One notable exception to accessory after the fact liability arises when family members are involved. Some statutes exempt family members from accessory after the fact liability. This exemption is due to the difficulty associated with proving that family members acted with the necessary knowledge and intent to conceal criminal activity as opposed to simply engaging in innocent family activities. For example, the parents of a teenager who returns to the family home after committing an armed robbery would probably not be considered accessories after the fact to the teen's crime. Presumably, the parents are simply engaging in the innocent activity of allowing their son to stay in the family home rather than acting with the intent to conceal his criminal activities. In any event, there would be serious difficulties with attempting to establish the parents' knowledge and criminal intent, given the nature of normal family interactions.

CASE STUDIES

A Conspiracy to Kill

Conspiracy is largely a crime of the mind, a meeting of the minds to commit a criminal act. At common law, the crime of conspiracy required only that there be an agreement to commit an offense, coupled with the intent that the offense be committed. However, because of the inherent difficulties with proving criminal intent when the crime is primarily mental in substance, modern statutes have added the requirement of an overt act. As explained earlier in this chapter, the overt act may be something as simple as making a telephone call to procure the weapons necessary to complete the criminal conduct.

Conspiracy was one of the essential crimes charged against the defendants in what has been described as the nation's worst act of terrorism. On April 19, 1995, a massive truck bomb detonated, killing 168 people and injuring 500 in a federal building in Oklahoma City, Oklahoma. After a lengthy investigation, the government arrested Timothy McVeigh and Terry Nichols and charged them with murder and conspiracy to use a weapon of mass destruction. The conspiracy charge stemmed from the prosecution's allegation that McVeigh and Nichols masterfully planned the bombing as an act of terrorism against the federal government.

To prove the conspiracy charge in the Oklahoma bombing case, the government needed to demonstrate a connection between McVeigh and Nichols prior to the bombing along with concrete evidence that they intentionally agreed to carry out the bombing. Since most conspirators don't incorporate their criminal intentions into specific written agreements, the government's proof in this case necessarily consisted of circumstantial evidence of overt actions by McVeigh and Nichols that proved their conspiratorial agreement. For example, the government theorized that McVeigh and Nichols agreed to carry out their criminal conduct by constructing a lethal bomb containing a mixture of ammonium nitrate fertilizer and fuel oil, which would ultimately be loaded into a Ryder truck. To prove this theory, the government introduced evidence of telephone conversations between McVeigh and Nichols specifically planning to acquire the bombing materials. The prosecution also put forth evidence that Nichols gathered the ammonium nitrate needed to make the bomb, after which he and McVeigh mixed the bomb near Nichol's home in Kansas. During the investigation, the government also uncovered evidence that McVeigh and Nichols planned and executed robberies in order to finance the bombing plot. As explained in this chapter, the agreement to commit robberies might be considered a sub-agreement necessary to further the overall conspiracy to commit the bombing. Taken together, the overt activities of McVeigh and Nichols prior to the bombing indicate, at a minimum, an implicit agreement to construct the deadly bomb with the intent to use it as a weapon of destruction against the federal government.

With such compelling evidence of McVeigh and Nichols' conspiracy to use a weapon of mass destruction, the government was able to prove that McVeigh, who placed the bomb in front of the occupied Oklahoma City building, acted with the intent to kill the occupants in the building. Thus, in addition to a conviction for the conspiracy, McVeigh was also convicted of murder for eight of the deaths that occurred and was sentenced to death. Interestingly, however, his co-conspirator Nichols' case resulted in a much different verdict.

Although Nichols was charged with the same offenses as McVeigh, a separate jury convicted him of conspiracy to use a weapon of mass destruction and involuntary manslaughter. On its face, the verdict appears to be inconsistent and completely contradictory, because if Nichols intentionally conspired to use a weapon of mass destruction, it seems to follow logically that he intended the natural and probable consequences of his actions. In other words, if Nichols conspired to bomb the building, didn't he also intend to cause the deaths of the people in the Oklahoma City federal building that was targeted by the bomb? If that is the case, then how could a jury convict Nichols of only involuntary manslaughter? Involuntary manslaughter would, by definition, involve an unintentional death that occurs during the course of an unlawful act (in this case, using a weapon of mass destruction). Again, however, how could the resulting deaths have been unintentional if Nichols intentionally conspired to detonate the truck bomb in front of an occupied building?

One response to the inconsistency in the jury's verdict is that trial jurors are entitled to reach inconsistent verdicts, and their deliberations and conclusions will not be questioned. While there is certainly a possibility that the jurors in the Nichols' case misunderstood the evidence or the judge's instructions, because of the historical deference afforded jury decisions, their verdict will be considered valid in all but the rarest of circumstances. What remains then is to consider how the jury might have come to what appears to be a contradictory conclusion on Nichols' responsibility for the Oklahoma bombing tragedy.

Another explanation for the jury's verdict relates to Nichols' role in planning the bombing. Perhaps the jurors concluded that Nichols' participation in the conspiracy was limited in such a manner so as to preclude an intent to kill. That is, while Nichols might have assisted in the creation of the truck bomb, he may have believed that the bomb would be used merely as a method of terrorizing the government and not as a means to murder innocent citizens. If the jury believed that Nichols only conspired to create the bomb without the knowledge and intent that it be used to kill others, then they could conceivably convict Nichols of involuntary manslaughter in connection with the deaths. This is because the jurors could have concluded that he did not intend to kill, although several deaths resulted from his participation in a conspiracy to use the deadly truck bomb.

If the jury's verdict in the Nichols' case is accepted on its face, then the verdict illustrates that a conspirator may agree to participate in a conspiracy to commit a specific offense and yet may not have knowledge of or specifically intend some of the natural and probable consequences that result from carrying out the objectives of the conspiracy. But perhaps more important, this case also illustrates the extraordinary dangers associated with the crime of conspiracy. As described in this chapter, when two or more people come together to commit a criminal offense, they are often capable of engaging in more complex schemes; there is a much higher likelihood that their objectives will be accomplished because of the moral support inherent in the conspiratorial arrangement. In this case, Nichols and McVeigh were able to carry out a series of robberies to support their plot and acquire the necessary materials to manufacture a deadly truck bomb. Additionally, their conspiracy took place over several months and involved criminal activity in several states. It is unlikely that a single person would have been able to carry out this level of criminal activity and devastation. With the assistance of co-conspirators and accomplices, more complex criminal objectives become possible, thereby creating a greater likelihood that the criminal activity will be completed and the resulting social harm will be magnified accordingly.

The Crime of Covering Up

A person may be responsible for the criminal conduct of another if he or she assists, encourages or facilitates that conduct with the intent that the crime be committed. As discussed in the section on aiding and abetting liability, the assistance or encouragement must occur prior to or at the time the crime is committed. Furthermore, the person providing assistance need not be present during the commission of the offense, as long as he or she has provided some assistance or encouragement with the intent that the crime be committed. Occasionally, however, some individuals provide assistance after the crime has been completed. Although such assistance is a criminal offense, it is considered quite different from assistance provided before or during the offense. The unusual case involving figure-skating rivals Tonya Harding and Nancy Kerrigan helps illustrate the crime of assisting after the fact or, as it is referred to in some statutes, the crime of hindering the prosecution of an offense.

Nancy Kerrigan and Tonya Harding were both scheduled to compete in the U.S. Figure Skating Championships in Detroit. The competition for the title was expected to be intense and focus primarily on the two young women. Prior to the championship, immediately after one of Kerrigan's practices, a man approached her and struck her just above the right knee with a metal pipe, badly injuring her. With Kerrigan unable to compete in the event, Harding won the U.S. championship and a spot on the Olympic team.

A police investigation later revealed that several people, including Harding's husband, Jeff Gillooley, had conspired to injure Kerrigan. The three men who assisted with the plan and actually carried out the attack eventually pled guilty to a charge of conspiracy to commit second-degree assault. For his part in the fiasco, Jeff Gillooley pled guilty to one count of racketeering, which is a form of organized criminal conspiracy that generally involves engaging in a pattern of unlawful activity. In this case, Gillooley was involved or assisted in several crimes, including the actual assault on Kerrigan and the attempt to cover up the assault by destroying physical evidence. These offenses were all related and formed a pattern of unlawful activity involving the attack on Kerrigan by the same group of individuals.

In addition to pleading guilty, Gillooley also identified Harding as a member of the conspiratorial group that planned and facilitated the attack on Kerrigan. Later, a grand jury investigation of the other participants in the conspiracy concluded that Harding did in fact help plan the attack and used training money from the U.S. Figure Skating Association to pay for the injury to Kerrigan. According to the report, Harding's alleged motive was to enhance her chances to win the U.S. championship, which would in turn lead to greater endorsements and sponsorships. However, at the time the grand jury report was released, Harding had already reached a plea agreement with prosecutors and pled guilty to the lesser offense of hindering the investigation of the case. She was therefore immune from any further prosecution related to the assault on Kerrigan.

Despite some rather compelling evidence of Harding's guilt contained in the grand jury report, Harding insisted that she did not know of the plan to attack Kerrigan until after she returned from the U.S. championship competition. Harding admitted that after she discovered the conspiracy to injure Kerrigan, she took the affirmative step of plotting with Gillooley to assist in covering up the criminal conduct. For her role in assisting to cover up the crime after the fact and thereby hindering the efficient and effective prosecution of the crime, she was placed on supervised probation for three years, ordered to perform 500 hours of community service, pay $160,000 in fines and resign from the U.S. Figure Skating Association.

By admitting to hindering the prosecution, Harding acknowledged that she performed some conduct with the intent to hinder law enforcement authorities from apprehending, prosecuting, convicting and punishing those responsible for the attack against Kerrigan. Her conduct in assisting in the cover-up of the attack on Kerrigan significantly interfered with the ability of law enforcement officials to efficiently and effectively carry out their responsibilities. It is important to understand that simply failing to report criminal conduct to authorities does not rise to the level of punishable conduct. Thus, a person who merely has knowledge of criminal conduct and fails to report it will not be criminally liable since there is no legal duty to report criminal activities. Therefore, in the Harding case, if Tonya Harding had simply known about the criminal conduct of Gillooley and the others, she would likely have faced no criminal liability since liability for assisting a crime after the fact arises from engaging in some affirmative act to assist in the cover-up. The reason for the affirmative act requirement is that it provides a more clear determination of the intent of the individual. Therefore, most statutes that penalize hindering the prosecution or acting as an accessory after the fact require affirmative assistance such as harboring or concealing a suspect or preventing discovery or apprehension of a suspect by means of some type of deception. With such affirmative actions present, it becomes clearer that the defendant has moved beyond merely failing to inform authorities of criminal conduct and into the realm of affirmatively acting against the interests of efficient and effective law enforcement.

FOR FURTHER CONSIDERATION

1. Does the overt act of a conspiracy have to be a crime? Why or why not? For this question, it might be helpful to consider the reason for requiring an overt act in conspiracy prosecutions.
2. If two conspirators agree to commit a bank robbery and also agree not to injure anyone in the process, will both conspirators be liable if one of the conspirators decides to kill a security guard as they are escaping from the bank?
3. Can onlookers who stand by and vigorously cheer a person who is beating another person to death be charged with the death of the victim? What would the prosecutor have to prove with respect to the onlookers? Would there be any difficulties with this proof?
4. Would a gun shop owner who sells a weapon and ammunition to a visibly angry customer be liable for a murder that is committed by the customer using the weapon? How much would the shop owner have to know about the customer's plans?

6

Theft Offenses

The more laws and order are made prominent,
The more thieves and robbers there will be.

—Lao-tzu

Theft crimes were among the earliest and most serious offenses known to common law. To emphasize the seriousness of these offenses, the penalty for many kinds of theft at common law was death. As the law developed, new forms of theft were defined and penalties were structured so that the death penalty was gradually eliminated as punishment for theft convictions. The variety of factual circumstances that can lead to theft convictions will be explored in this chapter.

LARCENY

Larceny is the trespassory taking and carrying away of the personal property of another with the intent to permanently deprive the owner of the property. To secure a conviction for larceny, the government must prove the voluntary act (trespassory taking and carrying away) and the mental state (intent to permanently deprive). The government must also demonstrate that the property taken has value and was owned by a person other than the defendant.

Trespassory Taking and Carrying Away of Property

To be unlawful, the taking of property must be trespassory. This means that it must be accomplished without the consent of the owner of the property and in a manner that is inconsistent with the owner's continued possession of the property. Generally speaking, unless property has been abandoned, someone owns it, whether it is in tha person's actual physical possession or not. Ownership of property grants the owner the right to use the property in a reasonably unrestricted manner. When another person exercises control over the property that is inconsistent with that right, then that person has committed a trespass against the property by interfering with the lawful owner's continued right to possess and enjoy the property. A trespassory taking can occur by physically removing property from the owner's possession or by using an animal, mechanical or digital device specifically designed for that purpose (e.g., a computer).

The "carrying away" of property is satisfied by the slightest movement of the property as long as the property is reduced to the actual possession of the person unlawfully taking it. Although the "carrying away" element is a fairly minimal requirement, it provides further proof of the defendant's intent to unlawfully remove the property from the owner's possession.

An additional requirement for a larceny conviction is that the property must be "valuable." The value requirement is easily met, and most statutes simply provide that the property must have a minimum value of one cent. Normally, the degree of larceny charged will increase depending upon the value of the property taken. Thus, the taking of property over a certain dollar amount will be considered grand larceny and punished more harshly, while anything below a certain amount will be petty larceny and punished accordingly.

Over time, the definition of property has undergone significant change to incorporate new kinds of property that may be the subject of larceny. At common law, the definition of property was limited to personal property that could be physically taken and carried away. The definition did not include real property or property that was somehow attached to the land. The common law definitions also did not include certain intangible items of property such as labor and services. Gradually, however, larceny statutes were modified specifically to include these forms of property. As a result, modern larceny statues are generally comprehensive enough to cover the theft of most forms of tangible and intangible valuable property.

Lost, Misplaced or Abandoned Property

At the time of the unlawful taking and carrying away, the defendant must intend to permanently deprive the lawful owner of continued enjoyment and possession of the property. In other words, there must be specific evidence that the defendant intended to steal the property from the lawful owner, as opposed to borrowing it or taking it based upon a mistaken belief that the property is abandoned. For example:

Larry Lightfingers and his friend are walking on a downtown street when they see what appears to be a wallet lying on the sidewalk. Upon closer examination, Larry discovers that the wallet contains $500 in cash as well as a driver's license and other information identifying the owner of the wallet. Larry's friend suggests that they immediately contact the owner to return the wallet and the cash. Larry scoffs at this suggestion, places the $500 in his pocket and discards the information identifying the wallet owner. Is Larry guilty of larceny?

To be convicted of larceny, the taking and carrying away must be trespassory, that is, without the owner's consent. This means that the property must belong to someone other than the defendant, whether or not it is in the actual possession of the owner at the time of the taking. In this example, although the owner of the wallet wasn't physically present and the wallet appeared to be lost, there is some evidence that the wallet was not completely abandoned. If at the time of finding the wallet, Larry has actual knowledge or a reasonable means for locating the true owner of the wallet, then the fact that Larry failed to contact the owner or make any effort to restore the wallet to its true owner may constitute a trespassory taking. In other words, the fact that Larry took the money and discarded the identifying information provides strong evidence of his intent to treat the property in a manner that is inconsistent with wallet owner's continued property interest in the wallet and its contents.

Whether property is truly abandoned or simply lost or misplaced is a matter to be determined by examining the circumstances of finding the property. If there is some indication of ownership either on the property or that could be reasonably inferred from the surrounding circumstances, then it is likely that the property has not been abandoned and the true owner can be located. In that case, a person who finds the property is required under most statutes to make a reasonable effort to restore the property to its rightful owner.

Intent to Permanently Deprive

The defendant, at the time of the trespassory taking and carrying away, must intend to permanently deprive the true owner of the property. This intent is also referred to as the intent to steal. Proving this intent typically involves examining the defendant's conduct as it relates to the trespassory taking and carrying away of the property. If the defendant treats the property in a manner that is inconsistent with the true owner's continued enjoyment and possession of the property, then that voluntary act provides strong circumstantial evidence of the defendant's intent to permanently deprive the owner of continued possession and use of the property. The major issue that arises in these cases involves determining when the defendant's voluntary act of taking and carrying away has progressed enough so that the intent to permanently deprive is sufficiently manifested. Consider the following example:

Sheila Shoplifter enters a department store and proceeds to try on several blouses in the women's department fitting room. Sheila finds one that she likes, but discovers that she cannot afford to pay for the blouse. At that point, Sheila decides to remove the price tag from the blouse, put it on and place her own blouse over the new blouse before leaving the fitting room. She then calmly walks around the store for several minutes before being apprehended by a security guard just as she is approaching the exit door. Can Sheila be convicted of larceny?

When Sheila removed the price tag and placed the new blouse under her own clothing, she evidenced an intent to treat the department store's property in a manner that was inconsistent with the storeowner's continued possession of the property. While it is certainly true that Sheila was permitted to try on the clothing, she did not have permission to remove the price tag and wear the blouse around the store concealed beneath her own clothing. Sheila's conduct exceeds the limited permission granted by the storeowner to examine and try on the property in the store. Additionally, the fact that Sheila appeared to be proceeding to the exit and had bypassed opportunities to pay for the blouse indicates that she intended to permanently deprive the storeowner of the property without paying for it. Based upon Sheila's voluntary actions and intentional mistreatment of the store's property, it may be inferred that she had the necessary intent to steal the blouse. Note that Sheila doesn't have to exit the store to be guilty of larceny. As long as she has exhausted the last opportunity to pay for the property, her intent to steal can be demonstrated even though she is still inside the store.

Occasionally, when caught with the goods, shoplifters will immediately offer to pay for the items and may, in fact, have the financial ability to do so. However, once the intent to steal has been demonstrated (i.e., by concealing the property and/or exhausting the last opportunity to pay), a subsequent offer to pay cannot negate the intent. This means that once there is a voluntary act (a taking and carrying away of the property) combined with the mental state (intent to steal), the social harm sought to be avoided by the crime of larceny is complete. A subsequent offer to pay is insufficient to remove this social harm, but it may serve to mitigate the defendant's punishment after conviction.

In some instances, a person may take property without the owner's consent, but with the intent to use it temporarily and thereafter restore it to the owner. If at the time of taking, there is no intent to permanently deprive the owner of the property, then it would appear that the necessary intent for larceny is not present. However, the intent must be examined in the context of the intended "temporary" use of the property. If the person taking the property intends to treat it in a manner that will make its restoration to its lawful owner highly unlikely, then there may be sufficient circumstantial evidence of an intent to permanently deprive the owner of the property at the time of the taking. Such circumstances might include, for example, taking property without the owner's consent and intentionally exposing it to dangerous or destructive circumstances.

Finally, a person may take property from another under the mistaken belief that he or she is entitled to take the property. For example, a person may take property with the mistaken belief that the owner has consented to the taking. In these situations, if the mistake by the taker is reasonable, it will negate any criminal intent to permanently deprive the owner of the property. The taking is simply an honest mistake. All of the surrounding circumstances must be evaluated, however, to determine if it was reasonable for the taker to have such beliefs with respect to the treatment of the property. If the beliefs are unreasonable, then the intent to steal may be established based upon the taker's treatment of the property.

EMBEZZLEMENT

The crime of *embezzlement* is similar to larceny in the sense that property must be taken without the owner's consent and with the intent to permanently deprive the owner of the property. The main difference between the crimes of larceny and embezzlement is that the embezzler usually has lawful possession of the property at the time of the taking. (Note that lawful possession does not mean ownership of the property.) In most cases of embezzlement, the owner of the property has entrusted the embezzler with care, custody or control of the property for a limited purpose or period of time. Embezzlement often arises in the employment context, when an employer gives an employee limited possession or control of certain property and the employee begins to treat that property in a manner that is inconsistent with the employer's limited grant of possession or control. To illustrate:

Ike Invoice is employed by the ABC Company as a purchaser. As part of Ike's job responsibilities, he purchases computer equipment for ABC and approves invoices that are submitted to ABC for payment for the computer equipment. After approving the invoices, Ike sends them to ABC's accounting department, where they are later paid with ABC funds. One day, Ike decides to purchase several computer items for his personal use. When the invoices for these computers arrive, Ike approves them as if the computers had been purchased for ABC and forwards the fraudulent invoices to ABC's accounting department, where they are later paid by ABC. Ike continues this practice for several months until an audit of the company's finances reveals his scheme.

In this example, Ike is guilty of embezzlement. His employer, ABC, gave him limited authority and control to purchase computer equipment for ABC, not for his personal use. When Ike exceeded the scope of his lawful authority over ABC's property, he was acting without the owner's (ABC's) consent. By causing invoices for his personal property to be paid with ABC's funds, Ike committed a trespassory taking against ABC's property with the intent to permanently deprive ABC of the funds used to pay for his personal property.

To summarize, the crime of embezzlement is an extension of the crime of larceny designed to cover instances when the taker has lawful possession or custody of the property for a limited purpose and uses the property in a manner that exceeds the scope of that lawful authority with the intent to permanently deprive the owner of the property.

ROBBERY

Robbery is yet another extension of the crime of larceny. To prove robbery, generally the government must demonstrate that the defendant took and carried away the property of another with the intent to steal and with the use or threatened use of force. The use or threat of force must take place in the victim's presence and must compel the victim to part with the property. The necessary force can take many forms, ranging from verbal threats to display of a weapon to physical force. Depending upon the type of force used, the degree of robbery that is charged and the corresponding punishment will be more or less severe. For example, a defendant who uses a deadly weapon such as a gun to cause the victim to part with property will usually receive a more severe charge (e.g., armed or aggravated robbery) than a defendant who grabs the victim by the collar and demands money. Since robbery is a larceny with the additional element of force, if there is no force or threat of force at the time of the unlawful taking, the crime is simply a larceny from the person and not a robbery.

EXTORTION

The crime of *extortion* might be referred to as the close cousin of robbery. Historically, the crime of extortion involved using one's political office or power to obtain unlawful payments. Today, most extortion statutes require that the force or threat of force be somehow conveyed by the defendant to the victim for purposes of taking property from the victim. As distinguished from the crime of robbery, however, the force doesn't have to be immediate or take place in the victim's presence. For example, the force or threat of force might be conveyed to the victim via a telephone conversation, a letter, or a third party. Additionally, the force doesn't have to take the form of a threat to the victim's personal safety. It could, for instance, be a threat to the victim's relatives or a threat to harm the victim's reputation. Once again, the force or threat of force must be used to compel the victim to exchange something of value, although the force or threat does not have to be immediate or in the presence of the victim as long as it is somehow conveyed to the victim.

BURGLARY

At common law, the crime of *burglary* required breaking and entering into the dwelling of another at night with the intent to commit a felony once inside the dwelling. Since this definition was much too specific to cover all of the factual variations surrounding the crime of burglary, the definition was gradually expanded to allow for different degrees of burglary depending upon the circumstances of the crime.

Breaking and Entering

The crime of burglary requires that the defendant unlawfully break and enter onto the premises. While the term breaking and entering can encompass the typical breaking (or picking) of a lock to gain entry, it can also include more subtle forms of breaking such as bypassing or fraudulently obtaining a security code in order to unlawfully gain entry. Additionally, certain circumstances can constitute breaking and entering simply because the defendant entered or remained on the premises without the consent of the owner. For example, entering the unlocked or open door of a residence can be considered breaking and entering even though the defendant technically did not have to break into the premises. The mere fact of entering without permission is sufficient to constitute breaking and entering. Similarly, if a person secretes himself and remains on the premises of a department store after closing in order to unlawfully take property, that conduct would also be considered breaking and entering. Again, the breaking and entering would occur because the defendant remained on the property after the established business hours without the consent of the owner.

Dwelling of Another at Night

Today, the *dwelling of another* can either be a home or a business and may or may not be occupied at the time of the breaking and entering. Additionally, a burglary may occur during the day. Although there is no longer a specific requirement that the breaking and entering occur at night in a dwelling, punishment for the offense is likely to be more severe if it does. This is because at night in a dwelling, there is a greater likelihood that the occupants of the dwelling will be present and suffer some harm as a result of the unlawful breaking and entering.

With the Intent to Commit a Felony

Breaking and entering onto the premises is the voluntary act element in the crime of burglary. The mental state component that accompanies this voluntary act is the specific intent to commit a crime once inside the dwelling. Many jurisdictions require that this intended crime amount to a felony. Therefore, when the defendant is breaking and entering the premises, he must have the specific intent to commit some type of criminal offense (e.g., larceny, robbery or a sexual assault) once inside the dwelling. It is important to understand that the defendant doesn't actually have to commit the offense once on the premises. It is sufficient for purposes of the crime of burglary if he breaks and enters with the specific intent to commit the criminal offense. Consider the following:

Barney Burglar waits patiently until an elderly woman leaves her home early one morning. Barney believes that the woman has lots of money hidden inside her home and intends to break into her home to steal it. As soon as the woman leaves, Barney approaches the back door and breaks a glass window to gain entry. Once inside, Barney begins opening and rifling through drawers and file cabinets. Suddenly,

Barney notices a very large German shepherd running toward him and immediately flees out the back door. Is Barney guilty of burglary?

Although Barney didn't take any money or other property after gaining entry into the elderly woman's home, he is still guilty of burglary. All that is required for the crime of burglary in this example is that Barney break and enter into the home with the intent to steal (or the intent to commit some type of crime while on the premises). There is no requirement that he actually commit the crime once inside the home. In fact, if he commits the crime while on the premises, he can be charged with two crimes. So, in the example above, if Barney had taken money from the home, he could be charged with burglary and larceny.

Occasionally, difficulties will arise in proving that the defendant had the intent to commit a crime on the premises, particularly if the defendant is somehow prevented from completing the criminal act once on the premises. As with most criminal law cases, the defendant's intent to commit a crime once on the premises can be demonstrated by circumstantial evidence. In the Barney Burglar example, Barney's specific intent to steal once inside the home can be demonstrated by examining his actions once inside the home. After breaking and entering, Barney began looking around and opening drawers and file cabinets before his activities were interrupted by the German shepherd "security system." This is strong circumstantial evidence of Barney's intent to unlawfully take property from the owner of the home after his unlawful entry.

RECEIVING STOLEN PROPERTY

Often, in property theft offenses, the defendant takes property with the intent to sell it to others in order to convert the property to cash. This unlawful practice creates a black market economy in which stolen goods are bought and sold at markedly reduced prices. To aid in undermining this underground exchange of stolen goods, the criminal law proscribes receiving stolen goods. To be guilty of *receiving stolen property*, a person must know that the property is stolen and intend to receive it as such. Implicit in this requirement is that the person receiving the stolen property is not the original thief, but is receiving stolen property from the person who stole it. To illustrate:

Cindy Shopper is walking on a downtown street one afternoon. A young man suddenly approaches her and tells her that he has excellent deals on brand new, expensive brand-name watches. When Cindy asks where she might view these watches, the young man removes several from his coat pocket and shows them to her. Cindy is somewhat surprised by this, but carefully examines the watches and purchases one for $30 cash. Cindy, a watch connoisseur, knows that her new purchase is a brand-name watch that would ordinarily sell in a retail store for at least $500. At the time of the purchase, Cindy also notices what appear to be personalized engraved initials on the back of the watch, but decides that the engraving can be removed with a little scrubbing. Is Cindy guilty of receiving stolen property?

To determine Cindy's liability for receiving stolen property, her knowledge and intent at the time of the purchase must be evaluated. A careful examination of the circumstances surrounding the watch purchase will be extremely helpful in providing insight into Cindy's knowledge and intent. First, the fact that Cindy was approached on the street by someone selling watches from his coat pocket strongly suggests that this is not the run-of-the-mill retail transaction. Further, the fact that the watches are being sold at a price that is significantly below their retail value (and Cindy knows this) is a strong indication that they may be stolen and that the seller is trying to get rid of them as quickly as possible. Finally, the fact that the watch Cindy purchased contained personal engraving is strong evidence that the watch may have been owned at some point and is not "brand new." Taken together, all of these facts provide fairly strong circumstantial evidence that Cindy knew the watch was stolen and intended to make the purchase despite the stolen character of the property.

FRAUD AND FALSE PRETENSES

The crime of fraud or false pretenses requires that the defendant make a false statement of past or present fact that induces the victim to relinquish title to property. Additionally, the defendant must have the intent to defraud the victim.

False Statement of Past or Present Fact

For the crime of fraud or false pretenses, the defendant must make a *false statement of past or present fact* as distinct from a statement or promise related to future activities. The requirement that the statement be related to past or present fact allows the statement to be evaluated for its truth or falsity. In other words, when trying to determine the defendant's fraudulent intent, statements of past or present fact can be measured against actual circumstances to determine if those statements are true or false. In contrast, statements of future actions or promises of future conduct cannot be measured because the outcome is uncertain, and the truth or falsity of the statements or promises cannot be evaluated until the particular time for the events has elapsed. Moreover, even though the statement or promise of future conduct may eventually turn out to be false, it is difficult to determine whether at the time the defendant made the statements, they were intended to be false or whether the defendant was merely being overly optimistic about the course of future events. For example, assume that a used-car salesman encourages a customer to purchase a vehicle by stating that the vehicle will be a "classic" in ten years and will double in market value. If the customer purchases the vehicle and many years later discovers that the vehicle is really just an average car and unlikely to increase in value, can the salesman be convicted of fraud? The answer is probably "no." At the time of the transaction, the salesman made statements concerning possible future events or occurrences. There would be no way to measure the truth or falsity of the statements at the time they are made with enough certainty to conclude that the salesman was acting with fraudulent intent. In fact, it is more likely that the salesman was giving his personal opinion or engaging in the common sales strategy of "puffing," that is, using slightly exaggerated statements to encourage customers to purchase products. While it is true that this sort of puffing can cross the border into fraudulent conduct, usually the statements must be of past or present fact so as to permit some way to measure the actual truth or falsity of the statements.

Relinquishing Title to Property

For the crime of fraud or false pretenses, the false statements must induce the owner to part with *title to the property*. Typically, the victim of a fraudulent transaction hands over money to the defendant. In these transactions, the victim fully intends that the defendant have complete title to the money and therefore intends to part with title to the property. The requirement that the defendant obtain title to the property fills a gap left open by larceny statutes, which only cover circumstances in which defendants obtain possession of property, as opposed to title.

Intent to Defraud

At the time of the false statement and the transfer of title, the defendant must also intend to defraud the victim. Generally, if the defendant has made a knowingly false statement of past or present fact that has induced the victim to part with title to property, there is strong circumstantial evidence of the defendant's *intent to defraud*. In other words, it is likely that most people would not knowingly make false statements and encourage others to rely upon them and part with property based upon the statements if they didn't have the specific intent to defraud. Nevertheless, the defendant's intent must be examined and proven in light of all the surrounding factual circumstances to ensure that the false statement was not a simple mistake or a misunderstanding.

Bad Check Statutes

One common and sometimes controversial example of the crime of false pretenses is writing bad checks. The theory of criminal liability for writing bad checks is that at the time the check is written, if the defendant does not have sufficient funds to cover the amount of the check, then the defendant is making a false statement of present fact. In these transactions, usually the owner of the property who receives the check parts with title to the property in exchange for the check (e.g., obtaining groceries at a grocery store). Thus, the owner parts with title to property in reliance upon the check (the false statement). The question in these cases is whether there is clearly an intent to defraud. If the check writer intends to place the money into his account before the check is presented for payment at the bank, then theoretically he does not have the intent to defraud the owner of the property. That is, at the time of the transaction, the check writer intends to exchange money for the property even though the money is not currently available in the account. On the other hand, if at the time the false statement (the check) is made in exchange for title to the property, the defendant knows that funds will never be available to cover the check, then it is clear that the defendant has acted with the intent to defraud.

Another way to analyze bad checks under the crime of false pretenses is to consider the check a promise to pay at a future date rather than a false statement of present fact. If it is considered a promise that the bank will honor the check at a future date when the check is actually presented to the financial institution for payment, then this conduct would fall outside the boundaries of the crime of false pretenses since the crime does not cover future promises. Perhaps anticipating or, in some cases, addressing this potential outcome under false pretenses statutes, most states have enacted statutes that specifically cover the crime of writing bad checks. Most of these statutes do not have a requirement that there be an exchange of property in reliance upon the bad check, but simply require that the check be presented with knowledge that the account has insufficient funds. Additionally, most of the statutes allow the check writer a grace period of usually ten days to pay the check once the bank has dishonored it. If the check writer does not remedy the situation within the grace period, then that fact will provide strong circumstantial evidence of intent to defraud.

CASE STUDIES

Theft by Computer

At common law, the theft of personal property was considered a serious felony. The definition of property was based upon the economic considerations of the time and encompassed most forms of tangible personal property. As the economy expanded, the definition of property similarly expanded to embrace new types of valuable property that could be the subject of theft. The trend of redefining property and the manner in which it can be "taken and carried away" continues today as criminals have begun utilizing modern computer technology to implement schemes to commit theft, one of the oldest crimes on the statute books.

Vladimir Levin worked out of a tiny office in St. Petersburg, Russia, as a programmer for a software company. His career aspirations were not limited to software programming, however, and it was subsequently discovered that Levin and his accomplices had developed and executed a scheme that eventually resulted in the theft of $10 million from Citibank, one of the country's largest financial institutions. Levin accomplished his scheme by surreptitiously transferring funds from Citibank customers' accounts in several countries into accomplices' accounts in the United States, Germany, Israel and the Netherlands. What is unique about Levin's crime is that he never left his dingy office in St. Petersburg and executed the entire scheme while sitting at his desk using an outdated computer. His actions represent an entirely new and sophisticated brand of theft by use of a computer.

With the advent of new types of computer technology and the vast array of sensitive financial information exchanged across networks everyday, it seemed only a matter of time before thieves infiltrated and abused these networks for their own unlawful financial gain. This brand of online theft is potentially more devastating because it is less easily detected than traditional bank robberies and thieves are capable of covering their "wireprints" effectively, leaving authorities with little or no concrete information as to the culprits' identities or geographic locations. Further, because the criminal conduct can be accomplished quickly, quietly and at any hour of the day, it is not unusual for these kinds of theft crimes to go undetected for a lengthy period of time. Of course, a longer delay in discovery increases the likelihood that the thieves will be able to commit similar crimes against the same institution. In other words, the delay provides a "window of opportunity" for more undetected criminal conduct.

Although the details of the Citibank scheme will likely never be made publicly available (for fear that others might be tempted to duplicate the criminal conduct), some basic information is known about the operation of the scheme. First, investigators acknowledge that Levin was somehow able to obtain very specific and confidential information concerning Citibank's security system, including customer identification and password information. With this information, Levin then accessed customers' accounts and wired millions of dollars from those accounts to the accounts created in the names of his accomplices. The accomplices then withdrew the illicit funds and, acting as couriers, transported the money to banks in other locations. The scheme was discovered when Wells Fargo Bank noticed a suspicious account containing a large amount of recently deposited money. Authorities eventually arrested a Russian national when she attempted to withdraw funds that had been unlawfully transferred from a Citibank account to the Wells Fargo account. All of the conspirators were arrested and convicted, including Levin, and all of the stolen funds were recovered except $400,000.

The traditional definition of larceny would probably not encompass this kind of theft for several reasons. First, the historical notion of "taking and carrying away" focused upon removing property from the possession or constructive possession of the owner. Thus, the "taking and carrying away" requirement specifically targeted the physical removal of the property. In many cases of computer crime, the theft is accomplished literally by means of pressing keys on a keyboard. The thief never physically touches the property. Additionally, the traditional notion of property was limited to tangible personal property, which would probably not be broad enough to cover the digital manipulation of numbers that represent property which occurred in the Levin case.

Statutes addressing crimes committed with computers have now been enacted in most jurisdictions. These statutes make it a crime to unlawfully access a computer or computer network for any purpose, including theft of property. Also, the definition of property in many theft statutes has been expanded to include taking valuable property by means of wire transfers. While many believe that these statutes have helped deter the spread of computer crimes, the true impact of these new statutory weapons is difficult to measure because victims are often reluctant to come forward and reveal the details of computer crime to authorities. Financial institutions, which are often targeted by these schemes, generally place a premium on consumer confidence and balk at notifying law enforcement authorities when their security systems have been breached for fear that consumers will lose confidence and take their business elsewhere. Therefore, most victims of these crimes prefer to deal with the issues quietly and internally. This is particularly true when the perpetrator of the offense is an insider or the theft is a direct result of the company's lax security policies. In these instances, the institution would rather seek private restitution from the thief or simply suffer the financial loss. The Citibank case was unusual because Citibank reported the suspected criminal conduct to authorities after noticing that money was disappearing from customer accounts. After Citibank's disclosure, the combined efforts of the FBI, Citibank officials and Russian law enforcement ultimately led to the apprehension of Levin and his accomplices. It is hoped that Citibank's frank disclosure in this case will serve as a model to other financial institution victims of computer crime.

Just as financial institutions can take security precautions to prevent criminals from walking in and using weapons to commit robberies, they can also take steps to enhance security in an effort to prevent theft by computer. Such prevention can include, among other things, establishing a secure computer network by changing passwords frequently, using encryption, erecting network firewalls and establishing multiple levels of authentication. These preventive measures go a long way toward increasing security by limiting authorized access to the network and requiring several levels of verification and authentication even for those with authorized access. However, because the Internet is essentially an unregulated global network of computers, it is virtually impossible to protect against every type of attack. As those familiar with security issues in the computer industry are quick to acknowledge, as long as a computer is attached to the Internet, it is exposed and can never be truly secure.

Theft by Receiving Stolen Property

As explained earlier in this chapter, those who steal items of property do so with the intent to exchange the stolen goods for cash in the thriving underground market for stolen goods. While the person who actually takes the property is guilty of larceny, those who acquire the property after the theft with knowledge of its stolen character are guilty of the crime of receiving stolen property. By attaching criminal liability to the act of receiving stolen property, the criminal law aims to deter this conduct and thereby remove the "demand" for stolen goods. The theory is that if there is no demand for the stolen goods, then those who "supply" the goods might be similarly deterred from committing thefts.

The crime of receiving stolen property often involves proof by circumstantial evidence. This evidence typically focuses on the recipient's knowledge of the stolen character of the property and his intent to possess the property despite its stolen character. Although the market for stolen goods is usually relegated to the secret underground economy, these illicit transactions can also arise in other, rather unusual circumstances.

Gregory Thomas was arrested for shoplifting merchandise at a Dayton's store in Minnesota. As Thomas was being questioned by police, he began disclosing details about the people who hired him to shoplift. Thomas eventually identified a wealthy family from Roseville, Minnesota, as his "employers" and told police that the family regularly provided him with a shopping list of items to steal and would then pay him a discount rate for the items when he acquired them. The family members allegedly involved in the unlawful scheme were Gerald Dick, a dentist, his wife, Judy, their son James, a former professional football player, and their daughter Stacy, an attorney. When police learned of the Dicks' scheme, they came up with a scheme of their own. Specifically, the police had Thomas (who was fully cooperating with the police) call the Dicks and tell them that he had stolen merchandise available and ready for delivery. As expected, Thomas was immediately invited to come to the Dicks' home. When Thomas arrived at the home, several members of the Dick family were present and purchased the goods. The Dicks were later arrested and charged with attempting to receive stolen property and conspiring to receive stolen property. At the time of the arrest, the police seized $400,000 worth of property believed to be stolen, including several items of expensive crystal and clothing.

At trial, the prosecutor revealed that Gregory Thomas, an admitted crack addict, had a long-standing relationship with the wealthy Dicks, who were apparently motivated by pure greed to acquire the stolen property. With the confession by Thomas and the "transaction" arranged by the police to catch the Dicks in the act, the evidence against the Dicks appeared to be overwhelming. The prosecution's case suffered a setback, however, when the judge excluded critical evidence in the case because of an unlawful search of the Dicks residence by the police. Throughout the proceedings, all of the Dicks denied knowledge of the stolen character of the property and also argued that they had been entrapped by the police. The jury eventually convicted only Judy Dick, who, based upon the evidence, appeared to be the ringleader of the scheme, that is, she had knowledge that the property was stolen. Gerald Dick and daughter Stacy were both acquitted, and charges against James Dick were dismissed during the trial due to evidentiary problems. Judy Dick was sentenced to fifteen days in jail and ordered to pay a $5,000 fine for attempting to receive stolen goods.

In reaching the guilty verdict against Judy Dick, the jury apparently considered several pieces of circumstantial evidence. For example, it appeared that Thomas dealt primarily with Judy in arranging these transactions. In fact, it was Judy who invited him to come to the Dicks' home immediately on the night Thomas called with stolen items as part of the police sting operation. Judy's husband and daughter also testified during the trial that they knew Judy was meeting with a "suspicious person" the night of the police sting operation, and each of them tried to avoid the situation. Ironically, this testimony may have at least indirectly implicated Judy in the scheme. Finally, there was the fact that Judy negotiated markedly reduced prices for the obviously expensive merchandise. Although one piece of evidence alone may not have been sufficiently indicative of Judy's knowledge and intent to receive stolen merchandise, taken together the facts paint a picture of Judy Dick as a person who had knowledge of the stolen character of the merchandise and an intent to acquire the property despite this knowledge. Again, although the police believed (and the prosecution alleged) that the entire Dick family was involved in the scheme, the evidence admitted at trial simply did not support such a conclusion.

A related criminal law concept raised by the Dick case is the issue of entrapment. Were the Dicks entrapped when the police asked Thomas to call and offer the Dicks stolen merchandise? Generally speaking, if individuals are already predisposed to commit certain offenses, the police do not entrap them by simply providing an opportunity to commit the offense. In this case, Thomas called the Dicks (as he had apparently done many times in the past) and offered them the opportunity to purchase the stolen goods. Thomas was immediately invited over and the transaction took place. There was no evidence that Thomas had to urge or insist upon a meeting with the Dicks that night, nor did the Dicks seem shocked or surprised to be presented with the opportunity to acquire the stolen goods. Indeed, there was evidence that Thomas had a long-standing relationship with the Dicks in which he repeatedly supplied them with stolen merchandise, long before the police became involved in the situation. In other words, the police did not plant the idea of receiving stolen property in the Dicks' minds, nor did they appear to cajole or harass them to commit the offense. The police (through Thomas) merely provided an opportunity to commit the offense, which the Dicks readily accepted.

The fact that the police were involved in the final transaction with the Dicks does however raise an interesting issue with respect to the stolen character of the property. When Thomas took the merchandise to the Dicks' home the night of the sting operation, he did so with the knowledge and consent of the owner of the property, Dayton's department store, and with the cooperation and participation of the police. In order for property to have a "stolen character," it must be taken and carried away from the owner without consent. If the owner consents to the taking, then the property is not stolen, and anyone who buys or receives it cannot be charged with actually receiving stolen property. However, the buyer or recipient in such a sting operation can be charged with *attempting* to receive stolen merchandise. This is because the crime of attempt focuses on what the defendant believed about the circumstances rather than the actual circumstances. Therefore, in a case of attempting to receive stolen property, if the defendant believed that the property was stolen and took a substantial step toward acquiring the property, then that conduct is sufficient for the crime of attempting to receive stolen property. The fact that the property wasn't actually stolen is irrelevant to this attempt because attempt crimes focus specifically on the defendant's conduct and beliefs rather than external circumstances. Judy Dick was convicted of attempting to receive stolen property because on the night of the sting operation, she believed the property was stolen and made an effort to acquire it despite her beliefs as to its stolen character.

Finally, the Dick case raises an issue with respect to punishment and white-collar criminals. Judy Dick spent very little time in jail and paid a fairly small fine when considering the total value of the stolen goods she apparently received. Were her wealth and status determining factors in setting her punishment? Perhaps. But this case also illustrates that in some instances of white-collar crime, the same wealth and status that may impact sentencing decisions can be quickly eroded by the humiliation, moral stigma and social ostracism that often accompanies a criminal trial. For some, this loss of esteem is by far the worst punishment.

FOR FURTHER CONSIDERATION

1. Has a larceny occurred if a customer pays for an item in a store and receives more change back than she is entitled to have but chooses not to return the extra change? Consider how the elements of larceny would apply to this example.
2. Many companies that discover employee embezzlement prefer to deal with the matter "in house." That is, they usually choose simply to fire the

embezzling employee rather than turn the case over to the authorities for prosecution. Why would companies choose not to seek prosecution in these cases? What are some costs and benefits to companies that do elect to prosecute embezzling employees?

3. Assume that on a camping trip you find a bag of money partially buried deep in the woods with a label on it that says "Acme National Bank." Would you be committing larceny if you decided to keep the money? Would it make a difference if you decided to keep the money because you are deeply in debt and about to lose the family home? Also, could you be charged with receiving stolen property? Why or why not?
4. Why do people who are intelligent, successful and wealthy commit crimes? Certainly it can't be because of the "usual" circumstances offered for embarking upon criminal conduct (e.g., bad environment, broken families, lack of education). Identify reasons that might make crime attractive to middle- and upper-class citizens. Also, consider what types of punishment might be most likely to deter these people from engaging in criminal conduct.

7

Criminal Law Defenses

Insanity is often the logic of an accurate mind overtasked.
—Oliver Wendell Holmes

In every criminal trial, the government is constitutionally required to prove its case against the defendant beyond a reasonable doubt. Additionally, defendants in criminal cases have a constitutional right to be free from compelled self-incrimination. Taken together, these concepts mean that in criminal cases, the government must independently investigate, obtain and present evidence against defendants. Criminal defendants are not required to speak or otherwise respond to the government's case against them, and the government shoulders the entire responsibility for proving its case.

Notwithstanding these prosecutorial responsibilities and constitutional protections, many criminal defendants voluntarily choose to present evidence during a criminal trial in response to the government's case. Such evidence might challenge the government's *case-in-chief* and/or attempt to present an excuse or justification for the defendant's behavior. Evidence challenging the government's case-in-chief will usually seek to demonstrate that the government does not have sufficient evidence to prove one or all of the material elements of the crime (i.e., the act, the mental state, causation and social harm) beyond a reasonable doubt. In challenging the government's case-in-chief, a defendant might also introduce evidence designed to prove that the government has charged the wrong person. This is known as an "alibi" defense, and the defendant will typically present evidence in the form of witness testimony that establishes that he could not have committed the crime because he was elsewhere at the relevant time of the offense. Finally, a defendant may also counter the government's case-in-chief evidence by vigorously attacking the accuracy and credibility of government witness testimony. By using these strategies, a criminal defendant is essentially challenging the government to meet its constitutional burden and prove its case beyond a reasonable doubt. But if a defendant is under no obligation to present a defense or even speak during a criminal trial, why would any defendant voluntarily choose to present a defense? Why not simply remain silent and put the government to its proof?

One reason may be that the defendant is innocent of the offense charged and wishes to present his or her story to the judge or jury. While the government has an obligation to collect evidence and prove its case, it is certainly under no obligation to present evidence favorable to the defendant during the trial. Another reason may be that the prosecution has amassed a compelling amount of evidence pointing to the defendant's guilt, and the defendant believes it would simply be too risky to allow that evidence to be offered at trial without challenge. Finally, in the face of overwhelming evidence of guilt, the defendant may wish to present evidence that his or her conduct at the time of the offense was either justified or should be excused. A defense offered to justify or excuse the defendant's conduct is known as an *affirmative defense*. By presenting an affirmative defense, the defendant is admitting that he or she engaged in the conduct charged, but is offering an excuse or justification for the behavior. In other words, the defendant is arguing: "Yes, I did it, but I have an (excuse and/or justification) for my conduct." When offering an affirmative defense, courts have determined that it is fair to place the burden of proof on the defendant because the defendant is raising the defense and is likely to have the most relevant evidence available to support the defense. Affirmative defenses are controversial because the defendant admits engaging in the conduct charged, but is asking to be partially or completely relieved of responsibility or punishment. Yet, many of these defenses remain popular precisely because, for defendants, they represent an opportunity to secure an acquittal or at least a reduced punishment despite the admission of responsibility. This chapter will focus on some of the more popular affirmative defenses.

THE INSANITY DEFENSE

The *insanity defense* is one of the best-known and most controversial affirmative defenses in criminal law. Although it seems that the defense is utilized on a widespread basis, in fact the insanity defense is used in no more than 3 percent of criminal trials and is rarely successful. The perception that it is frequently used is perhaps a by-product of the intense media attention that often surrounds criminal cases when the insanity defense is raised. The defense also attracts attention because it forces the criminal justice system to squarely confront the issue of how mental illness impacts the notion of moral blameworthiness. That is, how do we punish, if at all, the criminal defendant who commits an atrocious act, but does not know the nature of that conduct or cannot distinguish between right and wrong at the time of the criminal conduct? Is this defendant morally blameworthy and deserving of punishment? Or, should the conduct be excused and the defendant given treatment and appropriate rehabilitation so that he or she will no longer present a danger to society? These questions present extraordinarily difficult choices in our criminal justice system, particularly against the backdrop of horrific crimes, grieving relatives and the limitations and skepticism often associated with the idea of "rehabilitation" as punishment.

With the insanity defense, the criminal law seeks to ensure that a defendant is punished according to his level of moral blameworthiness by establishing specific criteria for presenting the defense. Those criteria will be discussed in the following sections.

Mental Disease or Defect

A defendant presenting an insanity defense must first demonstrate that he or she suffered from a mental disease or defect at the time of the offense. Although many state statutes refrain from specifically categorizing mental diseases or defects, generally, a mental disease or defect is defined as a severe, abnormal mental condition that grossly and demonstrably impairs a person's perception or understanding of reality. Thus, mental diseases or defects would include such commonly diagnosed mental illnesses as schizophrenia, multiple personality and bipolar disorders. However, mental diseases or defects typically do not include conduct that is manifested only by repeated criminal or otherwise antisocial conduct or conduct that is the result of voluntary intoxication. Therefore, a person who repeatedly engages in criminal activity just for the fun of it without remorse or who drinks to the point of intoxication and engages in criminal conduct would not be a likely candidate for the insanity defense.

Evidence of the defendant's mental disease or defect is usually presented in the form of psychiatric testimony. Prior to trial, as soon as the defendant gives notice of intent to use the insanity defense, psychiatrists for the defendant and for the government will examine the defendant to determine if, at the time of crime, the defendant's conduct was so grossly abnormal that it significantly impaired the ability to understand his or her actions or to distinguish between right and wrong. To make this determination, psychiatrists will attempt to reconstruct the events surrounding the crime. Of course, it is helpful to the defense if the defendant was seeking psychiatric help at the time of the offense or had already been diagnosed with a mental illness. Such treatment or diagnoses would provide some circumstantial evidence that the defendant may have been exhibiting abnormal behavior at or near the time of the offense, although this evidence would not be considered conclusive proof of a mental disease or defect.

When examining the defendant's conduct for evidence of a mental disease or defect, it is important to maintain a focus on the time period surrounding the criminal conduct because the criminal law is concerned only with the defendant's mental state at the time of the offense. Therefore, proving that the defendant suffers from a mental disease or defect at the time of trial is of little relevance unless the defendant's mental condition can be positively traced back to the time of the offense. (Of course, suffering from a mental disease or defect at the time of trial raises issues with respect to the defendant's ability to participate adequately in his or her own defense. However, those issues are beyond the scope of this book.) After considering all of the evidence gathered and presented by both sides, it will be left to the judge or jury to make the determination as to whether the defendant had a mental disease or defect at the time of the offense.

If, and only if, the defendant is able to sufficiently prove a mental disease or defect at the time of the offense, then his or her behavior will be further analyzed to determine if it meets the remaining criteria for the insanity test in effect in the particular jurisdiction. There are four different tests for insanity currently in use throughout the United States: The M'Naghten right-wrong test, the M'Naghten right-wrong test plus the irresistible impulse component, the American Law Institute (ALI) test, and the federal test. These tests are discussed in the following sections.

M'Naghten Right-Wrong Test

The M'Naghten right-wrong test requires the defendant to prove that, as a result of a mental disease or defect, he did not know the nature and quality of his actions or that if he did, he did not know right from wrong. As previously explained, the first step for any insanity defense is to demonstrate the existence of a mental disease or defect. If the defendant fails to prove that he suffered from a mental disease or defect at the time of the offense, then the insanity defense will fail at the first step. However, once a mental disease or defect is established, under the M'Naghten test the defendant must demonstrate that, as a result of this mental disease or defect, he either did not know the nature and quality of his actions or did know, but did not know right from wrong. These two alternatives are known as the two prongs of the M'Naghten test. A defendant will only have to prove that his conduct meets one of the prongs of the M'Naghten right-wrong test to satisfy the insanity defense.

M'Naghten's First Prong: Nature and Quality of Actions

The first prong of the M'Naghten test requires the defendant to prove that he did not know the nature and quality of his actions. This means that at the time of the offense, as a result of a mental disease or defect, the defendant simply did not know what he was doing. For example:

Dan Daze has been suffering severe paranoiac delusions and believes that his neighbor and close friend, Stan, is an alien who was sent to Earth to murder him. Based upon this belief, Dan barricades himself in his home and arms himself with several weapons in preparation for what he believes is an impending attack by Stan, the "alien" assassin. After not seeing or hearing from Dan for several days, Stan decides to check on him. As Stan unlocks the door to Dan's home, he is suddenly gunned down by Dan, who is wearing camouflage and yelling, "All aliens must die." When the police arrive, Dan insists that he just killed an alien assassin who was trying to attack him.

In this example, Dan would likely prevail on the first prong of the M'Naghten test. If it is initially demonstrated that his paranoid delusions arise from a mental disease or defect, then it appears that as a result of that mental disease or defect, Dan thought he was killing an alien. Dan did not know that he was actually murdering his close friend and neighbor, Stan, who had innocently come to check on Dan's condition. In other words, Dan did not know the nature and quality of his actions. If Dan prevails on this prong of the M'Naghten test, he will prevail on the insanity defense, and there is no need to consider the second prong of the test. On the other hand, if a defendant knows the nature and quality of his actions (i.e., fails the first prong of M'Naghten), then the second prong of the test permits further consideration of the defendant's conduct.

M'Naghten's Second Prong: Right versus Wrong

Defendants who know the nature and quality of their actions at the time of the offense may still prevail on the insanity defense if they can prove that as a result of a mental disease or defect, they did not know right from wrong. To illustrate, let's change the facts of the Dan/Stan example.

Assume now that Dan knows that it is his close friend and neighbor, Stan, entering his home. In fact, Dan specifically called Stan and asked him to come over. Unbeknownst to Stan, Dan had a vision the week before in which he was commanded by God to murder Stan in cold blood. Dan had been having delusions about murdering Stan for several months, but recently, a voice clearly told him that killing Stan was the right thing to do and that he had to act quickly in carrying out this "sacred mission." As Stan walks in the door, Dan kills him in accordance with the instructions he received from the vision.

Although Dan knows the nature and quality of his actions (i.e., that he is killing his neighbor and close friend Stan in cold blood), it appears that as a result of his psychotic visions, he cannot distinguish right from wrong. Dan's visions and voices "instruct" him to kill Stan and, as a result of his psychotic delusions, Dan is unable to exercise appropriate judgment with respect to this inherently unlawful behavior. If it is demonstrated that Dan was unable to distinguish right from wrong as a result of his psychotic visions, then he can prevail on the second prong of the M'Naghten test, even though he knew the nature and quality of his actions.

Some Problems with M'Naghten

The M'Naghten test measures a defendant's ability to understand what he is doing and evaluate how that conduct comports with legal and moral standards. The test has been criticized, however, for its failure to address the defendant who knows the nature and quality of his actions and can distinguish right from wrong but, by virtue of a mental disease or defect, is simply unable to control that conduct. There was a growing concern that the M'Naghten test placed too much emphasis on mental ability and ignored volitional impairment or the inability to control one's conduct. To compensate for this shortcoming in the M'Naghten test, many states added a third prong to the test, the "irresistible impulse" component.

M'Naghten Plus the Irresistible Impulse

The irresistible impulse prong is an addition to the M'Naghten right-wrong test and is intended to address impulsive conduct that is driven by a mental disease or defect. This prong covers conduct that cannot be controlled by the defendant as opposed to conduct that the defendant simply refuses to control. Problems arise when trying to determine the difference. That is, if a defendant knows the nature and quality of her actions and knows right from wrong, how is it logically possible that she cannot control her conduct? Is it more likely instead that the defendant simply did not control her conduct at the time of the offense? Or, stated another way, how much of the defendant's conduct at the time of the offense was driven by free will and choice rather than by a mental disease or defect? In jurisdictions that have added the irresistible impulse prong, these will be difficult questions for the judge or jury to grapple with when faced with an insanity defense based upon "irresistible impulse." Because of the difficulties associated with making these fine distinctions, many jurisdictions have not added the irresistible impulse prong to the M'Naghten test.

The American Law Institute Insanity Test

The American Law Institute (ALI) test was designed to address several other perceived shortcomings of the M'Naghten test. The ALI test provides that a person is not responsible for criminal conduct if at the time of such conduct, as a result of a mental disease or defect, that person lacks substantial capacity either to appreciate the criminality (wrongfulness) of his conduct or to conform his conduct to the requirements of law. The test further provides that the terms "mental disease or defect" do not include an abnormality manifested only by repeated criminal or otherwise antisocial conduct.

The most notable differences between the M'Naghten test and the ALI test are the phrase "lacks substantial capacity" and the exclusion of repeated criminal or antisocial conduct from the definition of mental disease or defect. Use of the phrase "lacks substantial capacity" makes the ALI test much broader than the M'Naghten test. Rather than requiring that the defendant be completely unaware of the nature and quality or wrongfulness of his actions, the ALI test asks only whether the defendent "lacks substantial capacity" to appreciate the wrongfulness of his conduct or conform to his conduct to the requirements of law. This means that the mental disease or defect does not have to completely incapacitate the defendant, who may be able to prevail on the insanity defense even though retaining some ability to think, perceive and/or control his conduct.

By excluding behavior manifested only by repeated criminal or otherwise antisocial conduct from the definition of mental disease or defect, drafters of the ALI test were seeking to draw a more clear distinction between mental diseases and defects and other forms of abnormal or psychopathic behavior. In defining mental diseases and defects, there was a concern that certain types of psychopathic behavior were not truly mental diseases or defects, but merely manifestations of more extreme variations along a spectrum of normal behavior. Because repeated criminal conduct and certain types of antisocial conduct are considered variations of normal behavior, they fall outside the boundaries of mental disease or defects. Defendants manifesting this type of behavior would not be entitled to use the insanity defense in jurisdictions that have adopted the ALI test.

The Federal Test

In response to the concern that the prevailing insanity tests were "too loose" and allowed defendants to escape punishment too easily, Congress enacted a federal test for the insanity defense. The federal test provides that the defendant must prove by "clear and convincing evidence" that at the time of the offense, as a result of severe mental disease or defect, he was unable to appreciate the nature and quality or the wrongfulness of his conduct.

In some respects, the federal test is more stringent than the ALI or M'Naghten test. First, the federal test requires proof that the mental disease or defect is severe, presumably creating an even higher hurdle for the defendant since in addition to demonstrating a mental disease or defect, the defendant must also prove that it is of a severe nature. Second, the federal test introduces a clear and convincing evidentiary standard, which means that the defendant must now produce a significant amount of credible and highly persuasive evidence to establish the insanity defense. Finally, the federal test returns once again to the requirement that the defendant be completely unable to understand the nature and quality or wrongfulness of his actions. A defendant who merely "lacks substantial capacity" would not be able to prevail under the federal test. The federal test is applicable in criminal cases that arise in federal courts.

Presenting an Insanity Defense

A defendant who chooses to present an insanity defense must notify the government prior to trial that he will use the defense. Both the defense and prosecution will then seek to have the defendant examined by psychiatrists, who will eventually be called upon to provide testimony at trial as to the defendant's mental state at the time of the offense.

At trial, the case begins with a presumption that the defendant is innocent and sane. The government begins first by presenting evidence that the defendant committed the crime. At the conclusion of the government's case-in-chief, the defendant presents evidence seeking to establish that he is not guilty by reason of legal insanity. By offering such evidence, the defendant is attempting to overcome the presumption of sanity and will be required to present enough credible evidence to have the insanity defense submitted to the judge or jury for consideration. After the defendant's presentation of evidence, the government will have an opportunity to challenge or rebut the defense evidence on the insanity issue and usually does so by presenting the testimony of psychiatrists to contradict the defendant's evidence. At the conclusion of the case, as in any criminal trial, the judge or jury must decide whether the government has proven its case beyond a reasonable doubt. In insanity defense cases, this inquiry will focus specifically upon whether the government has sustained its burden of proof despite the presentation of evidence on the insanity defense.

After reviewing all of the evidence, the judge or jury in an insanity defense case may return with one of several possible verdicts depending upon the particular jurisdiction. First, they may return a guilty verdict, which means that the government has proven beyond a reasonable doubt that the defendant committed the offense. A guilty verdict also means that the judge or jury rejected the insanity defense, and the defendant will be sentenced just as any other criminal defendant convicted of the same offense.

Second, the judge or jury could return with a verdict of not guilty, which means that the government did not prove its case beyond a reasonable doubt, and the defendant is completely acquitted and free to leave. A verdict of not guilty does not mean that the jury believed the insanity defense. It simply means that, for whatever reason, the government failed to prove each of the essential elements of the crime beyond a reasonable doubt. In that event, just as in any other criminal case, the defendant is completely acquitted.

Third, the judge or jury could return a verdict of not guilty by reason of insanity, which means that the defendant has prevailed on the insanity defense. The defendant is not free to leave, however, and is committed to a mental institution until he can demonstrate that he no longer presents a danger to society. The period of commitment is completely indefinite and could, in fact, last longer than any period of incarceration that the defendant might have received if convicted of the crime.

Finally, in some jurisdictions, the judge or jury could return a verdict of guilty but mentally ill. This verdict essentially represents a compromise because the defendant is considered responsible for the crime committed and is given a sentence as if ordinarily convicted of the crime. However, because it is also determined that the defendant was mentally ill at the time of the offense, he will be allowed to spend some of his incarceration period at a mental facility receiving treatment for his illness. If the defendant is cured of the mental illness during the term of the sentence, then he must still serve out the remainder of the sentence in a regular prison facility. If the defendant is not cured, he cannot be held longer than the term of the sentence and must be released from the mental facility, unless there are subsequent proceedings for a civil commitment.

Insanity Defense Distinguished from Diminished Capacity

A defendant raising a defense of *diminished capacity* is usually seeking to demonstrate that because of some type of mental or emotional abnormality or disturbance, he did not have the necessary mental state to commit the crime charged. As a result, a defense of diminished capacity is significantly different from the insanity defense both in substance and outcome. More specifically, the evidence of a defendant's mental condition in a diminished capacity case usually falls short of what is necessary to prove a mental disease or defect under the insanity defense tests. The diminished capacity defendant is thus precluded from presenting an insanity defense because of an inability to meet the "mental disease or defect" requirement. The diminished capacity defense allows a defendant to nevertheless use evidence of his abnormal mental condition to attack the prosecution's case-in-chief. In other words, the defendant may argue that he could not have possessed the mental state charged by the prosecution because he was suffering from an abnormal mental condition at the time of the offense. If the judge or jury believes the defense of diminished capacity, then the defendant will usually be convicted of a lesser crime than originally charged (e.g., a defendant might be convicted of voluntary manslaughter instead of intentional murder). The defense of diminished capacity is therefore not a complete defense such that the defendant will be acquitted of the crime charged if the defense is believed. Nor does it usually allow the convicted defendant to be "sentenced" to a mental health facility, because the diminished capacity defendant is not considered legally insane. Instead, acceptance of a diminished capacity defense usually means that the defendant will be held partially responsible for the crime because of his abnormal mental condition and, accordingly, he will receive a reduced punishment when convicted.

SELF-DEFENSE

If believed, a defense of *self-defense* presents a complete justification for the crime charged. This means that if the judge or jury believes that the defendant acted in self-defense, he will be completely acquitted of the criminal charges. Self-defense is typically presented in criminal trials when the defendant has been charged with murder or manslaughter. When presenting this defense, the defendant essentially argues that he used reasonable force to defend himself from an imminent unlawful attack and that he reasonably believed that such force was necessary to repel the attack. Depending upon the nature of the imminent unlawful attack, in some instances self-defense will permit the use of deadly force. Deadly force is force by whatever means that is highly likely to cause death or serious bodily injury to the victim. Consider the following example:

Ed and Doug have a heated argument one evening and have to be separated in order to avoid a physical altercation. The next day, as Doug is backing out of his driveway, he sees Ed rapidly approaching from behind the vehicle with a gun in his hand and yelling angrily. Doug fears that Ed has "gone over the edge," and decides that he needs to act quickly. Doug puts his car in reverse and quickly backs the car in the direction of Ed, who is still yelling and approaching with the weapon. Doug hits Ed with his vehicle and Ed falls to the ground, where he hits his head on the concrete and is killed by the impact. Is Doug guilty of murder for the death of Ed?

While it is true that Doug is responsible for Ed's death, Doug will likely have a compelling argument for self-defense considering the factors necessary for the defense. Doug was the victim of an imminent unlawful attack since Ed was rapidly approaching Doug's vehicle with a deadly weapon drawn. Assuming that Ed had no lawful authority to approach Doug with a deadly weapon, the attack upon Doug was imminent, unlawful and apparently intended to be deadly. Further, based upon what Doug is able to observe from Ed's aggressive behavior (coupled with Doug's knowledge of their confrontation the night before), Doug actually believes that Ed is going to use deadly force since Ed is approaching in a threatening manner with a deadly weapon drawn. Under the circumstances, it is also likely that a reasonable person would believe that Ed is going to use deadly force against Doug. Considering all of these circumstances then, Doug is justified in using reasonable force to repel Ed's attack. In this case, since it appeared that Ed was about to use deadly force (a gun), Doug would likely be permitted to meet deadly force with deadly force. Therefore, using his car as a weapon to repel the attack would probably be considered reasonable and appropriate force under the circumstances, and Doug will not be criminally responsible for Ed's death.

This example illustrates the application of several necessary factors for using deadly force in self-defense: (1) the attack must be imminent, unlawful and potentially deadly; (2) the person using self-defense must actually believe that deadly force is necessary to repel the attack; and (3) when considering all of the surrounding circumstances, it must be reasonable to believe that deadly force is necessary to repel the attack. What if Doug actually believed that Ed was going to attack him using deadly force, but it turns out that Doug's belief is not reasonable? In other words, what if a reasonable person would not have believed that deadly force was necessary under the circumstances? To illustrate:

Assume once again that Doug is backing out of his driveway. In his rearview mirror, he sees Ed casually approaching from the rear of the vehicle. Although Ed does not have a weapon drawn, Doug assumes that Ed is coming to "settle the score" from the heated argument they had the night before. Doug decides to back his car into Ed to prevent what Doug believes is an imminent, unlawful and deadly attack by Ed. Ed is knocked to the ground by the force of the vehicle and killed. It is subsequently determined that although Ed was still angry with Doug, Ed did not have a weapon of any kind as he was approaching Doug's car. Is Doug criminally responsible for Ed's death?

In light of all the circumstances surrounding the previous night's argument, Doug may actually have believed that an unlawful attack by Ed was imminent and that deadly force would be necessary to repel the attack. The pivotal question, however, is whether it was reasonable under the circumstances for Doug to have such a belief. Given the fact that Ed was casually approaching and did not appear to have a weapon, would a reasonable person have believed that deadly force was necessary under the circumstances? The answer is probably no. Even though Doug may have actually believed that an unlawful and deadly attack was imminent and that he needed to respond with deadly force, it is unlikely that these beliefs were reasonable under the circumstances. Instead, Doug overreacted and is now limited to what is known as an "imperfect self-defense." That is, while he honestly believed deadly force was necessary, his belief was unreasonable in light of the surrounding circumstances. Doug will therefore be criminally responsible for Ed's death, although he will probably face reduced charges of voluntary manslaughter, an unlawful killing without malice aforethought rather than intentional murder charges. This is because there was no malice involved in Doug's conduct since he honestly believed that deadly force was necessary, and that belief, rather than any malice toward Ed, motivated Doug's actions.

Defendant as Aggressor

To properly raise a defense of self-defense, a defendant cannot be the aggressor. This means that the defendant cannot instigate an altercation and then claim self-defense when the victim of his attack responds to his aggression with force. To illustrate, let's change the facts of the Doug/Ed encounter slightly.

Assume now that Ed is once again rapidly and angrily approaching Doug's vehicle with a weapon drawn. Doug sees Ed and, fearing an imminent use of deadly force by Ed, Doug begins backing his car in the direction of Ed. Ed now becomes afraid for his own life as the car is moving rapidly in his direction and shoots at Doug in an attempt to prevent Doug from running over him. One of the bullets strikes Doug, instantly killing him. Is Ed criminally responsible for Doug's death or can he use a defense of self-defense?

Since Ed instigated the incident when he angrily approached Doug while displaying a deadly weapon, Ed should have expected that his use or threat of deadly force would be met by equivalent deadly force by Doug. Ed cannot claim self-defense for shooting Doug when, in fact, Ed caused Doug to use deadly force against him in the first place. Does this mean that if Ed is the aggressor and instigates the encounter, he must simply stand by and allow Doug to use deadly force against him? In other words, if Ed approaches Doug with a weapon drawn and, in response, Doug begins to back his vehicle into Ed, does Ed have no alternative but to suffer the fate of being run down by Doug simply because Ed started the altercation? Or, can Ed somehow try to prevent Doug's use of deadly force, as he did by shooting Doug?

Under the law of self-defense, a person who is the aggressor is not entitled to use deadly force to repel an attack unless he first retreats and gives an indication that he is no longer a threat to the victim. If the victim persists in responding to the aggressor after the aggressor retreats, then the aggressor may respond with deadly force. To apply this analysis to the example, consider that, Ed, the aggressor, began the encounter by approaching Doug with a deadly weapon drawn. If Doug responds with deadly force by backing his vehicle into Ed, Ed may not respond to this use of deadly force by Doug, unless Ed first retreats and gives an indication that he is no longer a threat to Doug. Therefore, before firing his weapon at Doug, Ed should have put the weapon away and conveyed to Doug that he no longer intended to use deadly force and retreated from the scene. Then, if Doug continued to pursue Ed with his vehicle, Ed would be entitled to use deadly force because Ed is no longer a threat to Doug, and Doug has in effect become the aggressor by pursuing Ed after Ed has retreated.

There are at least two ways a defendant can become the aggressor. First, as in the example, a defendant who starts an altercation is considered the aggressor and may not claim self-defense if his aggression is met with deadly force unless he first retreats. Second, a person who escalates an encounter can become the aggressor. So, for example, if an encounter begins with the use of nondeadly force by the aggressor, and the victim responds with deadly force, the victim, by responding with deadly force, becomes the aggressor because he has escalated the encounter to the level of deadly force. The person who escalates the encounter would not have a valid self-defense argument since it is almost never considered reasonable to use deadly force in response to a nondeadly attack.

Retreat

As discussed, a person who instigates an encounter by using deadly force must first retreat before using deadly force to defend himself from a responsive deadly force attack by the victim. In some jurisdictions, the retreat doctrine is much broader, such that a victim who is initially threatened by an aggressor with deadly force must "retreat to the wall" before he may respond with deadly force. This means that the victim of an imminent, unlawful and deadly attack must do everything possible to avoid using deadly force, although he does not have to go so far as to place himself in greater danger (e.g., running into a busy intersection to avoid a gun-wielding aggressor). Also, a victim of a deadly attack does not have to retreat in his own home. The law does not force a person to flee the safety of his home in order to avoid an unlawful attack. The "retreat to the wall" doctrine is used in only a few jurisdictions, and most continue to adhere to what is known as the "true man" rule, which means that a person threatened with deadly force can stand his ground and respond with deadly force.

DEFENSE OF OTHERS

A person may use reasonable force to defend another person who is the victim of an unlawful attack. If the victim is threatened with or subjected to the use of deadly force, then the person coming to his defense may use deadly force in response. Problems arise when the person coming to the aid of a victim misinterprets the situation and uses force that is inappropriate under the circumstances. For example, a person may encounter two people engaged in a physical altercation and decide to step in and use deadly force to defend one of the parties. If it turns out that the victim of the attack would not have been entitled to use deadly force, then the person coming to his assistance would not be justified in using such force either, regardless of his perception of the situation. In this instance, the person offering assistance is said to "stand in the shoes" of the victim, and if the victim would not have been able to use deadly force during the encounter, then any person coming to his assistance will not be entitled to use such force either. Indeed, the person offering assistance may be criminally liable if his unjustified use of force results in harm to another.

A few jurisdictions allow a person coming to the aid of another to use force according to his perception of the circumstances. Therefore, if a person comes upon a situation and reasonably believes that deadly force is necessary to aid one of the participants in the encounter, then the use of such force will be considered appropriate even if it is later determined that the victim of the attack would not have been entitled to use such force. This interpretation of the right to defend others is intended to encourage third parties to offer assistance to those who may be endangered by violent unlawful attacks without worrying that they will be subjected to criminal liability for coming to the aid of another.

DEFENSE OF PROPERTY

Deadly force may not be used to protect property under any circumstances. The reason for this is simply that human life should be valued over real or personal property. Nonetheless, some jurisdictions have enacted "make my day" laws. These controversial statutes allow homeowners to use whatever level of force is necessary against intruders who enter the home and threaten to use any type of force against the homeowner or anyone in the home. Although these statutes do not permit the homeowner to use force merely to protect his property, they do allow the homeowner to insure safety within his home when someone enters the home with the intent to use force against him or other occupants in the home.

INTOXICATION DEFENSE

A defendant may use a defense of voluntary *intoxication* to prove that she did not have the necessary intent to commit the crime charged. When presenting this defense, the defendant is claiming that her mind was so affected by drugs or alcohol that she could not form the required intent to commit the crime or, in some cases, could not perform the voluntary act required by the criminal statute. The intoxication defense is very controversial because of the general belief that a voluntarily intoxicated person should be responsible for the consequences of her actions. Nevertheless, in many jurisdictions, the defendant's state of voluntary intoxication may serve as a defense if it prevents her from forming the necessary intent to commit a particular offense. The defense is sometimes limited, however, and in some jurisdictions the defendant may only present a defense of voluntary intoxication when charged with crimes that require specific intent. So, for example, if a defendant is charged with the crime of larceny (a specific intent crime), she may present an intoxication defense to show that, because of her intoxication, she could not form the specific intent to steal. The theory is that while the defendant might be generally aware of her conduct, her mind is too clouded by alcohol or drugs to think about and form the specific intent to permanently deprive the owner of the property as required by the larceny statute.

Even when limited to demonstrating lack of specific intent, the intoxication defense is still very controversial. As indicated earlier, the controversy is based, in part, on the fact that the law should strongly discourage individuals from becoming intoxicated to the point of engaging in criminal conduct. Allowing an intoxication defense, even in limited circumstances, significantly interferes with this deterrence objective. There is also a realization that rather than preventing the formation of intent to commit a crime, alcohol may indeed embolden some individuals to engage in criminal activity. For these reasons, a few jurisdictions have completely eliminated the defense of voluntary intoxication even for crimes that require proof of specific intent. Again, the theory is that defendants who become voluntarily intoxicated should be responsible for the consequences of their actions.

Involuntary intoxication, however, remains a valid defense to criminal conduct. Involuntary intoxication can occur, for example, when a person erroneously takes more than the proper dosage of medication or becomes unusually and unexpectedly intoxicated by an amount of alcohol that would not have such an effect on the average person. Under such circumstances, if the intoxicated state is truly involuntary and unexpected, then the person is not considered responsible for any resulting criminal conduct because, in fact, the person did not act voluntarily and/or with the necessary mental state.

SYNDROME DEFENSES

In some cases, a defendant charged with a criminal offense will offer evidence of a particular syndrome as a means for explaining conduct at the time of the offense. One of the more popular *syndrome defenses* is the battered woman's syndrome. Usually, in these cases, the battered woman, after a period of serious emotional and/or physical abuse, strikes out and kills her abuser. Self-defense is generally not an option in such cases because the killing often takes place when there is no threat of an imminent attack. Yet, the battered woman is indeed striking out against her abuser and the years of abuse. If she is prevented from using a defense of self-defense because there was no imminent unlawful attack, then her conduct looks very much like a premeditated, deliberate and intentional killing, with very little in the way of excuse or justification. In an effort to offer an explanation for her conduct and to place the judge or jury in her shoes at the time of the offense, the defendant may present evidence of the battered woman's syndrome. Offering evidence of this syndrome helps answer the question that inevitably arises in these cases: "Why didn't she simply leave the situation rather than killing her abuser?" The battered woman's syndrome allows the defendant to introduce evidence that battered women often feel emotionally and financially trapped by their abusive situations and are in constant fear that their abusers will violently attack with little or no advance warning. Thus, the syndrome evidence is offered to explain why the defendant decided to act when she did and how she did. In that sense, the battered woman's syndrome is not presented as a defense to the crime in the strict sense. Instead, it is offered as an explanation for why the defendant may have been thinking and acting as she did at the time of the offense. From the defense perspective, it is hoped that this evidence will engender compassion from the judge or jury when deciding the defendant's fate and will ultimately result in a reduced punishment.

Another example of syndrome evidence is the rape trauma syndrome. The government, during a rape prosecution, may offer evidence to help explain why the rape victim may not have acted as expected after the rape incident occurred. In some instances, a rape victim does not report the crime immediately and may even react calmly after the incident. The rape trauma syndrome helps the judge or jury to understand the victim's conduct by explaining that some victims may be under such severe shock that they may be physically and emotionally incapable of confronting the circumstances of the rape. The rape trauma syndrome explains that although rape victims may act in a manner that appears outwardly calm, they are in fact suffering from the severe trauma of rape. Of course, the court must take special care to insure that rape trauma syndrome evidence is not used to prove that, in fact, a rape occurred. Instead, the evidence should be limited to explaining why the victim may not have behaved as "expected" in light of the charges being made against the defendant.

Another popular example of syndrome evidence is the "Vietnam veteran syndrome," which is sometimes referred to as post-traumatic stress disorder (PTSD). In these cases, the defendant offers specific evidence to demonstrate how his traumatic combat experiences have affected his ability to cope with and respond appropriately to everyday noncombat circumstances. Again, a defendant offering this type of evidence is attempting to place the judge or jury in his shoes to help them understand his peculiar perspective at the time of the offense. With that unique understanding, it is hoped that the judge or jury will be somewhat compassionate when determining the appropriate punishment for the offense committed by the defendant.

MISTAKES

One of the basic maxims of criminal law is that ignorance of the law is no defense. This means that defendants may not escape criminal liability by claiming that they did not know that their conduct violated the law. The rationale for this is that the law is knowable and citizens should therefore be encouraged to discover the law rather than avoiding knowledge and using ignorance as a defense. There is, however, one notable exception to this general rule.

In some jurisdictions, ignorance of the law (or *mistake of law*) may serve as a defense if the defendant sought knowledge or advice from a person or entity with official authority to interpret the law and it is subsequently determined that this official interpretation was incorrect. This qualifies as an exception because the circumstances indicate that the defendant made a good faith effort to discover the law and should not be penalized if it turns out that the advice or information concerning the law was inaccurate.

Entities with official authority to interpret the law include courts, legislatures, administrative agencies and law enforcement authorities. Attorneys are not among those considered to have official authority to interpret the law because of the concern that, in some instances, attorneys might be tempted to provide any "official interpretation" that the paying client wants to hear.

A defendant who makes a *mistake of fact* may have a valid defense in some cases if the mistake is reasonable under the circumstances. For example, in a sexual assault case, if the defendant mistakenly believes that the victim consented to sexual intercourse, then the defendant has made a mistake of fact. When the defendant raises this defense at trial, the judge or jury will have to examine all of the facts related to the incident to determine if the defendant's mistake of fact was reasonable in light of all of the surrounding circumstances. If the mistake as to the victim's consent was reasonable, then the defendant could not have intended to sexually assault the victim. Thus, a mistake of fact can serve to negate the necessary mental state for the offense.

A defense of mistake of fact may also be valid if it negates the specific intent necessary for a crime. For instance, if the defendant takes property under the mistaken belief that it has been loaned to him by the owner, then he probably cannot be successfully prosecuted for the crime of larceny. Larceny requires a taking and carrying away of the property with the intent to permanently deprive the owner of the property. If the defendant honestly, but mistakenly, believes that the property had been loaned to him, then he cannot have the specific intent to unlawfully and permanently deprive the owner of the property—a necessary element for a larceny conviction. Again, whether the defendant has in fact made an honest mistake will be evaluated by examining all of the surrounding circumstances.

CASE STUDIES

The Case for Insanity

Insanity is a legal term of art that defines the circumstances when a defendant who has committed a criminal offense will be excused from traditional punishment standards because of his mental state at the time of the offense. As explained in this chapter, the insanity defense allows a defendant to argue that because of a mental disease or defect, he did not know the nature and quality of his actions, did not know right from wrong, or could not control his conduct at the time of the offense. As a prerequisite for raising the insanity defense, the defendant must demonstrate that he suffers from a mental disease or defect. This proof almost always involves competing psychiatric testimony from the prosecution and the defense concerning the defendant's mental state. Proof of a mental disease or defect alone is not enough, however. The defendant must also show that the mental disease or defect directly impacted his conduct at the time of the criminal offense. This proof generally requires an examination of the circumstantial evidence surrounding the unlawful conduct.

Jeffrey Dahmer was arrested in July 1991 and was eventually charged with fifteen counts of intentional homicide. During the investigation, when the police searched Dahmer's apartment, they found skulls and frozen body parts, which were apparently the remains of his many victims. After questioning by police, Dahmer provided a lengthy and detailed confession in which he explained that he was trying to find the perfect "zombie type" sex slave and took his search too far by murdering, dismembering and cannibalizing his victims.

Prior to trial, perhaps due to the compelling evidence of his guilt, Dahmer offered a plea of guilty but mentally ill. Thus, jurors hearing the trial evidence in Dahmer's case did not have to determine his guilt or innocence. The sole task for the jury was to determine whether Dahmer was legally insane at the time of the offenses. If the jury determined that he was legally insane, then his punishment would consist of commitment to a mental institution rather than incarceration in the traditional prison setting.

As anticipated, Dahmer's assertion of the insanity defense launched a multitude of psychiatric examinations that attempted to determine his mental state at the time of the offenses. Although his horrific behavior appeared to be the type of conduct that could only be committed by an insane person, for purposes of criminal law Dahmer's conduct would nevertheless have to meet the strict requirements of the insanity defense test. That is, it would have to be demonstrated that Dahmer suffered from a mental disease or defect and that as a result he either did not know the nature and quality of his actions or did not know right from wrong or could not control his conduct.

Not surprisingly, the psychiatric testimony was contradictory and somewhat inconclusive. The failure to arrive at clear and consistent results in these types of psychiatric examinations results from an effort to reconcile the incompatible disciplines of psychiatry and law in an attempt to determine moral blameworthiness. In this context, psychiatry and law are incompatible because the aim of psychiatry and psychology is to identify abnormal behaviors and pursue a course of treatment. Often, these abnormal behaviors are neither static nor easily defined or categorized. Yet, definition and categorization are precisely what the legal insanity test requires. Moreover, the legal insanity test focuses upon specifically defined behavior at a particular point in time—the time of the offense. Thus, confusion and inconclusiveness become the norm in insanity defense trials as lawyers attempt to use imprecise psychiatric terms to precisely define and categorize the defendant's criminal conduct at a particular point in time. Another reflection of the incompatibility of psychiatry and criminal law is revealed by examining the objectives of both. Psychiatry seeks to evaluate abnormal behavior for the purpose of establishing a treatment plan, whereas in the criminal law, the behavior is evaluated to determine moral blameworthiness and punishment. Thus, in an insanity defense trial the trier of fact is asked to take psychiatric information that is typically used for the diagnosis and treatment of mental illness and make a determination as to the defendant's criminal liability, using specifically worded legal tests. This can be a particularly daunting, if not impossible, task for jurors who have no prior knowledge of either psychiatry or the law.

The psychiatrists in the Dahmer case reached several different conclusions concerning Dahmer's mental state. In various opinions, they concluded that he suffered from paraphilia, necrophilia, alcoholism and an antisocial personality disorder. The psychiatrists all agreed, however, that based upon the contents of Dahmer's confession, he knew the nature and quality of his actions and could distinguish right from wrong at the time he committed the offenses. That is, Dahmer knew that he was torturing and killing young men and knew that his conduct violated the law. Therefore, the jury's task was to determine if Dahmer suffered from a mental disease or defect that prevented him from controlling his conduct.

After listening to days of testimony detailing Dahmer's criminal behavior, which was variously described as "unusual," "bizarre," and "Satanic," the jury rejected the insanity defense and found Dahmer guilty on all fifteen counts of murder. By rejecting the defense, the jurors found that Dahmer was legally sane and morally blameworthy for his criminal conduct. It is important to understand that the jury's determination did not mean that Dahmer was not suffering from a mental illness. Indeed, the horrific nature of his criminal behavior strongly indicates that he was a deeply disturbed individual. However, the jury only determined that insofar as the criminal law test for insanity, Dahmer's conduct did not meet the legal requirements. This seemingly inconsistent finding once again illustrates the different and sometimes incompatible focus of psychiatry and the criminal law.

Dahmer's case represents one instance in which the insanity defense was unsuccessful. In fact, it is the rare criminal defendant who uses and succeeds in proving an insanity defense. Interestingly, however, in some criminal trials, the insanity defense becomes an issue precisely because it is not used.

Colin Ferguson used a weapon to kill six people and wound nineteen others on a Long Island commuter train. Ferguson had no apparent motive for the shootings and his actions appeared to be a random act of violence. Prior to trial, Ferguson's assigned attorneys suggested that he pursue an insanity defense at trial. Ferguson rejected this suggestion and promptly fired his attorneys. Instead, Ferguson chose to represent himself during the trial and conducted a most unusual defense, which included harshly questioning those he was accused of injuring and ranting about conspiracy plots against him. Ferguson's arrogance and insistence that he was not the shooter, despite numerous eyewitnesses, intensely angered many of the victims and trial observers who believed that Ferguson's representation of himself made a mockery of the criminal justice system. Ultimately, Ferguson's bizarre defense of himself failed miserably, and he was convicted of the charges against him.

Although many believed that Ferguson's trial and defense of himself turned the criminal justice system into a circus, the fact is that criminal defendants have a constitutional right to represent themselves in a criminal trial. The Sixth Amendment to the Constitution has long guaranteed the right to counsel as well as the corresponding right to serve as one's own counsel. This guarantee is scrupulously observed by courts because improper denial of the right can lead to the reversal of a conviction. Judges are therefore very wary of denying a criminal defendant the right to self-representation. In some cases, though, it becomes clear that defendants are unable to represent themselves competently because of their mental state. The court is then torn between recognizing the right to self-representation and ensuring that defendants have a competent and effective defense throughout the trial. To mitigate some of the harm that might result from allowing mentally unstable defendants to represent themselves, courts usually assign legal counsel to assist them. Counsel is then available to offer advice and guidance and even to take over the defense if for some reason defendants are unable or unwilling to proceed.

Ironically, the decision to allow defendants to represent themselves may establish grounds for appeal if the defendants are convicted. The defendants' main argument on appeal is, of course, that they were not mentally capable of standing trial or conducting their own defense and the trial court erred by allowing them to do so. The appellate court is then placed in the anomalous position of determining whether defendants received competent self-representation at trial in spite of their own mental instability. By providing competent back-up legal counsel for these defendants during trials, the trial courts can go a long way toward preventing these kinds of anomalies.

Self-Defense or Murder? The Battered Woman's Defense

Self-defense in criminal law is ultimately a matter of reasonableness. Defendants who intentionally commit criminal acts may be acquitted of the crimes if they acted based upon an actual and reasonable belief that they were confronting an imminent, unlawful and deadly attack. In these cases, the trier of fact must determine not only what the defendants believed, but whether that belief was reasonable under the circumstances. When considering the notion of reasonableness in the context of self-defense, the question is: "Given all of the surrounding circumstances, would a reasonable person have believed there was an imminent threat of serious bodily injury?" If the answer to that question is "yes," then the defendants' behavior is considered reasonable under the circumstances, and the defendants are not deemed morally blameworthy for their conduct. If the answer is "no," however, then the defendants' actions are considered unreasonable, and they will face punishment for their unlawful behavior.

Over the years, there has been significant controversy as to how the notion of reasonableness in self-defense should be defined. Specifically, in cases of battered women who kill their abusive spouses, should the women's prior history of abuse be considered when determining whether they acted reasonably at the time of the killing? The answer to this question is an unqualified "yes," according to those working on behalf of the Battered Women's Clemency Project in several states. The Battered Women's Clemency Project, which is composed primarily of volunteers, files clemency petitions seeking early prison release for battered women who have been convicted of killing their abusers. The Clemency Project selects cases in which they believe the convicted women are most deserving of mercy.

For example, in Florida, after years of abuse in a ten-year marriage, Jewell Gibson confronted her abusive husband and shot him to death in front of several witnesses. The shooting occurred shortly after her husband had brutally beaten her. After the beating, Gibson simply decided that she had endured enough and took steps to end her husband's life. Gibson was eventually convicted of second-degree murder and sentenced to twelve years in prison. Similarly, in a case in Michigan, Geraldean Gordon killed her husband while he slept. Over the course of their marriage, her husband had repeatedly beaten and raped her. Gordon was convicted and sentenced to 18–35 years in prison for killing her husband.

In each of these cases, the Clemency Project has determined that these women are worthy candidates for early release from prison because they killed after enduring years of physical and mental abuse. Those working with the Clemency Project contend that the issues and effects of long-term domestic violence were not adequately taken into account during the trials of these women because, until recently, the legal system was not sympathetic to issues surrounding domestic violence. Since these issues were not properly accounted for during the trials of Gibson and Gordon, the Clemency Project volunteers petition to request consideration of these issues as a basis for clemency and early release from prison.

As might be expected, the efforts of the Clemency Project are extremely controversial because in each instance the criminal conduct of the women involved was deliberate and intentional. Moreover, at the time of the killing, the women were not acting in self-defense because they were not defending themselves from imminent deadly attacks. Thus, the killings occurred when there was no immediate threat of attack. At trial, without an adequate legal basis for a claim of self-defense, women accused of murder under these circumstances must somehow attempt to place the jurors in their unique frame of reference at the time of the killings.

By introducing evidence of the battered woman's syndrome, the defendant is asking the jury to consider the circumstances of past physical and emotional abuse when determining whether the defendant's conduct was reasonable under the circumstances. In other words, because the threat of serious bodily injury was not imminent in these cases, the jury is asked to consider the reasonableness of the defendant's conduct in light of the years of abuse that occurred rather than any threat that may or may not have been imminent at the time of the killing. Jurors are also told that after years of abuse, battered women often have a heightened awareness and fear of danger, and they are often capable of predicting when their abusers are going to explode in an abusive rage. Additionally, battered women typically feel a strong sense of isolation and an inability to escape their abusive situations. Because of this unique frame of reference, at the time of the killing, the defendant/abuse victim is striking out to prevent further abuse. From the defendant's perspective, the act of killing is a reasonable response even though there is no imminent threat at the time. Thus, the battered woman's syndrome defense asks the jury to step into the shoes of the defendant and consider the reasonableness of her actions from that perspective. If the jury believes that the defendant's conduct was reasonable under the circumstances, then the defendant is acquitted of all charges. If, however, the jury considers the conduct unreasonable, then the defendant could be convicted of voluntary manslaughter or first- or second-degree murder depending upon the nature of her intentional conduct during the killing.

Those who oppose the use of prior domestic abuse evidence in these cases argue that it impermissibly expands the definition of self-defense, which should remain limited to instances when the threat posed is imminent and deadly. If self-defense can be argued in cases when there is no actual imminent threat, then there is a grave concern that such a practice might result in open season on abusers instead of encouraging abuse victims to seek nonviolent remedies for their circumstances. Of course, similar arguments are advanced when organizations such as the Clemency Project attempt to secure early release for women convicted of killing their abusers. Some believe that since these women have been convicted of intentional murder, they should serve the sentence provided for their unlawful conduct. So far, efforts such as those by the Clemency Project have met with limited success. Nevertheless, these organizations continue their work with the hope that as issues related to the effects of long-term violent domestic abuse become more widely recognized, society in general will become more sympathetic to the plights and desperate choices of women whose lives are overshadowed by violence.

FOR FURTHER CONSIDERATION

1. What is a reasonable perspective in self-defense cases? Should we look at reasonableness from the defendant's perspective, or should we define a standard that applies to all cases? For example, assume that a man murders an Asian gentleman who rings his doorbell one day asking for directions. At trial, the defendant offers a defense of self-defense, arguing that he is intensely afraid of Asians because of prior bad experiences with them. When evaluating the defendant's conduct, should we consider what a reasonable person would have done under the circumstances, or what a reasonable person with an intense fear of Asians would have done under the circumstances? What are the implications of tailoring the reasonableness test to the defendant's characteristics in self-defense cases?
2. Why are defendants who prevail on the defense of self-defense acquitted of the crime, while those who prevail on the insanity defense are sent to mental institutions? Isn't there a social harm in both cases? Why do we treat these two defendants and defenses differently?
3. Although voluntary intoxication is not a defense in some cases, should a person who suffers from alcoholism be entitled to raise an insanity defense? Is a chronic alcoholic engaging in a voluntary act when drinking? Or is chronic alcoholism a mental disease or defect that impacts the defendant's ability to know right from wrong or control his conduct?

8

Miscellaneous Criminal Offenses

> Had I a hundred tongues, a hundred mouths, a voice of iron and a chest of brass, I could not tell all the forms of crime, could not name all the types of punishment.
>
> —Virgil

This chapter will explore a variety of unrelated criminal offenses that occur with varying degrees of regularity in the American criminal justice system. Since these crimes don't quite fit within any categories of the other chapters, they are set forth separately in this chapter to familiarize readers with the essential elements and issues that may arise when these offenses are charged or prosecuted. The crimes discussed in this chapter are kidnapping, arson, assault and battery, and drug and weapons offenses.

KIDNAPPING

A *kidnapping* occurs when the defendant either secretly confines the victim against his will or transports the victim from one place to another by force, threat of force or deceit with the intent to secretly confine the victim against his will. The essential elements of proof in a kidnapping case focus upon the defendant's knowledge and intent and the secret and nonconsensual nature of the victim's abduction and/or restraint. In some jurisdictions, the crime of kidnapping also requires that the defendant abduct or restrain the victim for a specific purpose, for example, to obtain a ransom or to engage in nonconsensual sexual activity with the victim.

Knowledge and Intent

The defendant in a kidnapping case must act with knowledge that his restraint or abduction of the victim is unlawful. This means that the defendant must act with a conscious awareness that his conduct is unlawful and determine to proceed with the conduct despite this awareness. As in other criminal cases, proof of the defendant's knowledge and intent may be based upon circumstantial evidence. Typically, the circumstantial evidence of knowledge and intent in kidnapping cases involves consideration of several factors including the presence or absence of a preconceived unlawful plan by the defendant, the nature and duration of the restraint or abduction and the defendant's own belief as to the nature of his conduct. For example, if the defendant argues that he believed that the victim consented to the restraint, then that belief is a factor to be considered when evaluating the defendant's knowledge and intent concerning the unlawful nature of the restraint. Ultimately, the judge or jury will determine the issues of knowledge and intent by carefully considering all of the factual circumstances, including the defendant's credibility on the issue of consent.

Abduction or Restraint and Secret Confinement

The act of kidnapping may be accomplished by either restraining the victim at a particular location (e.g., the victim's own home or office) or by abducting and transporting the victim to another location for the purpose of secret confinement. As a practical matter, the element of abducting and transporting the victim to another location can be demonstrated by very little physical movement. For example, forcing the victim to walk half a block to a vacant apartment might be considered "abducting and transporting" the victim from one place to another. Further, although the confinement must be secret, it can take place in an outdoor location or in a vehicle, as long as the victim is somehow shielded from the public and thereby unable to seek help. Consider the following:

Early one morning, Zack waits outside a coffee shop for an unsuspecting victim. As a young woman approaches the shop, Zack rushes up to her, tells her that he has a weapon in his pocket and instructs her to calmly accompany him into the coffee shop. When Zack tells the woman that she will be killed if she attempts to warn anyone, the frightened young woman, fearing for her life, does exactly as Zack instructs. Zack orders the woman to sit in a corner booth where he tells her that he wants her to withdraw a large sum of money from her bank account. They wait in the coffee shop for an hour until a nearby bank opens. Zack then accompanies the woman into the bank and stands beside her with his weapon concealed as she withdraws the money. The two then exit the bank together. Once outside, Zack grabs the money and tells the woman they are going to walk several blocks to a travel agent where she will purchase a plane ticket for him with her credit card. Again, the young woman complies. Once the ticket is purchased, Zack flees into the crowd with the money and the ticket. Was the young woman kidnapped?

Although it is clear that the young woman was detained against her will by the threat of force, she was never "secretly" confined. Since Zack and the woman were always in public places where assistance might have been provided, there was no secret confinement. However, since Zack did in fact restrain the young woman against her will, it is likely that he can be prosecuted for the crime of unlawful restraint, which is a lesser included offense of kidnapping and does not require proof of secret confinement. (Of course, Zack will also be criminally liable for the robbery he committed while unlawfully restraining the woman.)

Against the Victim's Will

The abduction or restraint element of kidnapping must occur without the consent of the victim. The victim's lack of consent may be demonstrated by direct or circumstantial evidence. If the victim is able to testify and denies that she consented to the restraint or abduction, then that is direct evidence of lack of consent. Beyond that, the lack of consent must be demonstrated by circumstantial evidence. Use of a weapon, threats or actual physical force by the defendant before or during the abduction or restraint provides some evidence of the victim's lack of consent. Lack of consent may also be demonstrated in instances when the victim is induced by fraud or somehow rendered helpless in order to effectuate the abduction or restraint. For example, if the defendant directly or indirectly administers a drug to render the victim unconscious so as to more easily abduct and transport the victim to a secret location, the abduction will be considered against the victim's will since the defendant is inducing and taking advantage of the victim's helpless condition. The age of the victim may also affect the lack of consent. Some state statutes contain provisions establishing a presumption that children under a certain age lack the necessary maturity to give knowing consent. Children are thus deemed incapable of giving consent, without regard to whether they may have actually given consent. This type of statutory provision makes it easier for a prosecutor to prove that children have been abducted against their will in instances when the children are enticed by strangers and appear to voluntarily accompany their abductors.

Kidnapping as a Separate Offense

An issue that often arises in kidnapping cases is whether the act of kidnapping can be separated from any underlying criminal conduct that may have been committed as part of the kidnapping. This question arises because some crimes by their very nature require that the victim be unlawfully detained for a period of time. Therefore, to charge the crime of kidnapping, the act of detention must be clear and distinct from the underlying offense. If the detention is an integral part of the underlying offense, then it merges with that crime and may not be charged as a separate offense. To illustrate:

Consider again the example of Zack and the young woman. Assume now that Zack approaches the woman just as she is entering the bank to make a withdrawal. He displays a weapon and demands that she withdraw a large sum of money from her account. Zack accompanies her into the bank and oversees the transaction. Once outside the bank, Zack forces the woman to drive two miles to a crowded area where he immediately jumps out of the car and disappears into the crowd. Would this be considered a kidnapping and a robbery?

The answer to this question would likely depend upon several factors. One factor will be the length of time the young woman was restrained by Zack. The less time, the more the unlawful detention appears to be merely incidental to another crime—in this case, an armed robbery. In the example, Zack approached the woman just outside the bank and restrained her only long enough to obtain the cash and get transportation to a safe place a short distance away from the bank. Another factor to consider is whether the detention or abduction creates a significant danger to the victim independent of that posed by the underlying offense. Again, in this example, Zack detained the woman only long enough to "get the money and run." It does not appear that the brief detention by Zack posed very much in the way of additional danger over and above the dangers normally associated with an armed robbery. Based upon these factors, the detention of the young woman seems to be merely incidental to the main crime of armed robbery, which Zack intended. In other words, to accomplish his objective of robbery, Zack had to briefly detain the young woman. Since it was a very brief detention and did not pose significant additional danger, however, it is unlikely that the detention will yield a separate kidnapping charge, although there is clearly a case for armed robbery.

Child Abduction Statutes

One of the tragic side effects of broken families is child custody battles. Occasionally, during one of these custody disputes, a noncustodial parent, without proper legal authority, abducts a child from the custodial parent. With the rise in parental abductions, it became clear that kidnapping statutes were inadequate to address this problem for several reasons. First, although the abducting parent may in fact have been acting without proper legal authority when taking the child, the parent's knowledge and intent (essential elements for the crime of kidnapping) are, at best, difficult to prove. Most abducting parents believe they are acting in the best interests of their children and do not intend to harm them. Another difficulty involves the secrecy of the confinement. Although the custodial parent and the authorities may be unaware of the location of the child, the abducting parent may indeed be living openly with the child in another jurisdiction.

Given the inherent difficulties that arise when trying to fit these types of child abductions into typical kidnapping statutes, many legislatures enacted separate child abduction statutes. These statutes specifically address the conduct of parents who take their children without legal authority. The term "without legal authority" generally refers to an intentional violation of a valid court order regarding the custody arrangement. These statutes cover various types of unlawful conduct ranging from circumstances when a parent intentionally conceals a child to situations when the parent simply removes the child from the lawful custodian or the jurisdiction of the court. In some jurisdictions, abducting parents may be allowed to present a defense to the charge of child abduction by arguing that they honestly believed that the abduction was necessary to protect the health and welfare of the child. Of course, just as with any other defense, the defendant will be required to present specific facts and circumstances to support this belief.

ASSAULT AND BATTERY

Simple Assault

The crime of *assault* can range from simple assault, which is usually a misdemeanor offense, to first-degree assault, in which the defendant causes serious physical injury to the victim. A simple assault is generally defined as an unlawful attempt to injure the victim, coupled with the present ability to commit the violent act. This means that the defendant acts in a threatening manner toward the victim and takes steps toward accomplishing the goal of injuring the victim. Under these circumstances, although the defendant does not actually physically harm the victim, the defendant's threatening conduct nevertheless causes the victim to be in reasonable fear of receiving a physical attack (a *battery*). When examining whether the defendant's conduct rises to the level of a simple assault, several factors must be considered. First, words alone, no matter how abusive or threatening, are not sufficient to constitute an assault. The criminal law does not punish people for having bad thoughts or expressing them to others. If criminal liability were premised on words alone, it would simply be too difficult to prove that the defendant uttered the statements with the intent to carry out a crime as opposed to bluffing or joking with the victim. There must be some other conduct accompanying the words to assist in determining and proving the defendant's actual intent. Other conduct evidence might include threatening gestures that accompanied the defendant's words, the presence of a weapon and/or the physical proximity of the defendant to the victim. Consider the following example:

Don Driver stops for a red light at an intersection and observes a person rapidly approaching his vehicle from the rear. What Don doesn't know is that the approaching motorist, Rob Rage, is angry because he believes Don cut him off earlier in traffic. Rob approaches Don's vehicle quickly with what appears to be a tire iron in his hands. When Rob is directly outside of Don's car window, he begins swearing, using extremely abusive language and shaking the tire iron at Don. Rob angrily tells Don that he is tired of people cutting him off in traffic and is going to make Don pay for his inconsiderate actions. After making this threat, Rob reaches for Don's car door handle. Fortunately for Don, the traffic light changes to green and he is able to safely proceed through the intersection. Did Rob assault Don?

Rob's conduct very likely amounted to a simple assault. Rob used threatening words coupled with conduct that indicated his present ability and intent to carry out his threat. The fact that Rob carried a potentially dangerous weapon as he approached Don's car and reached for the door handle provides strong circumstantial evidence of Rob's intent to make Don pay for cutting him off in traffic by inflicting serious bodily injury upon Don. Additionally, Rob's threatening conduct was sufficient to place Don in reasonable apprehension of a battery (unlawful physical contact). Reasonable apprehension means that Don must actually believe that a physical battery is about to occur and that belief must be reasonable in light of all of the surrounding circumstances. Whether Don actually believed a battery was imminent would be demonstrated by his testimony as to any personal fear at the time of the incident. Then, whether Don's actual fears are in fact reasonable would be determined by examining the circumstances of the encounter and considering whether a reasonable person in the same situation would have been afraid that a physical battery was about to occur. In this case, Rob's threatening language and visible anger, coupled with the fact that he brandished a dangerous weapon while reaching for Don's door handle, would likely create a reasonable apprehension that Rob intended to inflict a battery upon Don.

Other circumstantial factors that may be considered when determining whether a victim's fear of a battery is reasonable include the relative sizes of the victim and defendant and any previous relationship between the defendant and victim that might have contributed to the atmosphere of fear.

Assault with Intent to Inflict Serious Bodily Injury

In some cases, the defendant's threatening behavior may actually result in bodily harm to the victim. In most jurisdictions, the seriousness of the victim's injury will determine the degree of the assault charge. For example, if a defendant acts with intent to cause serious physical injury to the victim and does, in fact, cause such injury, he may be charged with assault in the first degree. The serious injury, in most cases, is caused by the defendant's intentional use of a deadly weapon or dangerous instrument against the victim. However, a serious injury may also result when the defendant engages in reckless conduct that creates a grave risk of death to the victim (e.g., operating a motor vehicle in a reckless manner).

A deadly weapon or dangerous instrument may include "traditional" weapons such as guns and knives, but may also include "nontraditional" items that can be used in a dangerous manner such as bricks, tire irons, boiling water, heavy boots, and vehicles. The selection and use of such deadly weapons or dangerous instruments to attack victims usually provides strong circumstantial evidence of defendants' intent to cause serious physical injury to their victims.

One question that frequently arises in assault cases is whether the victim has suffered a physical injury that is serious enough to warrant a charge of first-degree assault. Generally speaking, to constitute a serious physical injury, the injuries must create a substantial risk of death to the victim. When determining whether the victim has suffered a serious physical injury, the trier of fact will be required to consider the nature of the injury, any required hospitalization or surgery, the likelihood of future complications and any permanent injury, disfigurement or disablement to the victim.

In many first-degree assault situations, because the defendant's conduct is so life-threatening and creates such a substantial risk of death to the victim, the government may also charge the defendant with attempted murder. For attempted murder, the government must prove that the defendant intended to kill the victim and took a substantial step toward accomplishing that objective. For example, if the defendant angrily and viciously wrestles the victim to the ground and begins pounding the victim's head into the concrete pavement (a dangerous instrument), this conduct would likely be considered first-degree assault. However, the same conduct might also warrant a charge of attempted murder if the nature of defendant's conduct demonstrates an intent to kill (e.g., using a dangerous instrument such as concrete) and a substantial step toward accomplishing that objective (e.g., pounding the victim's head into the concrete). The defendant's intent to kill can be demonstrated circumstantially by examining the type of weapon used as well as the nature and extent of the victim's injuries.

Assault with Intent to Commit Other Criminal Offenses

A defendant may cause injury to a victim during the course of and in furtherance of the commission of another offense. For example, a defendant may initially intend to commit a robbery and during the robbery attempt, he may cause physical injury to the victim. In that case, the defendant may be charged with assault with intent to commit robbery. This charge covers conduct that occurs when the defendant causes some level of injury to the victim in the process of furthering another crime. To illustrate:

Robber approaches Victim with a gun and demands money. When Victim hesitates, Robber hits him over the head with the gun and begins to search his clothing for money. When Robber hears the sound of other people approaching, he quickly leaves the scene without the money.

In this example, Robber did not complete the robbery because he did not take and carry away any of the victim's property. He did, however, have the intent to commit a robbery and caused injury to the victim while furthering the commission of that crime. Robber's conduct would thus constitute an unlawful assault that took place during the course of and in furtherance of a failed robbery attempt. Note also that these same facts could also give rise to a charge of attempted robbery since Robber had the intent to take the victim's money by force and took a substantial (although unsuccessful) step toward accomplishing that objective.

ARSON

The elements of the crime of *arson* include using an incendiary device or explosive with the intent to cause damage to property or vehicles. An incendiary device is one that is designed to explode or produce combustion upon impact. Property can include buildings, whether occupied or not, as well as items attached to the ground such trees and shrubbery. Additionally, since a significant number of arsons are committed for the purpose of collecting insurance proceeds, many arson statutes specifically criminalize "burning for profit" conduct.

When proving the elements of arson, the government must first demonstrate that the fire or explosion was caused by a human act rather than, for example, an electrical malfunction. Once it is determined that the fire was caused by a human act, the government must then prove that the fire was started with the specific intent to damage property as opposed to an act of carelessness (e.g. carelessly discarding a match or cigarette). Of course, each of these elements may be demonstrated by circumstantial evidence. Using careful arson investigation techniques, fire officials can usually determine the origin of a fire or explosion. For example, if the investigation reveals that the fire began with the aid of an accelerant (such as gasoline) not typically located on the premises, then that provides some circumstantial evidence that the fire may have been started unlawfully.

Linking the defendant to the incendiary device and proving the necessary mental state may be accomplished by showing that the defendant had the means and opportunity to commit the crime. For instance, the government may present evidence that the defendant purchased large quantities of gasoline or other materials to make an explosive or incendiary device shortly before the fire. Or, they may present witnesses who observed the defendant near the location of the fire shortly before it occurred.

Proof of a motive can also significantly bolster the government's circumstantial evidence in an arson case, although it is not an element of the crime. Proving the basis for a motive to unlawfully burn property might require examining the defendant's financial condition and potential to collect insurance proceeds. Additionally, in some cases, an unlawful motive might be revealed by exploring prior disputes or threats by the defendant against the owner of the property or the property itself. Each of these facts alone may not be sufficient to establish defendant's guilt. But, when taken together, they may paint a strong circumstantial evidence picture from which the judge or jury may draw inferences as to the defendant's intent to unlawfully burn property.

DRUG OFFENSES

Most drug statutes make it a crime to knowingly manufacture or deliver or possess with intent to manufacture or deliver controlled or counterfeit controlled substances. *Controlled substances* include, among other things, heroine, cocaine, morphine, methamphetamine, LSD and marijuana. Possession of controlled or counterfeit controlled substances may be actual physical possession or "constructive" possession. *Constructive possession* means that possession will be implied if the defendant has the intent to possess the illicit substance and maintains control and dominion over the premises where the controlled substances are located. The mere presence of controlled substances on defendants' premises is not enough, however, particularly if it is a location that is well traveled or occupied by others. There must be sufficient proof that the defendants had knowledge of the presence of the controlled substances and intended to possess the substances even though they may not have been in their physical possession. Thus, if the controlled substances are located in an area of the defendants' home or car, where they have exclusive dominion or control, this may constitute possession by the defendants, by virtue of the location of the drugs on the defendants' private property.

In drug-dealing cases, if defendants are apprehended before the actual delivery of the controlled substance, proof of intent to deliver controlled substances is generally demonstrated by circumstantial evidence. The most compelling circumstantial evidence on this issue is the amount of controlled substance defendants have in their possession at the time of arrest. The larger the amount, the more likely it is that the defendants intended to deliver some portion of it to others, rather than keeping it for personal use. Even if the defendants possess a small amount of the controlled substance, they can still be convicted of possession with intent to deliver, but much more circumstantial evidence will be necessary. Thus, in addition to possession, the government might be required to produce evidence of contacts or appointments made for purposes of delivering the controlled substances. Other circumstantial evidence of possession with intent to deliver might include the type of packaging used for the controlled substance, large sums of money or weapons in the defendants' possession or the presence of other drugs or drug paraphernalia in the area.

If there is insufficient evidence of intent to deliver, then defendants can still be charged with the lesser offense of possession of a controlled substance. Simply proving that the defendants had knowledge of the controlled substance and that it was in their immediate and exclusive control is sufficient for a charge of drug possession. Note here again that knowledge of the controlled substance alone is not enough. The defendants must also have immediate and exclusive control over the controlled substance. Just as in the case of possession with intent to deliver, simple possession of a controlled substance may either be actual or "constructive."

Interestingly, most drug offense statutes also make it crime to possess with intent to deliver or merely possess *counterfeit controlled substances*. At first glance, this seems an unusual criminal offense because counterfeit substances don't cause any real social harm. Nonetheless, one rationale for these provisions is that they allow the government to bring cases against defendants in instances when undercover officers pose as drug purchasers and buy counterfeit controlled substances instead of the "real thing." Without statutes outlawing delivery or possession of counterfeit controlled substances, the drug seller could not be prosecuted because what he sells the undercover officer is not actually a controlled substance as defined by the statute. A similar result would occur if the officer arrests an individual for simple possession of drugs only to later discover after testing that the drugs are in fact counterfeit.

One of the major difficulties associated with prosecuting defendants for delivery or possession of counterfeit controlled substances involves distinguishing between possession of innocent substances and possession of counterfeit controlled substances. In other words, how can we tell whether the defendant intended to possess counterfeit cocaine or was merely possessing an "innocent" substance such as flour? Generally, the counterfeit substance must be packaged and presented in such a manner that a reasonable person would believe that using the product would produce an effect similar to that of the actual controlled substance. Some factors that will be considered when charging the defendant with delivery or possession of counterfeit controlled substances include the type of storing and packaging used for the counterfeit substance, any representations made by the defendant as to the nature of the substance, and whether the defendant was attempting to exchange the counterfeit substance for something of value. Further, to avoid dismissal of the indictment for failure to charge the appropriate crime, it is no defense to a charge of selling counterfeit controlled substances that the defendant thought they were actual controlled substances. This means that a defendant who may have been misled as to the authenticity of the substances will not be able to escape prosecution.

Finally, the penalty provisions for drug offenses typically impose lengthier sentences depending upon the amount of controlled or counterfeit controlled substances manufactured, delivered or possessed by the defendant. Many statutes also provide for enhanced penalties if the defendant is convicted of delivering or possessing with intent to deliver controlled or counterfeit controlled substances to persons under the age of 18 or if the defendant engages in such conduct within certain distances of specified locations such as schools, churches, nursing homes and public housing facilities.

WEAPONS OFFENSES

Almost every state and the federal government have enacted statutes that regulate the possession, carrying, use, sale, manufacturing, importing and exporting of deadly weapons. Deadly weapons are typically defined as instruments that can be used or are intended to be used to cause death or serious bodily injury. Deadly weapons may include firearms, knives and explosives. Although the Second Amendment to the United States Constitution provides a right to bear arms, the government may, in certain instances, reasonably regulate the possession or use of firearms. Such regulations are usually designed to protect the health, welfare and safety of citizens who might be harmed by the uncontrolled possession and use of deadly weapons.

Some of the same issues that arise in drug possession cases also become relevant in weapons possession cases. For example, one may unlawfully possess a weapon either actually or "constructively." Just as in the area of drug possession, constructive possession means having both knowledge of the weapon and the intent and ability to exercise dominion and control over it.

Unlawful possession of a weapon may also enhance the charge and penalty if the defendant possesses or uses a weapon during the commission of another offense. For instance, if a defendant commits a sexual assault and uses (or in some cases merely possesses) a deadly weapon while carrying out the offense, then the defendant may be charged with the sexual assault and the weapons offense. The addition of the weapons offense increases the punishment imposed on the defendant and is intended to deter individuals from committing crimes while using or possessing deadly weapons.

As a condition of probation or parole, many states also prohibit convicted felons from possessing or carrying deadly weapons. If a felon is caught violating this statutory provision, that violation may result in revocation of parole or probation.

Some jurisdictions also provide for enhanced penalties if the possession or use of deadly weapons occurs on or within certain distances of educational settings or if weapons are sold or delivered to minors.

Concealed Weapons Statutes

A number of states have enacted statutes that permit individuals to lawfully carry concealed weapons. The permit process usually requires the individual to complete a background check that examines criminal and mental history. Most states also require concealed weapons licensees to participate in a firearms safety program and periodically renew the concealed weapons license.

CASE STUDIES

Sentencing Disparity and Crack Cocaine

Drug offenses are one of the most frequently prosecuted crimes in the criminal justice system. These prosecutions can range from simple possession charges against an individual to large-scale conspiracy and drug distribution charges against major drug-dealing operations. The government's widely touted "war on drugs" has spawned aggressive stances with respect to prosecuting drug offenses and has simultaneously given rise to controversial legislation and sentencing schemes designed to combat drug trafficking. Much of the recent controversy involves the statutory sentencing disparity that results from convictions for possession of crack cocaine and powdered cocaine.

Crack cocaine is a highly potent and less expensive derivative of powder cocaine. Pursuant to federal sentencing guidelines, a person possessing five grams of crack cocaine will face a mandatory sentence of at least five years in prison. In contrast, it would take possession of five hundred grams of powdered cocaine to yield a similar penalty for possession of that substance. The stated rationale for the disparity in the sentencing structure is that crack cocaine is a more addictive substance and is also more likely to be associated with violence. The reality is, however, that crack cocaine is also more likely to result in the prosecution, conviction and consequently lengthier sentences for black defendants. Statistics on prosecutions reveal that 90 percent of those convicted in federal courts for crack cocaine possession are black, while only 30 percent of defendants convicted of possession of powdered cocaine are black. Observers of the criminal justice system believe that this sentencing disparity unfairly targets black defendants for prosecution and subjects them to harsher punishments upon conviction. What is perhaps even more disturbing is that this disparity in prosecution and punishment exists despite the fact that studies have revealed that whites actually use crack cocaine at higher rate than blacks.

The government's prosecution and sentencing practices in cocaine cases have been challenged in court. In the case of *United States vs. Armstrong*, the government was ordered by a federal district court to explain statistics showing a sharp racial disparity in crack cocaine prosecutions. The racial disparity argument arose from the fact that in 24 crack cocaine cases represented by the federal public defender's office in Los Angeles in 1991, all of the defendants were black. The government refused to comply with the order to explain the statistics, and the case was eventually appealed to the U.S. Supreme Court.

In its opinion, the Supreme Court explained that the standard for proving selective prosecution is very high. (Selective prosecution is a process in which the prosecutor chooses to prosecute certain defendants for criminal conduct while foregoing prosecution of others for the same or similar conduct.) The Court first acknowledged that historically the prosecutor's discretion in the charging process is afforded a high level of judicial deference. This means that courts have traditionally been unwilling to formally inquire into the prosecutor's decision to prosecute or forego prosecution in any given case. The prosecutor is allowed utmost discretion. That discretion is not absolute, however, and if the prosecutor's decisions are challenged as discriminatory, then, according to the Court, the defendant must show that the government was motivated by a discriminatory purpose. Additionally, in order to obtain governmental statistics and explanations as to its policies in specific prosecutions, the Court concluded that the defendants would have to make a credible showing that "similarly situated" persons were treated differently by the government. In the context of crack cocaine prosecutions, to meet the "similarly situated" standard, the defendant would need to demonstrate that substantial numbers of white defendants fit the criteria for prosecution for crack cocaine possession under the federal statute but were nevertheless not prosecuted in the federal courts. Applying this standard, it might be difficult to prove selective prosecution and discriminatory purpose because many white defendants prosecuted for crack cocaine possession simply do not meet the federal standards for crack cocaine prosecution, which are much harsher than state standards. For example, the federal standards for a crack cocaine prosecution require several factors in addition to possession of the crack cocaine, including possession of a gun, previous offenses and/or involvement in organized criminal activity.

Those who challenge the government's rationale for imposing harsher punishment in cases of possession or distribution of crack cocaine argue that the rationale is merely a smokescreen for race-based enforcement of drug laws. This argument is supported, in part, by the fact that the majority of defendants sent to jail for drug offenses under federal guidelines are black even though 74 percent of all drug users are white. According to critics of the crack cocaine/powder cocaine penalty structure, this overall disparity in drug prosecutions indicates a willingness to aggressively arrest, prosecute and punish drug offenders in minority communities, while ignoring the growing problems of drug possession and abuse in suburban areas. Moreover, not only are minority communities specifically targeted, but the arrests and prosecutions tend to focus on those offenders who make multiple sales or purchases in order to guarantee even lengthier sentences upon conviction.

In response to the perception of unfairness and racial bias in the crack cocaine/powdered cocaine sentencing structure, many, including judges (who have to impose these sentences) and the Federal Sentencing Commission, have called for an equalization of the penalty structure. So far, these proposals for change have met with resistance from both the legislative and executive branches of government.

There is no doubt that drug dealing and drug possession have a devastating impact on the individuals and communities involved. There is also little doubt that many law abiding citizens in minority communities applaud the efforts of law enforcement in attempting to wage a war on the illicit drug trade that has spread like a malignant cancer throughout their communities. Nevertheless, one of the fundamental principles of our criminal justice system is that the punishment must fit the crime. As discussed in Chapter 1, this principle enhances the overall perception of fairness and justice in the system. When penalties for certain conduct seem unduly harsh and disproportionately impact certain groups of individuals, then not only do the individual defendants suffer, but everyone pays a price because the overall integrity of the system is undermined by the appearance of bias and unfairness. Ridding communities of unlawful drug activities is certainly a worthy goal. But even the worthiest goals must be carefully scrutinized for compatibility with the overarching principles of fairness and justice in the criminal justice system.

Parental Kidnapping

As discussed in this chapter, a kidnapping occurs when a person unlawfully abducts or restrains another without that person's consent. In many cases, the abduction is carried out for the purpose of extorting money from the victim or his relatives or, in some instances, for the purpose of committing other crimes against the victim such as sexual assault. In most kidnapping cases, there is significant circumstantial evidence that the victim was held against his will. Likewise, there is usually evidence that the defendant either harmed or intended to harm the kidnapping victim. But what happens in cases when the "kidnapper" is the parent of the "kidnapping" victim? If the child/victim willingly accompanies the parent, there is usually no evidence that the child was held without consent. Additionally, the abducting parent typically doesn't harm or intend to harm the child and, when caught, will often argue that taking the child was in fact in the best interests of the child. Given the unique factual circumstances surrounding parental abductions, traditional kidnapping statutes were not particularly suited to deal with these cases, and many parents were left without remedies when their children were unlawfully removed from their custody by noncustodial parents.

In 1978, Stephen Fagan and Barbara Kurth were divorced, and Kurth was awarded custody of their two young daughters. Fagan was very displeased with the custody arrangement and, in an effort to obtain custody of his daughters, attempted to demonstrate that Kurth was an unfit mother who drank heavily and failed to care for their children. When these attempts failed, Fagan took the girls on a previously arranged weekend outing and simply disappeared. After abducting the children, Fagan changed his name to William Martin, moved to Florida and told people that he was a doctor, lawyer, CIA agent and adviser to President Nixon. Fagan also told his daughters that their mother had died in a car accident.

Meanwhile, for several years, Kurth attempted to track down her daughters, spending thousands of dollars on investigative services. Kurth was forced to rely primarily upon private investigative services because, at the time, parental abduction of children was considered a "family matter" and law enforcement personnel were ill equipped to properly address this problem. After several years of searching in vain, Kurth exhausted her financial resources and ended her efforts.

In September 1997, after nineteen years, police advised Kurth that an anonymous tip had provided concrete information as to the whereabouts of her ex-husband and her daughters. Shortly thereafter, Fagan was arrested and charged with kidnapping his daughters, which carries a maximum ten-year prison sentence. In an interesting twist to the case, the daughters, now adults, have taken their father's side and have also leveled accusations against their mother for not doing more to locate them over the years and for turning their lives into a public spectacle when she finally found them.

As might be expected in a parental abduction case, there is no allegation that Fagan harmed the girls or that they were held against their will during the nineteen years they were in his custody. In fact, there is evidence that Fagan was an extremely attentive father and the girls willingly and happily lived with him. Given these facts, had there had been no change in kidnapping statutes over the past several years, it would be practically impossible to charge, much less convict, Fagan of kidnapping. Fortunately, kidnapping laws have been expanded to include the conduct of parents taking children in violation of lawful custody decrees. Under the new parental abduction statutes, there is no requirement that the parent have any intent to harm the child or that the child be held against his will. The sole criteria is that the child was taken in violation of a lawful custody decree. The purpose of modifying traditional kidnapping laws was to ensure that custody decrees granted in one state would be recognized as lawful and given full effect in other jurisdictions in the United States.

There have also been efforts to expand these protections on the international level since an increasing number of child abductions involve noncustodial parents unlawfully abducting their children and fleeing to foreign countries. To date, 49 nations, including the United States, have agreed to the Hague Child Abduction Convention. This treaty seeks to promote cooperation among foreign jurisdictions for the protection and safe return of abducted children. Despite this promising cooperative agreement, in some jurisdictions it is still practically impossible to obtain the cooperation of foreign governments. Patricia Roush learned this all too well as she engaged in a multiyear effort to be reunited with her daughters, who were abducted by their father and taken to Saudi Arabia. For more than a decade, Roush made numerous attempts to get her daughters back, including hiring a five-man rescue team that attempted and failed to kidnap the girls in Saudi Arabia. Roush also obtained federal and state warrants for the arrest of her ex-husband and an Interpol "Red Alert." She also solicited and received the signatures of numerous U.S. senators on petitions to the Saudi government requesting assistance in securing the safe return of her daughters. Sadly, these efforts have been unsuccessful because U.S. laws are simply not recognized in Saudi Arabia. Thus, Roush and other parents in her situation must often rely upon extralegal diplomatic efforts by the governments involved, which can take years and involve significant bureaucratic red tape.

To combat this problem, it is clear that laws related to parental abduction must now expand their reach beyond the borders of the United States in an effort to forge concrete agreements with foreign countries that provide for the recognition and enforcement of custody agreements and the prompt extradition of those who flee in violation of those agreements. This solution places the best interests of the children first and ensures that parents unlawfully abducting children cannot escape the law by fleeing to foreign jurisdictions.

FOR FURTHER CONSIDERATION

1. Stalking is a form of assaultive behavior in which the stalker engages in a course of conduct designed to harass, threaten or intimidate the victim. A course of conduct usually means a pattern of conduct that shows some evidence of continuing over time. Why do stalking statutes require a "course of conduct?" Does the "course of conduct" requirement mean that a stalking victim must suffer several threatening or intimidating incidents before the stalker can be charged with stalking? Should the gravity of the threats or conduct be a consideration rather than the "course of conduct?"
2. Parents who abduct their children from custodial parents often argue necessity. That is, they argue that it was necessary to remove the child immediately from a situation that presented a threat to the child's health and safety. Under what circumstances might it be necessary for parents to violate a lawful custody order and abduct children? Should those circumstances be limited or eliminated altogether? Are any policy goals promoted by allowing parents to argue a defense of necessity?
3. Should drug use and possession be considered a victimless crime? If a person is addicted to drugs and is arrested and convicted for drug use, aren't we punishing that person for the "status" of being a drug addict? You may wish to refer back to the case study on " 'Undesirable Conduct' and Criminality" in Chapter 1. Is drug addiction any different from alcohol addiction?

9

The Criminal Process

> Trial by jury, instead of being a security to persons who are accused, will be a delusion, a mockery, and a snare.
>
> —Lord Denman

THE ARREST

For a defendant, the criminal process usually begins at the time of arrest. An arrest indicates that the police have probable cause to believe that the person being arrested has committed a crime. Probable cause means that the police officer believes there is a "fair probability" that the suspect has engaged in criminal activity. Thus, the officer doesn't have to be certain that the suspect committed a crime in order to make an arrest. Probable cause may be developed by relying upon witness reports or observations of criminal activity or by conducting extensive police investigations into suspected illegal conduct.

Once arrested, the suspect is advised of his constitutional rights. These rights include the right to remain silent, the right to have an attorney present during questioning and the right to have an attorney appointed if the suspect is unable to afford one. The suspect is then booked, fingerprinted and photographed. As soon as possible after the arrest, the suspect is taken before a judge or magistrate and advised of the charges against him. At this time, the judge or magistrate may also make a determination concerning the pretrial release of the suspect. Depending upon the nature of the crime and the risk of flight, the suspect may either be detained without bail, detained pending the posting of a specific bail amount or released on his own recognizance, which means that the suspect simply promises to return to court for further proceedings in the case.

In some jurisdictions, the suspect may request a *preliminary hearing* at this point. During the preliminary hearing, the government is required to present evidence establishing that there is probable cause to believe that the defendant committed the crime. The defendant is also entitled to appear with his attorney to challenge the probable cause evidence. If the judge determines that there is insufficient evidence of probable cause, the case will be dismissed with no further proceedings. After a dismissal at the preliminary hearing stage, the government is free to continue its investigation and may refile charges against the defendant later if it believes that newly discovered evidence is sufficient to meet the probable cause standard.

THE INDICTMENT AND THE GRAND JURY PROCESS

In some cases, prior to an arrest, a grand jury will be convened to investigate suspected criminal activity. The *grand jury* is composed of a group of lay citizens who are charged with the responsibility for gathering information and determining whether probable cause exists to issue an indictment or formal charge against anyone. The grand jury has significant investigatory power and can subpoena witnesses and documents on a fairly broad scale as it carries out its functions. Subpoenaed witnesses must appear before the grand jury and bring any subpoenaed documents with them. Additionally, witnesses are not permitted to bring counsel into the grand jury room, although they may leave the room to consult with counsel on specific questions. Failure to comply with a grand jury subpoena may result in sanctions for contempt, which could include a period of incarceration until the witness agrees to comply with the grand jury request. These types of grand jury investigations often result in the issuance of an *indictment*, which then requires the police to formally arrest the person(s) named in the indictment. Grand jury investigations of this nature are particularly useful for investigating large-scale criminal activity that is often associated with white-collar crime (e.g., securities fraud, tax fraud). Again, because the grand jury has broad subpoena power and can demand testimony and documents, it can use relatively unrestricted investigative techniques that are, for the most part, constitutionally unavailable to law enforcement officers.

The grand jury process may also be used after the arrest of a suspect in some cases. Typically, these grand jury proceedings are initiated and led by the prosecutor who believes that a crime has been committed and presents the government's evidence against a specific suspect to the grand jury. Because the government's evidence is presented unchallenged, in all but the weakest cases, the grand jury finds probable cause to issue an indictment against the suspect.

Grand jury proceedings and the identities of the grand jurors are guarded with the utmost secrecy. The secrecy is intended to protect the grand jury in its fact-finding process by ensuring that grand jurors are free from external influences that might affect the impartiality of the decision-making process.

In some cases, in lieu of the grand jury indictment process, the prosecutor may file an *information* with the court. The information, which is used primarily in less serious cases, is a formal written statement of the charges against the defendant and serves the same purpose as a grand jury indictment. It is important to understand that neither the issuance of an indictment nor the filing of an information means that the defendant is guilty of the crime. These are merely formal statements of the charges that must be proven at trial.

ARRAIGNMENT AND PRETRIAL MOTIONS

Once the indictment or information has been issued or filed, the defendant is brought before the court to be formally charged with the crime. This proceeding is called the *arraignment*. During the arraignment, the charges are read in detail to the defendant, who is asked to formally enter a plea to the charges. At the arraignment, the court will also insure that the defendant is represented by counsel and may hear arguments for and against setting or reducing bail for the defendant's release pending trial.

If the defendant pleads guilty at the arraignment, the court will carefully question the defendant to determine whether the guilty plea is being made knowingly and voluntarily. The court is essentially seeking to ensure that no one has improperly coerced the defendant to enter a guilty plea. The court will also instruct the defendant that by pleading guilty, he or she is waiving the right to a trial and choosing to proceed immediately to the penalty phase of the criminal process. If the court is satisfied that the defendant is voluntarily entering a plea of guilty, a date will be set for sentencing. Defendants who do not choose to plead guilty at the arraignment will have their cases scheduled for trial during the arraignment proceeding.

Once a case is scheduled for trial, both the prosecution and defense begin to plan their strategies. The defense strategy may include challenging the government's collection of evidence against the defendant on constitutional grounds. To carry out this strategy, the defendant may file motions to suppress evidence, arguing that the evidence was seized in violation of the Fourth Amendment or that incriminating statements were obtained in violation of the Fifth or Sixth Amendment. Depending upon the outcome of these motions to suppress and the nature of the evidence suppressed, the government's case may not be able to proceed and the case against the defendant may have to be dismissed. For example, if a defendant is charged with narcotics trafficking and the narcotics evidence is successfully suppressed because of an unlawful search of the defendant's home, the government will not be able to proceed with the case because a crucial and necessary piece of evidence will be excluded from the case.

During the pretrial process, the government and defense have certain obligations with respect to sharing evidence. For example, the government is obligated to share information that tends to show that the defendant might not have committed the crime. Additionally, both sides must give notice of potential witnesses and experts to be called during the trial, and the defendant must provide notice as to whether certain defenses, such as the insanity defense, will be presented during the trial. This pretrial exchange of information is intended to allow both sides to fairly and adequately prepare and present their cases and avoid the disruption and surprise associated with "trial by ambush."

THE TRIAL

The Trier of Fact: Judge or Jury

The defendant may elect to have his case tried before a judge or a *jury*. If he chooses to have it tried only by a judge, then the judge hears all of the factual evidence, makes evidentiary rulings during the trial and renders a verdict at the conclusion of the case. If, however, the defendant chooses to have the case tried before a jury, then the jury selection process is the first phase of the criminal trial.

In most jurisdictions, potential jurors are selected from voter or license registration lists. From this broad pool, both the defense and prosecution attempt to identify jurors who can listen to the evidence in an unbiased fashion and render a verdict based solely upon the evidence submitted at trial. The process of questioning and selecting jurors is called *voir dire*. During this process, the defense, the prosecution and occasionally the judge will ask questions of potential jurors in an attempt to expose any biases or preconceived notions that might interfere with their ability to render a fair and impartial verdict. During the voir dire, each side (the defense and prosecution) may request that prospective jurors be excused from the case either for cause (e.g., bias) or, in limited instances, for no reason at all. Requesting that a juror be excused without providing a reason is known as exercising a peremptory challenge. Each side has a limited number of peremptory challenges and may use them to excuse jurors for practically any reason except race and gender.

Opening Statements

Once the jurors have been selected, the trial begins with *opening statements* by the government prosecutor. The defendant comes into the trial with a *presumption of innocence*, and the government has the burden of proving each of the material elements of the crime beyond a reasonable doubt. During opening statements, the prosecutor usually begins by explaining the government's theory of the case to the jury. The prosecutor will articulate how the government's evidence will establish that a crime was committed and that the defendant is the perpetrator of the crime. After the government's opening statement, the defense presents its opening statement and theory of the case. This is the first opportunity for the defendant to refute the government's theory of the case and set the stage for alibi or other types of defenses (e.g., self-defense, insanity). During the opening statements, no evidence is introduced, and each side explains its theory of the case in a narrative fashion.

Presentation of Evidence

After the opening statements, the presentation of evidence begins with the government's case-in-chief. Since the government carries the burden of proof, the prosecutor will begin by introducing evidence on each of the material elements of the offense in an attempt to establish the defendant's guilt beyond a reasonable doubt. The evidence presented is usually testimonial in nature and is introduced by calling witnesses to the stand. Evidence might also consist of documents, which will be introduced into evidence through witness testimony that verifies the authenticity and accuracy of the documents. Since most crimes are committed in secret with very few direct eyewitnesses, in most cases, the government must build its case piece by piece using circumstantial rather than direct evidence. Direct evidence is firsthand evidence of the defendant's guilt, such as a direct eyewitness to the crime or a voluntary confession by the defendant. With circumstantial evidence, however, the government introduces pieces of evidence from which the judge or jury may draw inferences as to the defendant's guilt. Thus, circumstantial evidence is much like the pieces of a puzzle. The government hopes that after the presentation of all of the circumstantial pieces of evidence, the judge or jury will put all of the pieces together and neatly conclude that the defendant committed the crime beyond a reasonable doubt. There is nothing unlawful or unconstitutional about building a criminal case based primarily upon circumstantial evidence. In fact, without the ability to use circumstantial evidence, the majority of crimes would likely go unprosecuted for lack of direct evidence of the defendant's guilt.

Throughout its case-in-chief, the government must produce evidence on each of the material elements of the offense. If, for example, the defendant is charged with the crime of larceny, the government must produce evidence that defendant (1) took and carried away (2) the personal property (3) of another (4) with the intent to steal. If the government fails to produce sufficient evidence on any of the material elements during its case-in-chief, then that failure is cause for *acquittal* of the defendant and a complete dismissal of the charges.

During the government's case-in-chief, the defendant will have an opportunity to cross-examine the government's witnesses. Through the cross-examination process, the defendant attempts to attack and discredit the government's case. Skillful cross-examination can be quite an effective tool for the defendant and, indeed, may significantly impede the government's efforts to prove its case. It is important to note that the defendant is under no obligation to cross-examine witnesses or even to speak during the criminal trial, and the government may not comment to the judge or jury on the defendant's failure to do so. As a practical matter, however, during a criminal trial the defendant remains silent at his own peril, particularly if the government is presenting a compelling case. If the government is able to produce legally sufficient evidence on each of the material elements during its case-in-chief, the case will continue and proceed to the presentation of the defendant's case.

During the defense phase, the defendant may present evidence to support his theory of the case. Additionally, if the defendant is presenting certain types of defenses, such as self-defense or insanity, the defendant will be required to produce specific evidence to support these defenses. Of course, the government will be permitted to challenge evidence and cross-examine witnesses produced by the defendant. A defendant in a criminal case is not required to testify and may not be called as a witness by the prosecutor. However, if the defendant chooses to testify, he will be subject to cross-examination by the government just as any other witness put forward by the defense. At the conclusion of the defendant's presentation of evidence, the government will have an opportunity to respond to the defense evidence in the rebuttal phase of the trial. During the rebuttal phase, government witnesses are presented to respond to the evidence introduced by the defendant. Once again, the defendant is entitled to challenge evidence and to cross-examine government witnesses presented during this phase.

Closing Arguments

At the conclusion of the presentation of evidence, each side "rests" and closing arguments begin. *Closing arguments* provide an opportunity for each side to summarize and emphasize the main points of the evidence presented during the trial. The prosecutor usually begins by discussing specifically each piece of evidence that proves the material elements of the case. One of the goals of this exercise is to remind the jury of the prosecution's strongest points and to explain, if necessary, any perceived weaknesses in the government's case. The closing argument for the defense has a somewhat different focus. Typically, the main goal is to highlight and hammer away at the weaknesses of the government's case. If the defendant has presented an alibi or any other defense during the trial, the closing argument will also emphasize these defenses as another way to neutralize the government's case.

Finally, the government will have the last word in the closing argument during the rebuttal. The closing rebuttal allows the government to refute statements made by the defense during its closing argument and to again emphasize the strongest points of the government's case. Overall, closing arguments are the last opportunity for both sides to persuade the judge or jury of the merits of their respective cases. Just as in the opening statements, no evidence is offered and closing arguments are presented in a narrative fashion.

Jury Instructions and Deliberation

After closing arguments, a judge who is deciding the case will simply take the case under advisement to determine a verdict. The judge knows the law and will apply it to the facts gleaned from the presentation of evidence during the trial. In contrast, if the case is being tried before a jury, then the judge must instruct the jury on the law to be applied to the case. For example, the judge instructs the jury on the appropriate burden of proof (beyond the reasonable doubt), the nature of direct and circumstantial evidence and the elements of the offense. The judge also specifically instructs the jury that they are to determine the facts of the case based solely upon the evidence admitted at trial, and then to apply the law to those facts.

After the *jury instructions*, the jurors retire to the deliberation room taking with them all of the evidence admitted during the trial. Although most of the jury *deliberation* process is secret, jurors usually begin by selecting a foreperson to lead the deliberations. Since criminal trials must be decided by a unanimous verdict, jurors might take a poll early in the deliberation process to see how many votes are for, against or undecided about the guilt of the defendant. Jurors will then begin to discuss the evidence and engage in a process of subtly persuading their fellow jurors of their beliefs. Throughout the deliberations, jurors may also ask to have certain points clarified or questions answered by the judge, particularly if there is a misunderstanding as to the applicable legal standards. Depending upon the nature and complexity of the trial and the evidence, the deliberation process could take hours, weeks or months. In high-profile and/or controversial cases, the jury may be sequestered during their deliberations so that they have no contact with information that might unfairly taint the decision-making process.

The goal of the deliberation process is to determine whether the government has proven the defendant's guilt *beyond a reasonable doubt*. This standard of reasonable doubt, which is constitutionally required in criminal cases, essentially means that after careful examination of all of the evidence, jurors do not feel an abiding conviction, to a moral certainty, of the truth of the charge. This definitional language, which is practically standard for jury instructions, has often resulted in confusion. Some jurors want to know exactly what constitutes an "abiding" conviction and/or by whose standard do we measure "moral" certainty? Nevertheless, many courts refrain from attempting to further define the term "reasonable doubt" for fear of further confusing jurors and ultimately tainting the outcome of the trial. Thus, jurors must rely upon the facts, the law and their collective wisdom when determining a defendant's guilt.

When considering the evidence and assessing reasonable doubt, jurors may evaluate only those facts developed during the trial and draw logical inferences from those facts. Jurors may not consider evidence that was not admitted at trial and may not interject their personal biases or predilections into the fact-finding process. Perhaps most importantly, jurors must understand that the standard "beyond a reasonable doubt" does not mean that they must be free of all possible doubt as to the defendant's guilt—just of reasonable doubt. This standard of proof is peculiar to criminal law and is the highest burden known to law, particularly since the defendant comes into the trial cloaked with a presumption of innocence. The rationale for this elevated standard of proof arises from the enormous stakes involved in a criminal trial. Because the criminal defendant faces the potential loss of liberty and the moral stigma attached to a criminal conviction, the government is required to establish proof beyond a reasonable doubt before society is willing to impose penalties that infringe upon the defendant's significant liberty and privacy interests.

The Verdict

At the conclusion of the deliberation process, if the jury has reached a unanimous *verdict*, they will advise the judge. The judge will then call all of the parties back to the courtroom to hear the jury's verdict. Once the verdict is announced, each juror is polled to assure that the verdict is indeed unanimous. If the verdict is acquittal, the defendant is free to go and, pursuant to constitutional double jeopardy standards, can never be tried for that particular crime again. However, if the verdict is guilty, the defendant may be taken into custody and, in some cases, will have to await sentencing at a later date. In some jurisdictions, the same jury that convicted the defendant will take part in the sentencing phase and determine an appropriate punishment. In other cases, after the verdict, the jury members are thanked for their service and excused. The judge later determines an appropriate punishment for the defendant.

In some cases, after considerable deliberation, the jury is unable to reach a unanimous verdict and will be deadlocked or "hung." When the jury reaches a point of deadlock, they will usually advise the judge, who will encourage them to continue the deliberations in hopes of reaching a unanimous verdict. Despite this encouragement, however, some juries are simply unable to reach a unanimous verdict, even after lengthy deliberations. Under those circumstances, the judge declares a mistrial and excuses the jury. If there is a mistrial because of juror deadlock, the government can elect to reprosecute the case and try for a more favorable outcome with a new jury. A mistrial due to a *hung jury* does not raise double jeopardy concerns because the original trial does not result in any final determination of the defendant's guilt or innocence; prosecuting the defendant again is considered merely a continuation of the previous trial.

CASE STUDY

Juries and Celebrity Criminal Trials

Question: What do O.J. Simpson and Snoop Doggy Dogg have in common? Answer: The jurors in each trial attended post-verdict celebrity parties toasting the "successful" conclusion of each defendant's criminal trial. Average Americans, who were previously unknown to these celebrity criminal defendants, were suddenly, as a result of public service, surrounded by media hype and the glitz and glamour of celebrity life. These post-verdict festivities represent but one aspect of the dilemma associated with the increasing criminal prosecutions of celebrity defendants. Just as in any criminal trial, celebrity defendants are cloaked with the constitutional right to a fair trial with an impartial jury of peers. However, given the unique circumstances that typically surround celebrity trials, the traditional jury trial mechanism may be inadequate to provide such impartial fact finding and decision making. More specifically, in celebrity cases, there is a genuine concern that the criminal trial process will be derailed by jurors who, despite expressions of impartiality, are nevertheless drawn to the enticements of potential post-verdict wealth and celebrity. This concern raises the question of whether fascination with celebrities is itself a form of juror bias or a basic human instinct that cannot be easily eliminated from the jury selection process.

As discussed in this chapter, the voir dire is a question and answer session designed to measure the pretrial opinions and biases of potential jurors. This process normally operates to filter out obvious instances of bias either favoring or disfavoring criminal defendants. However, in celebrity criminal trials the subtle influences of "association" with a celebrity and the potential for post-verdict "benefits" may operate as an indirect form of bias that affects prospective jurors' evaluation of the evidence. Clearly, this indirect form of juror bias can have consequences that may, in some instances, undermine the prosecution's right to a fair trial. In addition to proving the material elements of the crime beyond a reasonable doubt, the prosecution in celebrity criminal trials, must usually confront overwhelmingly favorable public sentiment and sympathy generated by the defendant's celebrity status. Thus, the prosecutor must walk the fine line between prosecution and persecution, particularly when the defendant is a beloved or admired public figure. Furthermore, at the trial stage, jurors enamored with celebrity status are often predisposed to filter much of the evidence in a manner consistent with maintaining the defendant's celebrity status. This rationalization process ultimately allows jurors to explain away unacceptable behavior and implicitly imposes a higher standard of proof on the prosecutor during the trial. Finally, during the deliberation process, jurors in celebrity criminal trials may be more likely to superficially evaluate the evidence and "rush to judgment" in an effort to realize potential post-verdict benefits. In light of these potential consequences and the significant societal interest in convicting and punishing offenders, how should the criminal justice system simultaneously accommodate the celebrity defendant's right to a fair trial, the prosecution's right to have its evidence interpreted through a prism of true impartiality and the basic human instinct to identify with and, in some instances, to embrace celebrity status?

The U.S. Constitution provides that a defendant in a criminal trial is entitled to a trial by an impartial jury selected from the state and district where the crime was committed. The jury trial mechanism was added to the criminal trial process to prevent oppression by the government and bring together the shared common-sense judgment of lay citizens to determine the defendant's guilt or innocence. While the Constitution and subsequent case authority provide the framework for the jury system, jury selection procedures are largely governed by the legislative process. For example, the federal jury selection process is governed by a specific federal statute, while each state has its own statutory provision. The names of potential jurors are usually selected from voter registration lists or actual voter lists, although on the state level name selection procedures may vary from voter lists to the "key man" system. The key man system is a procedure whereby jury commissioners select prospective jurors based upon their belief that those selected will meet statutory qualifications for jury service, which include, among other things, good moral character, a sound mind and no felony record.

Under most selection systems, once prospective jurors have been chosen, a judge determines whether a person is unqualified for, exempt, or entitled to be excused from jury service. Statutory reasons for disqualification include lack of U.S. citizenship, failure to meet the jurisdictional residency requirement, inability to read, write, understand or speak English, mental or physical infirmities or a pending felony charge or conviction in a state or federal court. Potential jurors may also be excused if the court determines that jury service may cause undue hardship or extreme inconvenience or if the potential juror is likely to be unable to render impartial service. The focus of this elaborate selection process is to maximize the likelihood that any given panel of jurors will be randomly selected, representative of the community and impartial. This outcome is frequently distorted, however, by the breadth of the statutory excuse provisions that allow avoidance of jury service. For instance, because juror compensation is minimal and because jury service may require significant time away from one's primary occupation, many citizens simply cannot financially afford to serve on juries. Thus, those citizens who remain on juries tend to exhibit similar socioeconomic and ideological characteristics, which may not be representative of society at large.

However, while avoidance of jury duty is one factor that plays a role in the unrepresentative quality of the pool of potential jurors, those jurors who are *not* excused from service may also undermine the representative nature of the jury pool. In other words, in highly publicized trials, prospective jurors may fail to present valid excuses in an effort to remain on the jury panel. Indeed, the "highly motivated juror" may be the first subtle manifestation of the impact of celebrity status on a criminal trial and may foreshadow that prospective juror's inability to be truly impartial.

As the first true measure of impartiality, prospective jurors must survive the voir dire process. During this process, the defense, the prosecution and the judge, through direct questioning of the prospective jurors, seek to detect actual or potential bias. Most questions probe potential jurors' backgrounds, education, beliefs and experiences. Additionally, prospective jurors are questioned as to their prior knowledge of or relationship to the defendant. In celebrity trials, the question of prior knowledge of the defendant with celebrity status is usually answered in the affirmative and is therefore not the most accurate measure of bias or a basis for exclusion from a celebrity trial. Instead, the more important inquiry relates to the prospective jurors' ability to overcome their previous knowledge of the celebrity defendant and reach a fair, impartial verdict. This line of questioning during the voir dire represents a critical point in the process for both the prosecution and defense because it provides the first insight into the possibility that the burdens of proof might be implicitly reallocated. For example, if a number of prospective jurors respond favorably or admiringly when queried as to previous perceptions of the celebrity defendant, this may signal that the prosecution, in addition to proving the elements of the crime, must also transform the "celebrity" into the "defendant." During this transformation, the prosecution must endeavor to avoid the appearance of attacking the celebrity figure. In other words, the prosecution must effectively convey the message to prospective jurors that "it's not personal." In contrast, voir dire provides the defense with an opportunity to personalize the defendant and bolster his credibility, reputation and celebrity status through carefully crafted questions.

Once the jury is empanelled, numerous circumstances may subtly influence celebrity-trial jurors and impact their ability to be truly impartial. Truly impartial jurors in a celebrity trial would likely possess the following characteristics: (1) a recognition of the influence of celebrity status, (2) an ability to distance themselves from the defendant as a celebrity, and (3) a willingness to reconnect with the accused as a defendant and view the evidence through this new prism. Thus, while jurors might initially convince themselves and others that they are capable of impartiality in a celebrity trial, this professed impartiality should be measured according to a "true impartiality" standard. Not surprisingly, true impartiality is often difficult to achieve, given the unique circumstances of celebrity trials. In fact, the ability to recognize or admit possible biases becomes even more difficult in a celebrity trial because prospective jurors, already engaged by the celebrity status of the trial, may be even less willing to acknowledge deep-rooted biases and, in some instances, may actively and convincingly disguise those biases.

The intense media scrutiny that accompanies celebrity trials is another major factor that may significantly impact a prospective juror's ability to be impartial. For example, to minimize the impact of media scrutiny in a celebrity trial, the court may impose gag orders on the attorneys and sequester the jury during the trial. Sequestration is an extreme remedy because it forces jurors to become virtual prisoners for the duration of the trial and, ironically, can result in heightened juror interest in what is occurring in the "outside world." Additionally, because some level of juror anonymity usually accompanies sequestration, media and public interest in the jurors' identity is also heightened. With only scant media reports concerning each juror's age, ethnic group and occupation, celebrity trial jurors attain an initial level of "celebrity" themselves simply by virtue of the mystery surrounding their actual identities. Again, the glare of the media spotlight and the special treatment may act as subtle influences on jurors' perceptions throughout the trial.

In the midst of all of the unique and unfamiliar circumstances, celebrity jurors become intensely aware that they are part of a history-making event, and each juror has the sense that he or she has a unique role in shaping history. That sense of responsibility carries with it certain benefits that can also impact true impartiality. For example, it might be difficult for jurors to ignore the media's thirst for knowledge and detailed information concerning various aspects of the trial. A celebrity juror, aware of certain monetary benefits associated with providing the media with specific post-verdict information, may become a "recorder" of trial events throughout the trial rather than an active participant in the jury trial process. In the role of recorder, the celebrity juror may begin to see the trial as a story unfolding with a beginning, middle and end. Thus, the juror becomes primarily focused on the development of a "storyline" rather than impartial and involved consideration of the evidence. Unfortunately, jurors who begin to informally or formally record trial events and view the evidence as aspects of a story may implicitly emphasize and deemphasize evidentiary matters in accordance with their desired plot development. Furthermore, meticulously recording trial events may impact juror interaction and deliberation in the sense that the recorder may have a tendency to become secretive and uncommunicative with fellow jurors. This partially results from a feeling of conflict between the juror's sense of duty and the simultaneous desire to play a role in the development of the "story" of the trial. Also, as a practical matter, the recording juror must necessarily feel removed from fellow jurors, since the other jurors are also a part of this developing storyline.

Perhaps the most troublesome aspect of a juror's inability to be truly impartial is the likelihood of elevating the standard of proof in a criminal trial. A fundamental principle of our criminal justice system is that the prosecution must prove each of the material elements of the offense beyond a reasonable doubt. As explained in the chapter, the term "beyond a reasonable doubt" has developed numerous meanings in the law. In its purest form, it means that the jurors must evaluate the evidence and apply the law in an impartial manner and assess whether, in light of all the evidence, they possess an abiding conviction, to a moral certainty, as to the truth of the charges. If reasonable doubt remains, they must acquit. Even without the aspect of celebrity, jurors often grapple with the troublesome concept of reasonable doubt. This definitional struggle may be exacerbated in a celebrity trial, as some jurors may tend to define and filter reasonable doubt in a manner that most accurately maintains the celebrity status of the defendant. The prosecution's burden may implicitly be elevated; and the government is thereby denied the right to a fair trial, because it must produce more evidence, both qualitative and quantitative, to persuade jurors of the defendant's guilt.

Some may question the prosecution's right to a fair trial, as much of the case authority in the area of criminal law focuses on the defendant's right to a fair trial. However, as numerous cases have held, the prosecutor, as representative of the people, is entitled to present all relevant and constitutionally obtained evidence against the accused. Moreover, it is not unreasonable to expect that once the government has presented such evidence, the jury will apply the reasonable doubt standard in a truly impartial manner. But, in a celebrity trial, for the reasons mentioned, "beyond a reasonable doubt" may effectively become "beyond any doubt." This may occur because the celebrity trial juror is still identifying with the accused through a prism of celebrity. From that perspective, the mere fact of celebrity is thought to somehow insulate the accused from criminal behavior. Rather than careful examination of the evidence, the critical question becomes, "Why would someone with such status, money and power throw it all away by engaging in criminal behavior?" Since most people find it difficult to reconcile horrific criminal behavior with a beloved or admired celebrity, even overwhelming evidence of guilt will seem implausible under the circumstances. Of course, this discussion is not to suggest that celebrities cannot receive a fair trial and be convicted of criminal conduct. Instead, it is intended to identify the numerous concerns and additional hurdles that can and do arise in celebrity criminal trials. To combat the potential for unfairness, extreme caution must be exercised from the outset of the trial to ensure that both the defense and the prosecution receive a fair trial. In the end, however, because of the nature of our lay jury system, we must rely upon individual jurors to conduct themselves according to appropriate legal standards and, with rare exceptions, accept their verdicts as evidence that our justice system is functioning according to constitutional and legislative design.

FOR FURTHER CONSIDERATION

1. After some criminal trials, when the jury verdict appears to be inconsistent with the known evidence, there are calls for modification or elimination of the jury trial system as we know it. In several European countries, judges are members of the jury panel in criminal trials and are available during deliberation to clarify points of law. Should we move to a system of requiring judges or "professional" jurors trained in the law to serve on juries? What are the costs and benefits of dispensing with our current system of providing a jury of one's peers?
2. Jury nullification refers to the power of the jury to ignore the judge's instructions and not apply the law if they believe that doing so would result in an injustice to the defendant. Jury nullification was widely used before the Civil War when juries refused to convict abolitionists who helped runaway slaves. Are there modern-day circumstances that would permit jury nullification? What are the implications for our system of justice if jury nullification becomes a widespread practice?

Glossary

Accessory after the Fact: A person who aids in concealing a completed crime or hinders law enforcement investigation of completed criminal activity.

Acquittal: A determination by the judge or jury that the prosecution has not met its burden of proving the defendant's guilt beyond a reasonable doubt. After an acquittal, the defendant is free to leave and cannot be criminally prosecuted for that offense again.

Affirmative Defense: A defense offered as a justification or excuse for the defendant's conduct. Self-defense and insanity are examples of criminal law affirmative defenses.

Aiding and Abetting: Encouraging or facilitating the commission of a crime by another with the intent that the crime be committed. A person who aids and abets another will be charged with the same offense as the person who committed the offense.

Arraignment: The formal proceeding after arrest during which the defendant is formally charged with the crime and asked to enter a plea to the charges.

Arson: Using an incendiary device or explosive with the intent to cause damage to property or vehicles.

Assault and Battery: An unlawful attempt to injure a victim coupled with the present ability to commit a violent injury (battery). An assault may range from a simple assault (without a battery) to a first-degree assault in which the victim suffers serious physical injury.

Attempt: The intent to commit a specific offense plus a substantial step toward the commission of that offense.

Beyond a Reasonable Doubt: The evidentiary standard necessary to convict a criminal defendant. Although this standard is somewhat difficult to define, it essentially requires the *trier of fact* to consider and evaluate all of the evidence to determine whether there is an abiding conviction, to a moral certainty, that the defendant is guilty of the crime charged.

Burglary: Breaking and entering into a structure with the intent to commit a crime on the premises.

Case-in-Chief: The portion of the criminal trial when the government presents its main case against the defendant. During this portion of the trial, the government is required to present evidence related to each of the material elements of the offense.

Causation: A basic concept of criminal law that identifies who or what is *morally blameworthy* by identifying which conduct or activity produced the harmful result.

Circumstantial Evidence: Evidence that tends to prove a fact and provides a basis from which the judge or jury can draw reasonable inferences that a particular fact or circumstance occurred.

Closing Arguments: A narrative summary of the evidence presented by the prosecution and the defense after the presentation of evidence in a criminal trial. Closing arguments are also sometimes referred to as closing statements.

Common Law: A body of legal principles that reflected the societal customs and values of a particular period. The common law developed primarily through the decisions of judges, as distinguished from enactments by state legislatures.

Conspiracy: An agreement between two or more parties to commit an unlawful act and an overt act in furtherance of that agreement.

Constructive: A legal fiction that allows the law to assign certain characteristics to conduct even though that conduct may not actually have those characteristics.

Controlled Substance: Drugs that are specifically regulated by law with regard to possession, manufacture or delivery. Some examples of controlled substances include heroin, cocaine, morphine, methamphetamine and marijuana.

Counterfeit Controlled Substances: An imitation drug designed to induce a reasonable person to believe that using the product will produce an effect similar to an actual controlled substance.

Deliberate: The act of considering the consequences of engaging in criminal conduct before going through with it. The term "deliberate" is used in conjunction with *premeditate* to describe the circumstances surrounding first-degree murder.

Deliberation: The process used by the jury at the conclusion of a criminal trial to weigh the evidence presented during the trial and determine the defendant's guilt.

Direct Cause: A factor that can be directly linked to producing a harmful result. Finding the direct cause is usually the first step in determining moral blameworthiness in criminal law.

Direct Evidence: Evidence that proves a fact without the need to draw inferences. In a criminal trial, direct evidence of the defendant's guilt would be a confession or an eyewitness to the crime.

Embezzlement: The taking and carrying away of property in one's care, custody or control with the intent to permanently deprive the true owner of the property.

Extortion: Taking property from another by threat or force. For extortion, threat may be to the victim's family, reputation or business and does not have to take place in the presence of the victim. The threat may be written or verbal and may be conveyed through a third party.

Extreme Reckless Disregard: Conduct that consciously ignores a substantial and grave risk that death might occur as a result of the conduct.

Felony: The serious crimes at common law such as murder, manslaughter, robbery, arson larceny and burglary. Today, felonies are usually distinguished from misdemeanors by the seriousness of the offense as well as the possibility of incarceration for more than one year.

Felony Murder: An unintentional death that occurs during the course of and in furtherance of a felony.

Grand Jury: A formal body of lay citizens given the responsibility and broad authority for gathering and evaluating evidence in order to determine if a crime has been committed and if charges should be filed against anyone. The grand jury may work independently or under the direction of the prosecutor.

Homicide: A generic term used to describe the taking of life. A homicide may be lawful (e.g., the death penalty in some jurisdictions) or unlawful (e.g., murder).

Hung Jury: A jury in a criminal trial that fails to reach a unanimous verdict after lengthy deliberations. A hung jury is sometimes also referred to as a *deadlocked jury*.

Indictment: A formal criminal charge filed against a defendant in serious cases. An indictment is issued by a *grand jury*.

Information: A formal criminal charge filed against a defendant in less serious offenses. An information is filed by the prosecutor's office.

Insanity Defense: An *affirmative defense* offered to show that, as a result of a mental disease or defect, the defendant did not have the ability to understand or control his conduct at the time of the criminal offense.

Intent: See **Mental State**.

Intoxication Defense: A defense offered to show that the defendant could not form the necessary mental state to commit a crime due to the influence of drugs or alcohol voluntarily or involuntarily ingested by the defendant.

Jury: The selection of lay citizens assembled in a criminal trial to hear evidence and ultimately determine the guilt or innocence of the defendant based upon that evidence and the relevant law. The jury is selected through the *voir dire* process.

Jury Instructions: The formal process by which the judge explains the relevant law and evidentiary standards to the jury prior to the *deliberation* process.

Kidnapping: Secretly confining a victim against his will or using force, threats or deceit to abduct or transport a person for the purpose of secretly confining him against his will.

Knowingly: A mental state in which the defendant is aware or practically certain that a particular outcome will occur as a result of his conduct.

Larceny: The taking and carrying away of the personal property of another with the intent to permanently deprive the owner of the property.

Legal Cause: The factor that is deemed *morally blameworthy* for a particular harmful result.

Malice Aforethought: One of four mental states necessary for the crime of murder. The four mental states are: intent to kill, intent to do serious bodily harm, *extreme reckless disregard*, and *felony murder*.

Manslaughter: An unlawful killing committed without *malice aforethought*.

Material Elements: The components of a criminal charge necessary to prove in order to obtain a conviction. Material elements typically include the *mental state*, the *voluntary act*, *causation*, and *social harm*. Each of the material elements of an offense must be proven *beyond a reasonable doubt*.

Mental State: The state of mind that the defendant exhibited at the time of the offense. With the exception of *strict liability* offenses, the mental state is a *material element* of proof in any prosecution.

Misdemeanor: A less serious criminal offense usually resulting in a penalty of less than one year in jail and/or the payment of a fine.

Morally Blameworthy: A term used to describe those who have violated the standards of the criminal law without excuse or justification.

Motive: The reason or purpose that drives the defendant's unlawful conduct. Although most defendants commit crimes with a specific motive in mind, it is not necessary for the prosecution to prove the motive during a criminal trial.

Murder: An unlawful killing committed with *malice aforethought*.

Negligence: Unconsciously disregarding a substantial and grave risk that death might occur under circumstances in which a reasonable person would have recognized the risk and avoided the conduct. In the criminal context, negligence is also referred to as criminal negligence so as to distinguish it from the civil law concept of ordinary negligence.

Opening Statements: The procedure at the beginning of a criminal trial when each side articulates what it intends to prove or discredit during the criminal trial.

Opening statements are presented in a narrative fashion and are sometimes referred to as *opening arguments*.

Overt Act: Minimal conduct performed in furtherance of a conspiratorial agreement. An overt act can be something as simple as a telephone call to obtain a weapon to commit the offense.

Precedent: A rule or series of cases that serves as a model or example for decisions in subsequent cases.

Preliminary Hearing: A court hearing shortly after an arrest to determine if there is probable cause to believe that a crime was committed and that the defendant committed that crime.

Premeditate: The act of thinking about committing a crime prior to carrying out the act. The term "premeditate" is often used in conjunction with *deliberate* to describe the necessary circumstances for a charge of first-degree murder.

Presumption of Innocence: The condition that exists from the time of arrest and throughout the criminal trial in which the defendant's innocence is considered a fact requiring no proof. The presumption of innocence is one of the strongest presumptions known to law.

Proximate Cause: See **Legal Cause**.

Purposely: A mental state in which the defendant acts with a specific objective and intent.

Rape: Sexual intercourse by force and without the victim's consent.

Reasonable Doubt: See **Beyond a Reasonable Doubt**.

Receiving Stolen Property: Knowing possession of stolen goods with the intent to possess such goods.

Recklessly: A mental state in which the defendant consciously disregards a substantial and unjustifiable risk that death or serious bodily injury might occur.

Self-Defense: The justifiable use of force to repel an imminent, unlawful use of force.

Sexual Assault: Sexual conduct performed by force and without the victim's consent.

Sexual Conduct: Sexual intercourse or sexual contact.

Social Harm: The injury inflicted upon victims and society as a result of criminal conduct.

Solicitation: Requesting or urging another to commit a crime with the intent that the crime be committed.

Statutory Rape: Sexual intercourse between an adult and a minor. Statutory rape is a strict liability offense.

Strict Liability: A standard that allows for a criminal conviction without proof of a mental state.

Substantial Step: Significant conduct in furtherance of the defendant's criminal intent. To reach the point of a substantial step, the defendant must be close in time, proximity and preparation to committing the offense.

Syndrome Defense: Evidence offered in a criminal trial to explain why the defendant acted as he or she did during the commission of the crime. A common syndrome defense is the battered woman's syndrome.

Trier of Fact: The role of the judge or jury in a criminal trial to determine the facts of the case based upon the evidence admitted during the trial.

Verdict: The final determination by the judge or jury with regard to the guilt or innocence of the defendant.

Voir Dire: The process of selecting jurors for a criminal trial by posing questions designed to reveal biases or partiality.

Voluntary Act: Behavior by the defendant that is performed as a result of free will and choice.

Bibliography

The following books were useful to me in preparing the historical portion of this book:

Freidman, Lawrence M. *A History of American Law.* Simon and Schuster, 1973.

Holmes, Jr., Oliver Wendell. *The Common Law.* Little, Brown and Company, 1881.

Kimball, Spencer L. *Historical Introduction to the Legal System.* West Publishing Company, 1966.

Additionally, during the years I have taught criminal law, I have relied upon the following codes, texts and treatises in shaping my own understanding of the criminal law.

American Law Institute. *Model Penal Code and Commentaries.* American Law Institute, 1962.

Dressler, Joshua. *Understanding Criminal Law.* Matthew Bender, 1995.

Fletcher, George P. *Rethinking Criminal Law.* Little, Brown and Company, 1978.

Lafave, Wayne R., and Austin Scott, Jr. *LaFave and Scott's Hornbook on Criminal Law.* West Publishing Company, 1986.

Moenssens, Andre A., Fred E. Inbau, and Ronald J. Bacigal. *Cases and Comments on Criminal Law.* 5th ed. The Foundation Press, 1992.

Index

Accessory liability, 100–102; accessory after the fact, 103, 107–8; as distinguished from conspiracy liability, 102; knowledge requirement, 101
Accomplice liability. *See* Accessory liability
Act. *See* Voluntary act
Aiding and Abetting. *See* Accessory liability
American Law Institute test, 137–38
Armed robbery. *See* Robbery
Arraignment, 177
Arrest, 175
Arson, 165
Assault, 161; first degree, 163; simple assault, 161–63; with intent to commit other crimes, 164
Assisted suicide, 56–58
Attempt, 97–100; required mental state, 98; substantial step, 99

Bad check statutes, 122
Battered woman's syndrome, 147, 152–55
Battery, 162
Beyond a reasonable doubt, 182, 188
Burglary, 117–19

Capital punishment. *See* Death penalty
Causation, 29–31; direct cause, 29; expert testimony to establish, 37–40; proximate cause, 30
Child abduction statutes, 161, 172–74
Common law, 1–3
Computer crime, 123–25
Conspiracy, 91–97, 104–6; agreement, 92; liability for, 96–97; overt act requirement, 91, 94; parties to, 91; scope of, 94; unlawful act requirement, 93; withdrawal from, 95–96
Criminal codes, 3–8; codification process, 3–5; common characteristics of, 5–6; federal criminal law, 6–7
Criminal procedural law, 7–8
Criminal trial process, 178–83
Criminality and undesirable conduct, 10–14

Date rape. *See* Sexual assault

Death penalty, 14–17
Defenses, 131–49; affirmative, 132; battered woman's syndrome, 147, 152–55; case-in-chief, 131; defense of others, 144; defense of property, 145; diminished capacity, 140; ignorance, 148; insanity, 132–40, 149–52; intoxication, 145–46; self-defense, 141–44; syndrome defenses, 146
Drug offenses, 166–68, 169–71

Embezzlement, 115–16
Entrapment, 127
Extortion, 117

Federal criminal law, 6–7
Federal test, 138
Felony murder, 43, 47–49
First-degree murder, 44–45
Fraud and false pretenses, 120–22; bad checks statutes, 122

Grand jury process, 176–77

Homicide, 43. *See also* Manslaughter; Murder

Ignorance of the law, 148
Indictment, 176
Insanity defense, 132–40, 149–52; American Law Institute test, 137–38; as distinguished from diminished capacity, 140; federal test, 138; mental disease or defect, 133–34; M'Naghten test, 134–37; procedural requirements, 138–40
Intent. *See* Mental state
Intoxication defense, 145–46
Involuntary manslaughter. *See* Manslaughter

Jury process, 178–78, 181–83; celebrity trial jurors, 183–89; deliberation process, 181; hung jury, 183; peremptory challenges, 179; selection process, 178, 185; verdict, 183; voir dire, 178, 186

Kidnapping, 157–61; child abduction statutes, 161, 172–74

Larceny, 111–15; carrying away, 112; intent to permanently deprive, 113–15; lost or abandoned property, 112–13; trespassory taking, 112

Malice aforethought, 43
Manslaughter, 49–56; adequate provocation, 51–52; as a defense, 53; as distinguished from murder, 43, 49, 58–61; cooling off, 52; heat of passion, 49; involuntary manslaughter, 54–56, 61–63; voluntary manslaughter, 49–54
Marital rape. *See* Sexual assault
Mental state, 22–29; extreme reckless disregard, 43, 46–47; intent to do serious bodily harm, 43, 46; intent to kill, 43, 44–45; intentionally, 27; Model Penal Code, 23–27; strict liability, 27–29; willfully, 27
Mistakes, 148–49
M'Naghten right-wrong test, 134–37
Model Penal Code, 5, 23–27; American Law Institute, 5
Motive, 45
Murder, 43–49; as distinguished from manslaughter, 43, 49, 58–61; extreme reckless disregard, 43, 46–47; felony murder, 43, 47–49; first-degree, 44–45; intent to do serious bodily harm, 43, 46; intent to kill, 43, 44–45; malice aforethought, 43

Premeditation and deliberation, 44–46
Punishment, 8–10; sentencing disparity, 169–71

Rape. *See* Sexual assault
Rape shield statutes. *See* Sexual assault
Receiving stolen property, 119–20, 125–28
Robbery, 116–17

Self-defense, 141–44; aggressors, 143–44; battered woman's syndrome, 147, 152–55; imperfect self-defense, 142; retreat, 144
Sex offender legislation, 75–76
Sexual assault, 65–74; date rape, 69–71, 76–80; marital rape, 71–72, 80–82; rape shield statutes, 74, 82–83; rape trauma syndrome, 79, 147; statutory rape, 72–74, 83–85
Social harm, 32; victimless crimes, 34–37
Solicitation, 87–90; innocent instrumentality, 90–91
Speeding. *See* Strict liability
Statutory rape. *See* Sexual assault
Stealing. *See* Theft offenses
Strict liability, 27–29

Theft offenses, 111–23; burglary, 117–19; by use of computer, 123–25; embezzlement, 115–16; extortion, 117; fraud, 120–23; larceny, 111–15; receiving stolen property, 119–20, 125–28; robbery, 116–17

Undesirable conduct, 10–14

Verdict, 183
Victimless crimes, 34–37
Voir dire, 178, 186
Voluntary act, 19–22; involuntary acts, 20–21; failure to act, 21–22; sleepwalking, 20–21, 32–34
Voluntary manslaughter. *See* Manslaughter

Weapons offenses, 168–69

About the Author

RANETA LAWSON MACK is a law professor at Creighton University School of Law and a legal consultant who does commentary for the broadcast media on current legal issues.

ISBN 0-313-30556-0
90000
EAN
9 780313 305566
HARDCOVER BAR CODE